GEHRING BESIDE HIMSELF:

More Selected Essays

by

Wes D. Gehring

BearManor Media.com

Typesetting and layout by PKJ Passion Global

Published in the USA by
BearManor Media
1317 Edgewater Dr #110
Orlando FL 32804
www.BearManorMedia.com

Softcover Edition
ISBN-10:
ISBN-13: 979-8-88771-621-3

Published in the USA by Bear Manor Media

To Sarah & Emily

MAE WEST:

The Woman Behind Diamond Lil

Mae West didn't just
Enter a room,
She dusted off all the
Corners on the way through.

If she had been
Born on the frontier
It would have been
A real wild, wild West.

As it was, '30s America
Found Mae ever so steamy,
Though some merely
Called her seamy.

When censors
Tried to keep at least
One foot on the ground,
Her observations were
horizontal.

Mae had so much "It"
That Clara Bow should
Have demanded a recount ...
Or a new nickname.

While built like a cast iron
Hour glass, Mae was male
In her mannerisms—especially
"Frank" in her suggestions.

Though seldom compared to
Rival Snow White, Mae admitted
To being as pure as
The driven snow ... until she
drifted.

Thus, Mae was more than
A mere sex symbol,
In time America called
Her a real life preserver.*

(Reprinted with permission from both *The Journal of Popular Film and Television*, Summer 1982; and Anthony Slide's 1988 anthology *The Picture Dancing on the Screen: Poetry of the Screen*.)

*During World War Two life preservers were known as "Mae Wests."

TABLE OF CONTENTS

ACKNOWLEDGEMENTS

This difference between the right word and the nearly right word is the same between lightning and the lightning bug.

— Mark Twain

I wish to express my gratitude once again to BearManor Media for publishing a second selection of my essays and giving them new life. Since they are drawn from a forty-plus year career, the cover is from an early memorable moment in a long academic life. I had just given a talk on Chaplin and dark comedy at a special gathering celebrating the 100th anniversary of his birth (1889-1989). Given it was by special invitation from the Paris-Sorbonne University, I was surrounded by delightful young "Charlies," and it was my first visit to the "City of Light," there was much to smile about. Plus, I have even neglected the topper, I just had a delightful conversation with Chaplin's oldest daughter and host, actress Geraldine Chaplin.

Fittingly, I want to also thank Ball State University for long supporting my adventures in writing, as well as the tab for this trip — which also doubled as a book research jaunt. (Actually, all my excursions double as fun fact-finding missions; ask anyone.) Regardless, since 1989 was also the Eiffel Tower's 100th anniversary, with an amazing nightly light show to match, it was as if the whole city was celebrating Chaplin's birthday. Fittingly for the romantic Chaplin, on screen and off, the Tower is sometimes nicknamed the "Beautiful Lady." Thus, 1989 Paris was definitely the place for this Chaplin devotee to be.

Oh yes, back to the thank yous. Since this text draws from works covering many years, to name every particular person of assistance is regrettably impossible. However, a few individuals merit special attention. Janet Warrner long provided editorial and proofing assistance. Kris Scott continues to perform many computer tasks — with a special ongoing thank you to her always helpful student staff. (One such staffer, Skye Allen, provided additional proofing.) Chris Flook covers the final preparation of stills (A few obscure ones were tracked down by Stacy Mulford.) Longtime mentor and friend Anthony Slide is forever encouraging. Also from LA, friends and sounding boards Joe & Maria Pacino continue to be delightful hosts of late night film discussions, as well as graciously letting me crash at their home. Plus, my family has always provided so much support, especially my daughters, Sarah and Emily. With a dad for a film professor, they have also grown into longtime movie assistants.

The many libraries are scattered over several countries. Yet, there are four pivotal constants, starting with the New York Public Library's main branch at Fifth Avenue and Forty-Second Street (guarded by the lions "Patience" and "Fortitude"). Fittingly, this is undoubtedly best known for film fans as a research mecca via the terrified librarian exiting at the start of the original *Ghostbusters* (1984). The other trio are: New York's Performing Arts Library at Lincoln Center, the Academy of Motion Picture Arts and Science's Margaret Herrick Library (Beverly Hills, California), and my home base Ball State University Bracken Library (especially its tireless interlibrary loan staff). Two Bracken "historians" merit special kudos, Elaine Nelson and James Shimkus.

These essays have been drawn from a number of publications whose interest made this text possible: *THALIA: Studies in Literary Humor* (University of Ottawa, Canada), *USA Today Magazine*, *TRACES of Indiana and Midwestern History*, *Indiana Social Studies Quarterly*, *FORUM* (BSU), *Elderhostel Journal*, and the *Indianapolis Star Magazine*. I own the copyright on all the essays, except for a special arrangement with *USA Today Magazine*. Consequently, I owe a special thank you to this journal's Publisher and Editor-in-Chief, Wayne M. Barrett, for permission between myself and "The

Society for the Advancement of Education, Inc. All Rights Reserved." I am primarily a freelance writer. However, since I wear several hats at *USA Today Magazine*, including Media Editor, columnist, and occasional essayist, special copyright arrangements have been made.

For consistency, some reformatting has been done concerning the different style sheets of various scholarly and mainstream publications over a forty-plus year period. Footnotes have been standardized for the scholarly pieces. However, the "casuals" (essays), such as for *USA Today Magazine*, retain in-text references. (All stills are from the author's public domain "press kit" collection.)

— Wes D. Gehring

AUTHOR'S PREFACE

> This is what I find encouraging about the writing trades: They allow mediocre people who are patient and industrious to revise their stupidity, to edit themselves into something like intelligence. They also allow lunatics to seem saner than sane.
>
> — Kurt Vonnegut

I have been a film professor for well over forty years, and thankfully I still do not feel like its past "last call" and the music has been turned off. Writing has done that for me. I write to better understand myself. While the process of self-discovery is never complete, it remains a joy to continue chipping away for more moments of clarity, however fleeting. Noel Coward once said "work is more fun than fun." That is how I feel about writing. The task is often criticized for its difficulty, such as W. Somerset Maugham's observation, "To write simply is as difficult as to be good." However, there's that fun factor again. Real writers enjoy mucking around in a paragraph for half the morning to discover just the right combination/arrangement of words.

This is my second collection of selected essays. Thus, I feel especially blessed, with a special thank you to BearManor Press. That first pass of selections was difficult to make. Ironically, this time around it was no easier. Besides a still sizeable original quality pool from which to choose, several prolific writing years had passed. Once again, each pick felt like a proverbial jump ball situation. Moreover, the first anthology had been pre-Covid. Consequently, this time around, from a personal perspective, it was interesting to weigh not only the passage of time on my writing, but also the epidemic's impact. That is, sorting through some long-marinated essays can fascinatingly showcase a different you. Still, one's morphing of self is usually slow and steady as she goes. In contrast, Covid often made transitions more dramatic, as in "Hello mortality," even in a seemingly lighter piece, like "Wes' Trip to 1970 Beatle Land ..." While obviously meant as entertainment, it was also a touchstone to my grandchildren.

Plus, a couple points from my first anthology bear repeating. First, while I have been lucky enough to write many books, composing in the compressed form of an essay can often feel more exhilarating. Nothing is ever perfect. However, like Edgar Allan Poe, I frequently feel as if a shorter piece can up one's odds of precise intelligibility. Second, an anthology also represents a historical mercy mission. Yes, one's hard copy journal might find new life online. However, there is also a chance it will end up stacked in the garage, or out in the recycling bin. For a tactile person, an essay's life expectancy greatly increases in book form. And as an old school sort, I am very much a fan of William E. Gladstone's observation:

> Books are a delightful society. If you go into a room filled with books, even without taking them down from their shelves, they seem to speak to you, to welcome you.

Thus, to recycle a James Thurber book title, *Welcome to My World*.

— Wes D. Gehring

PART ONE:

FILMS

BUTCH CASSIDY AND THE SUNDANCE KID

Forgotten Basics About a Classic

Robert Redford (left), Katharine Ross, and Paul Newman on the set of *Butch Cassidy and the Sundance Kid* (1969).

Fifty years ago *Butch Cassidy and the Sundance Kid* (1969) opened. Recently a major publication showcased an article which keyed on the critical storm which greeted the inclusion of the song "Raindrops Keep Fallin' on My Head." The whimsical ditty carried the sound track while Butch (Paul Newman) gave Sundance's girlfriend Hetty (Katharine Ross) a ride on his bicycle. The Burt Bacharach and Hal David tune went on to turn into a Number One Billboard Hot 100 hit for a month, and later won a Best Song Oscar. (Bacharach earned another Oscar for the *Butch Cassidy* score).

After reading the essay I immediately thought of the documentary, *Gore Vidal: The United States of Amnesia* (2013). Why? The article was about how prior to the picture's release, neither 20th Century Fox (which bankrolled the movie), nor at least one of the major stars wanted it included ---- "How did the song fit with the film? At the time there was no rain." Yet, other than simply noting "Raindrops" was kept in *Butch Cassidy* at the insistence of director George Roy Hill (1921-2002, who later won an Oscar for directing Newman and Redford in *The Sting,* 1974), no one seemed to have a clue on either why Hill kept the song, or a reason behind its success.

This is where the amnesia factor really kicks in. Does no one do any research anymore? Yes, I am *now* a film professor. However, in 1969 I was just a college freshman trying to keep up with the current movie releases, and the PR machine material behind hits like *Butch Cassidy.* Therefore, if one simply liked the film, the answers to the aforementioned questions were pin balling around everywhere at the time, from countless print publications then in existence, to a focused television coverage of only three or four stations in most markets. Indeed, there was even a popular documentary at the time narrated by Hill ---- *The Making of Butch Cassidy and the Sundance Kid* (1970).

So why "Raindrops?" The long run of Western film success was on the wane. From roughly 1940-1965 one out of every American films was a horse opera! Plus, Westerns ruled much of television programing during this time. Throughout the early 1960s over twenty sagebrush sagas played on the small screen in *prime time*. Bob Hope joked, "Before I can turn on my TV I have to brush the hay off."

The surest sign that a genre has run its course is when it begins to be milked dry by parodies. For example, through the 1930s and World War II the horror genre was riding high. However, by the late 1940s suddenly it was *Abbott and Costello Meet Frankenstein* (1948), or *Abbott and Costello Meet the Killer Boris Karloff* (1949). During the 1960s the same thing was happening to the Western, with spoofs like *Cat Ballou* (1965, with Jane Fonda and Lee Marvin), or Don Knotts in *The Shakiest Gun in the West* (1968). Lee Marvin's parody was so effective he copped an Oscar for dual roles as a drunk and his twin desperado with an artificial metal nose.

In *Butch Cassidy*, Hill wanted a subtler form of spoofing, sometimes referred to as "parodies of reaffirmation." They are often confused with the genre being undercut, and produce a fascinating tension between broad comedy such as Butch doing bicycle tricks during "Raindrops" for an appreciative Ross (before he hits a fence), and the darker side of a true Western ---- the freeze frame ending deaths of Butch and Sundance.

Plus, keep in mind the basic parody anti-Western components of *Butch and Sundance*. They are constantly running away from their antagonists (versus a normal confrontational shootout, as in *High Noon*, 1952). Indeed, my correspondence with William Goldman (whose screenplay won an Oscar for the film) revealed the greatest difficulty in getting 20th Century Fox to green light the project was their concerns over these seemingly cowardly antiheroes. However, the film is peppered with breaking other basic Western givens, from Butch never having been in a gunfight until late in the movie, to the duo not even being capable of shooing away the posse's horses as they once again run away. Moreover, maybe the most missed classic component derailed in *Butch and Sundance* is that a school teacher is part of the gang. Normally, the school marm comes from the East to help in settling the wild West.

"Raindrops," like the *Butch and Sundance* dialogue, attempted to have a contemporary feel to it, which helped give the film a more modern action adventure feel ---- not just being another Western. It avoided the later obvious musical broad parody of Mel Brooks' *Blazing Saddles* (1974), when classic Western singer Frankie Laine belted out his typical shot glass rattling over the top rendition of the title song.

"Raindrops" also fit the modern image immediately carved out by Ross in her co-starring role two years earlier, *The Graduate* (1967). However, given this instant clout, yet dealing with what Hill realized was a classic script (often later referenced in scriptwriting texts), Hill had a problem. He did not want to tamper with this brilliant script, which was partially inspired by another reaffirmation parody, Goldman's favorite film, *Gunga Din* (1939), which also has a cliff scene in it.

So how does one give Ross more screen time without major plot changes, or new dialogue scenes? How about using a few upbeat modern sounding songs, like "Raindrops," which allows her to interact with Butch and/or Sundance without messing with that script, even if she is the silent part of the team? Moreover, what is strange about this, in light of the aforementioned article, is that Hill was explaining all this at the time on TV and in print interviews, as well as his personalized *Making of Butch Cassidy and the Sundance Kid* documentary. Indeed, the unnamed star mentioned was briefly interviewed in the same film. Did he not tune in for the completed film and Hill's voice over?

Strangely enough, in the article which was the catalyst for this piece, a major film historian is also asked about "Raindrops," and he responds as if the film was created in a vacuum, "There's no reason the song should work, but it does; I can't explain. It's catchy, quirky with ethereal lyrics and unusual tempo. But it's so appealing. And when you're looking at those attractive people in a Western setting, it all comes together." I half expected *American Bandstand*'s Dick

Clark to suddenly appear before me with some Philadelphia teenager saying, "The song has a nice beat and you can dance to it."

Why did this unnamed historian not mention what was going on in the late 1960s? He was older than I was at the time. By modernizing *Butch and Sundance* via song and dialogue, was this so different from either *Bonnie and Clyde* (1967), or *Easy Rider* (1969), all of which played the anti-establishment period card, were partially driven by provocative use of music, and all had to have sacrificial death conclusions? Coupled to this disc jockey impaired historian, were the even more derailing final comments of the unnamed *Butch and Sundance* star (so-called) film expert, "Today, the song still works from the standpoint of nostalgia. All these years later, it still has resonance."

Nostalgia? The song worked then. Released before the picture, its two million plus sales did not take off until *after* the film opened! If the use of the song, and/or its lyrics seemed odd for a Western, look at how *Butch and Sundance* starts. Sundance is in a poker game and one of the players calls him a cheat and challenges him to a shootout ... until he realizes who he is up against. Suddenly, Butch arrives and offers a theatre of the absurd-like out. He tells the scared cowboy, "What would you think about inviting us to stick around ["What?"] You don't have to mean it or anything but if you'd just please invite us to stick around, I promise you we'll go." That is what happens, and the same eccentric tone follows. I would call Newman one existentialistic cowboy. (Also, like the contemporary tone of "Raindrops," one can see the same quality here.)

With an opening like that, even if this *United States of Amnesia* factor were not out there, can one honestly expect the film to follow, *Butch and Sundance*, is going to assume standard Western norms? As an addendum to my frustration over the article that is the mainspring for this essay, maybe an underlying Goldman point in my correspondence with him was his sense of wonder at the whole *Butch and Sundance* story. In real life, Butch was a divertingly humorous motor mouth. Sundance was a silent, sullen, dangerous soul. Yet they were best friends. The duo was cared for by a lovely schoolmarm. As cowboy bad men who had been successful in a nontraditional manner, when they found themselves in an unfriendly new century, the team moved to Bolivia to continue their trade.

They were unlike any other of our Western legends. Even their deaths are in question. Indeed, their alleged Bolivian graves have been exhumed to see if either one survived a shoot-out which makes the Alamo look like a walk in the park. Yet nothing is conclusive. Moreover, do we really want to know? Isn't Amelia Earhart's disappearance better for conspiracy business? The same applies here. Regardless, Lula Parker Betenson (with Dora Flack) wrote a book, *Butch Cassidy, My Brother*, which chronicled how her sibling somehow got away. The saga was provocative enough to even get Robert Redford to write the Foreword. Goldman had every right to be mesmerized by their story.

Thus, when one comes across the "Raindrops" lyric that "Nothing seems to fit," who is to say this song does not fit the movie? In fact, the "Raindrops" number, even with the modest amount of dialogue, is the closest thing to a romantic sequence in the movie. Thus, if one does not want to simply do the homework, one can still "read" the "Raindrops" bicycle ride as the one real romantic scene in the movie. This plays into how her relationship with the Newman and Redford is both complex and tragic, with her eventually leaving the two in Bolivia rather than see them both die. Of course, Newman's bicycle courtship does not have to be romantic when compared to the tone of Sundance's invitation for her to join them on their move to Bolivia, "You speak it [Spanish] good. And it'd be a good cover for us going with a woman ---- no one expects it ---- we can travel safer. So what I'm saying is, if you want to come with us, I won't stop you, but the minute you start to whine or make a nuisance, I don't care where we are, I'm dumping you flat."

The scene is so patently unromantic that Butch's immediate comment invariably generates a big audience laugh, "Don't sugarcoat it like that, Sundance ---- tell her straight." Be that as it may, I find it meaningful that in my correspondence with Goldman, he noted male camaraderie first when underlining his all-important *Gunga Din* influence on *Butch Cassidy*, "The camaraderie, the sadness of good men dying, the joy of what that film can do ... nothing has ever moved me as much as a kid as *Gunga Din*. It is still, my favorite [film]."

So, there you have it. Maybe the ultimate uniqueness of the "Raindrops" number, beyond the many forgotten facts lost to some current "historians," and I use the term loosely, is that the song sequence provides a rare charming moment in a story otherwise really about a Howard Hawks–like male bond in the work of George Roy Hill.

(Reprinted with permission from *USA Today Magazine*, November 2019. Copyright © 2019 by "The Society for the Advancement of Education, Inc. All Rights Reserved.")

BETTE DAVIS' *JEZEBEL* THROUGH A COVID LENS

Bette Davis, Henry Fonda, and *that dress* in *Jezebel* (1938).

If one had written about Bette Davis' *Jezebel* (1938) a year ago, it would have required taking an intellectual off-ramp to stop and ponder the many options. For example, this was her early Warner Bros consolation prize for not making the Scarlett O'Hara final cut for *Gone with the Wind* (1939). Moreover, by winning her second Best Actress Oscar (after 1935's *Dangerous*), this offered another sweet revenge writing alternative – cementing her position as *the* actress of the decade.

After all, as acid-tongued critic David Thomson suggested of Davis, how could a "far-from-pretty" woman with those "pulsing eyes" not be a better actress if she kept winning awards from those less intense Hollywood beauties. Plus, for much of *Jezebel*, she gave her largely feminine audience just what they wanted, playing a woman one loved to hate – a flute thin self-centered shrew. Indeed, her *Dangerous* Oscar was assumed to have been a makeup prize for not winning as the barbed-wired tongue whore who torments that nice Englishman (Leslie Howard) in *Of Human Bondage* (1934). Davis was not one to keep her emotions in a safety deposit box.

However, that was last year. The coronavirus can now even provide a gut-punch to *Jezebel*. The story revolves around the spoiled Southern belle Julie (Davis). She is about to be married to the young successful banker Preston "Pres" Dillard (Henry Fonda). The year is 1852. Pres' work periodically takes him to New York for the railway concerns he represents, a key plot point.

The movie begins upon the day of the Olympus Ball, *the* social event of the year. Unmarried women are expected to wear virginal white. When business keeps Fonda from accompanying Davis on a shopping trip, she decides her revenge will be to wear a brazen red dress to the ball. During Pres' business meeting his close friend and banking associate Dr. Livingston (Donald Crisp) expresses worry over recent yellow fever victims repeating the large scale outbreak of 1830. Pres supports Livingston, but their concerns are minimized by being told this is nothing to worry about. Fonda's comment about cleaning up the unsanitary conditions in the city are poo-pooed as unnecessary and maybe a product of his being up North too much.

With the business concluded, but before the Ball, it is made clear that Pres and Julie's relationship has long been threatened by her provocative behavior. Thus, when he calls for the crimson gowned Davis, she is unaware that their future is now over. However, Pres plays out his hand. The two are ostracized at the Ball, and when the dance begins the floor empties. Davis realizes her mistake, but Fonda forces her to dance. When the music stops, he makes the orchestra continue, and the duo dance alone. Upon respectfully taking Davis home, she slaps him and he cordially leaves for New York.

Davis is also loved by Buck Cantrell (George Brent), a wealthy likable character who has accepted her choice like a gentleman. However, he is old school South and feels nothing should change, including an honor code which makes dueling a social norm. Indeed, he is first introduced about to duel, something at which he never loses. As the picture progresses he comes to represent *the South stuck in amber* – nothing is to change, whether it is accepting yellow fever as a seasonal norm, to slavery. Change is for Yankees.

One year passes and Fonda returns… with a wife. Davis' hopes for a reconciliation are destroyed. She will soon use her power over Buck to orchestrate a revenge duel with Pres. However, it ironically fails and Buck is killed dueling Pres' brother Ted (Richard Cromwell).

Pres' return has been prompted by business and Crisp's growing concern about the fever. However, there are denials by secondary players like, "There is no more yellow fever then last year," or "a shot of bourbon" is all that is needed. Fonda's suggestions from the previous year that the city's often filthy streets might make a difference had met with the same response. Indeed, when Fonda again defends Crisp's warnings, Davis observes, "The doctor takes pleasure in frightening us."

Shortly after someone says it is necessary to continue "business as usual," Fonda collapses with the fever. Yet, even people with the fever want to continue doing business and keep a lid on what is happening. However, soon wagons of dead and dying are being taken from the city to Lazarus Island, and the city goes into a panic. One might think using the name Lazarus is a cruel joke, or a far-fetched wish – did not Jesus raise this man from the dead? One needs to know the complete story. Jesus knew of his friend's sickness but delayed visiting him, and Lazarus died. Both Mary and Martha rebuked Christ for not acting sooner. That was why Jesus brought him back to life.

Once the New Orleans of *Jezebel* acted it was too late, especially given its remedies. Since it was felt yellow fever was caused by bad air, instead of transmission by mosquitoes (and there is a high profile scene of Fonda being bitten), the city did what it always did – cannons were fired and barrels of tar were lit. The city was then quarantined by an 1850s version of the national guard, with people being shot if they attempted to leave.

Crisp's character was rebuked by his upper-class associates when the doctor reported Fonda's condition to authorities – which meant a trip to Lazarus Island. Crisp's response was essentially this should not be a poor man's affliction. However, those that escaped the city headed north for what had long been known as the safety of the "fever line." However, this essentially said it was an affliction of the poor, for there was no mobility for slaves and the impoverished. Plus, decades of an established "fever line" was a *do nothing some people are expendable tradition*. There is no bottom to what many people will do, regardless of the era.

Regardless, what about Jezebel Davis? Unlike her Biblical namesake, she finally decided to do something unselfish. Julie somehow convinces Fonda's New York bride that she should go to the dreaded island to care for Fonda. Davis' witchy character, who probably once double-dated with Simon Legree, made the arguably realistic claim that Fonda's wife did not know all the ways of the South, and if anyone could maximize such talents and save him, it would be her. Believable, or not, the bride bought it, and Davis went off to Oscarland, I mean martyrdom. Our last image of her is the only upright person in a trail of death wagons headed for the island. Many critics were with her for most of the narrative, but then became decidedly mixed. However, her three hanky movie base loved it all.

Forgetting Joan of Arc Bette, *Jezebel* was fairly accurate for its day. The year 1853 was New Orleans' worst outbreak of yellow fever since 1830. It was assisted by a huge year for cotton profits (making the city overcrowded with business people and celebrating their good luck.) It was also an unusually warm and long summer in which almost 8,000 people died.

However, this is the varnished perspective; these are the real reasons: First, warning signs were ignored. Second, business as usual kept a lid on it, and even attempted to work through it. Third, *Jezebel* people acted like they were different. (I seem to remember recent Covid comments like: "We're not the Chinese" and "People die from the flu every year.") Fourth, they were unprepared and ignored the signs. Finally, this was largely a poor person's affliction, because they were marginalized and not adequately cared for *before* the outbreak.

> "History is a gallery of pictures in which there are few originals and many copies."
>
>   — Alexis de Tocqueville

(Reprinted with permission from *USA Today Magazine*, May 2020. Copyright © 2020 by "The Society for the Advancement of Education, Inc. All Rights Reserved.")

LEO McCAREY'S *MAKE WAY FOR TOMORROW*:

The Film Orson Welles said "Would Make a Stone Weep"

Leo McCarey (circa 1940), with John Decker's painting of W. C. Fields as Queen Victoria.

There has been a TV commercial running for years which I cannot believe is still in some markets. It sounds like a pitch to find a great storage unit for mom. Plus, the assumption seems to be that poor old Dad has already left the building. As an aging Baby boomer, I have already gone through the many agonizing decisions to which the commercial crassly plays. However, the callous upfront manner in which it is presented sadly speaks to the age we live in.

However, the commercial also returns to the old fashioned approach to the family melodrama. In this scenario, the children, often grown children, cause older parents great psychological pain. *The* example to link "A Place For ..." up with is Leo McCarey's *Make Way for Tomorrow* (1937). It is a loose adaptation of Josephine Lawrence's novel *The Years Are So Long*. The film chronicles the story of an elderly couple (Victor Moore and Beulah Bondi) who lose their home and that none of their grown children have room for both parents. Separated for the first time in fifty-plus years of marriage, they are shunted about by the children. Ultimately, Moore's character will go live with a daughter in California, while Bondi (best known now as Jimmy Stewarts's frequent screen mother, including in *It's a Wonderful Life*, 1946), will enter an East Coast retirement home. As McCarey' daughter Mary later summed it up in a 1946 *Saturday Evening Post* article, "Why are children so mean to their parents?" While hardly applicable to Leo or his daughter, the director thought the property was both an excellent way to salute his parent's generation and create a cleansing catharsis over his grief at his father's death. Orson Welles later said of the film, "It would make a stone cry."

More than that, *even* critics cried! The *Chicago Tribune*'s Mae Tinsée was typical of this normally cynical circle: "It is one of the most genuinely moving productions I have ever seen; one of the most beautifully acted; one of the best directed. And ... I cried quietly all the way through it." Indeed, while the *New York Post* reviewer gave *Make Way* the newspaper's highest "movie meter" rating, he felt it was so sad it was hard to watch. The *Hollywood*

Reporter critic said, "It is so [movingly] lifelike as to mark a distinct departure from prevailing [happy ending] photoplay fashions."

This latter characteristic, a story told with brutal honesty, was a further source of critical praise for the director — so unlike the aforementioned rosy commercial. Regardless, the *New York Tribune*'s Howard Barnes observed, "McCary produced and directed the picture with courage, power, and imagination." The *New York Times* also used the term "courage" to describe Leo's decision to not sugarcoat old age. This directly clashes with the walk-in-the-park nature of the commercial.

For all the film's tearjerker traits, *Make Way* was not only a melodrama. That is, the movie also functions as a poignant love story of equal nontraditional dimensions. How often does this genre have a focus romantic couple where each partner is seventy-plus years old? This contrasts sharply with today's tendency to minimize the aging factor by using younger couples with gray spray-painted hair and not a liver spot in sight. Indeed, in today's youth culture, Oscar Wilde's *The Picture of Dorian Gray* has never been so topical.

McCarey most effectively showcases the *Make Way* love story in an extended sequence shortly before the end of the picture. Moore and Bondi steal five hours in New York away from their grown children before *one* of them has to catch that train to California. Though much of the couple's life had recently gone south, McCarey mercifully now grants them both and the viewer a much needed respite prior to that gut-wrenching train depot departure. While the couple's children had been less than ideal, this charming interlude is peopled with populist sorts more consistent with McCarey feel good types, from the comedy team he created, Laurel & Hardy, to *Ruggles of Red Gap* (which teams Charles Laughton and Charles Ruggles in a Laurel & Hardy fashion, 1935).

The plot catalyst for *Make Way*'s dose of decency had Moore and Bondi revisiting the New York hotel where they had honeymooned over a half century before. Befriended by a sympathetic hotel manager, he first signs for their drinks ("two old-fashions for two old-fashioned people"), and then orchestrates dinner and dancing at the hotel, with the pivotal introduction of the song, "Let Me Call You Sweetheart." Most importantly, however, the manager and staff (especially a thoughtful hat check girl, a friendly bartender, and a sensitive bandleader) treat the couple with the dignity they deserve — something that had been decidedly lacking until now. (The scene is even more moving now, with the underlining Covid suggestion that older people are just unfortunately expendable.)

The hotel's finale gives Moore the strength to phone his New York-based children and finally speak his mind, as well as warn them to stay clear of Grand Central Station; the couple will say their good-byes on their own. This eleventh-hour resiliency is also matched by at least one of the children (Thomas Mitchell), who recognizes the siblings and their spouses have been heels, and he keeps the others from crashing his parents' farewell. To put this in perspective, film historian Leland Poague wrote, "There is no more powerful image of courage in the history of cinema than the simple and heart-rendering close-up of Bondi on the railway platform as she watches her husband's train pull away." (On the soundtrack, one hears an instrumental rendition of "Let Me Call You Sweetheart.")

Years later McCarey would write a *Hollywood Reporter* article entitled, "Say It With Music." Without mentioning either "Let Me Call You Sweetheart" or *Make Way for Tomorrow,* his essay ultimately culminates with a movingly veiled reference to both. Sagely, McCarey observes, "Melody is the adjunct to romance in every land and in every age," and he takes a purely Leo perspective by keying on *senior lovers* — "sometimes aging couples' memories fly over a half century when they hear songs to which they danced when they were first sweethearts."

A melodramatic love story notwithstanding, *Make Way* would not be a McCarey movie without an undercurrent of comedy. Thus, the aforementioned tearful critic from the *Chicago Tribune* closed her review with the confession, "Some of the time I was laughing

WHILE I cried." The *Hollywood Reporter* even described the picture as a "gentle comedy of tender sentiment." Regardless, much of the humor is sandwiched into the hotel segment, including arguably the picture's funniest spot-on topic line. When the hotel manager realizes the couple had a large family he observes, "I bet they've brought you a lot of pleasure," to which Victor Moore's character deadpans, "I bet you haven't any children."

A close bond developed between the actors and crew on *Make Way*. But the comradery went beyond the normal populist spirit de corps forever fostered by Leo. Everyone became so absorbed in this story about elderly parents that there was never a sense of quitting time. The director's goal of honoring both his father's memory, and his parents in general, was equally embraced on a personal level by cast and crew alike. Indeed, Moore later wrote in the 1947 *Saturday Evening Post*:

> The extras, grips, cameramen and prop men were so moved that several of them told Beulah Bondi … that they had just written long-delayed letters to their parents. One old lady, after hanging up extras' clothes on a line, said to me, "You and Beulah are acting this. I'm living it.

Moore, maybe best known today for a small role in Marilyn Monroe's *The Seven Year Itch* (1955), would always consider *Make Way* his best and favorite role. As an addendum to McCarey, in the following decade the writer/director would win a basket of Oscars for the year's Best Picture, *Going My Way* (1944), a film that brings joy to the sometimes cantankerous senior priest Barry Fitzgerald, who wins a Best Supporting Actor statuette. Plus, if those earlier Orson Welles comments did not sound like the later dark filmmaker, keep in mind *Make Way* predated *Citizens Kane* (1941). Moreover, the ending of *Kane* arguably makes it Welles' only sentimental picture. That is, discovering "Rosebud" symbolized a *lost* childhood, one can forgive a lot in the title character that dies a lonely old man.

Besides Welles' amazing comment, a "well-done" fan letter from George Bernard Shaw, and *Daily Variety* calling it a "masterpiece," "Make Way" was a box office disappointment. Ironically, McCarey won a Best Director Oscar that year for *The Awful Truth*, (1937), a screwball comedy whose title might have also been used for "Make Way."

While candor can be a hard thing to face, certainly we are better than "A Place for …" Still, as the comedian said, "Insanity is hereditary. You get it from your children."

Tarantino's *ONCE UPON A TIME IN HOLLYWOOD ...*

&

Why a No Show Steve McQueen Would Have Negated Manson's Murders

Steve McQueen in *Bullitt* (1968), an action star in real life, too.

Every date has the potential to be a fifty-year milestone anniversary, but 1969 seems to have hit the mother load, from the moon landing to the Manson murders. Indeed, 1969 is even the year I graduated from high school, and my still favorite band, the Beatles, performed their last public performance at the impromptu rooftop jam above Abbey Road. In fact, a recent *New York Times* article (August 4, 2019) explored this rash of 1969 events and pontificated three key reasons for this growing fifty year phenomenon: all that color film footage with which to draw upon, a youth culture spotty on their history, and the commercial given – money.

Naturally, these events are normally celebratory, such as Woodstock also occurring in 1969. However, one recent filmmaker, Quentin Tarantino, has put a rather provocative revisionist twist on the subject in *Once Upon a Time ... in Hollywood...* (2019). The film slowly (over 189 entertaining minutes) eventually gets to the first Manson clan cult killings (August 1969). The most infamous element of the tragedy being the stabbing death of pregnant actress Sharon Tate and four friends, while her director husband Roman Polanski was in Europe filming.

However (spoiler alert), if one is revisionist Tarantino, who so enjoys tweaking history, bad things do not have to happen. This ranges from his Jewish American World War II soldiers taking out Nazis with Louisville Slugger baseball bats (such a nice American touch) and making "toast" of Hitler a year before he did it himself for a honeymoon in *Inglorious Basterds* (sic, 2009), or a slick-dressing slave/cowboy killing assorted racists in the pre-Civil War days of "Django Unchained" (2012).

Plus, one must remember the title of Tarantino's latest exercise in altering history, *Once Upon a Time ...*, which is how all those ultimately happy fairy tales begin. Moreover, if you are Tarantino, such a title telegraphs the filmmaker's joy in spoofing a sub-genre of movies – "the spaghetti western," à la 1968's *Once Upon a Time in the West*. Indeed, these Italian productions (normally shot in Spain for an American–like topography) had a revisionist slant, too. History was not so much changed, but prior to this Westerns were usually a white hat – black hat affair, with no need for a rooting score card. In contrast, "the spaghetti western" was served in several shades of moral gray.

However, what I have yet to see is any "butterfly effect" applied to Tarantino's films. If one is changing history, you might as well go all out. If you have been in a coma since 1969 (*one more item!*), when the phrase was first used metaphorically, the "butterfly effect" is when a minor change completely alters an already established complex series of events. (It is basic fantasy 101, if you are into that genre.) Regardless, the key point for applying the effect is that action actor Steve McQueen had been invited to a small gathering with Tate that evening.

I have written a biography of McQueen, and the actor seems to hover over Tarantino's movie. Its two stars, Leonardo DiCaprio and Brad Pitt, are variations of McQueen. DiCaprio begins the film as TV Western star Rick Dalton, in a part which heavily draws upon McQueen's small screen hit, *Wanted: Dead or Alive* (1958-61). From there, like McQueen, he moves into feature Westerns.

Pitt's character, Cliff Booth, is Dalton's stuntman double and best friend, who is quietly tough and likes to repair things. To flesh that out, if taken care of, mechanical things are more dependable than people. (A core McQueen belief.) Regardless, as a bad boy sex symbol, it also allows Pitt to take his shirt off while fixing a roof top antenna. This alone was enough to make several *Once Upon a Time* ... reviews sound more like beefcake Pitt had finally returned. All this could double for a McQueen press kit biography.

Regardless, since the film came out, countless PR blurbs, given McQueen's invitation, have stated he would have been murdered, too. Being a film professor, people also feel a need to inform me of this information. Having written a book on the actor, this tends to hurt my feelings. However, I will save that for another essay. Yet, after several such occasions, "the butterfly effect" is my rebuttal. If these people had not read my book, I could at least negate faulty fatal news about McQueen.

Steve McQueen was an ex-marine and kept himself in amazing shape. Because of a horrible childhood (the kind that James Dean liked to fabricate – I did a book on him, too), McQueen had a constant chip on his shoulder and enjoyed fighting. Though he had been trained in martial arts by Bruce Lee, he had no compulsion about fighting dirty. Also, given his angst-ridden youth, military training and a general distrust of people, McQueen was *always* very sensitive to his surroundings. He also collected and sometimes wore guns. Oh, and one final point, in a fight, gender was not a factor for him.

Given that this initial Manson kill squad was composed of three untested young girls (a fourth did not take part) and a less than imposing young man, and were armed only with knives and one 22-caliber pistol, do you really think they would have waltzed into the Tate compound with the same results if McQueen had been there? Unless you flatlined during the course of reading this essay, or still tend to rely on crayons, the correct answer is NO. Each Manson member would have quickly gone horizontal, with a substance resembling Guacamole sauce coming out of their ears. To borrow some period phrasing, we're talking *McQueen* here, *Steve McQueen.*

(Reprinted with permission from *USA Today Magazine* March 2020. Copyright © 2020 by "The Society for the Advancement of Education, Inc. All Rights Reserved.")

BULL DURHAM

&

Comic Reality in the Minors

Susan Sarandon and Kevin Costner in *Bull Durham* (1988).

No matter how good the film, there is always at least one scene which some viewer feels is a little too hard to believe. This is human nature, or call it universal relevance. One wants this special film to go beyond mind candy and tell us something all-inclusive.

However, the popcorn critic should always be wary about the nature of truth. What follows is an example of why *not* to second guess a scene in an inspired movie. The picture in question is *Bull Durham* (1988). Written and directed by Ron Shelton, the movie sports auteur, whose other sports themed films include *White Men*

Can't Jump (1992, with Woody Harrelson and Wesley Snipes as basketball hustlers), *Tin Cup* (1996, with Costner as a *go for it* golfer), *Driven* (1994, Nick Nolte playing an industrial-strength Bobby "throw that chair" Knight like college basketball coach), and *Cobb* (1994, Tommy Lee Jones as the elderly Ty machete-tongued Cobb).

Bull Durham covers the misadventures of the minor league baseball team the Bull Durham Bulls during a partial Single–A season. *Sports Illustrated* has called this the best baseball picture ever made. Whether one buys into this position or not, it is undoubtedly a top three pick, which also happens to be the ranking the *Movies Arts Film Journal* gave it against *all* sports movies! Plus, one has to love the research that went into it, since Shelton played twelve years of minor league ball, topping out at Triple-A. Thus, what could possibly not be to like? The scene in question involves a mound meeting between Kevin Costner's "Crash Davis," a veteran minor league catcher sent down to Single-A ball to nurture "Nuke," a young wild pitcher (Tim Robbins) for a shot at the "Big Show" (the major leagues).

The mound meeting is soon about everything but baseball, because a gang of infielders have joined in. Nuke is nervous because his dad is in the crowd. José (Rick Marzan) is upset because his girlfriend has put a hex on his glove, and to remove this bit of voodoo someone will have to cut the head off a live rooster. (The film, as in baseball, is peppered with examples of superstitious ballplayers.)

Another player is bemused that sexy Millie (Jenny Robertson), the most promiscuous baseball fan in Durham, is going to marry Jimmy (William O'Leary), the team's virginal religious innocent. (Crash immediately negates any negative comments be made on the subject.) Plus, no one knows what to get the couple for their baseball diamond wedding. So, when Robert Wuhl's bench coach finally comes out to check on this impromptu mound gathering, team leader Crash blurts out, as a manner of explanation, "We're dealing with a lot of shit!"

The nonchalant topper to this decidedly casual nongame atmosphere is when Wuhl's character does *not* get upset, as one might expect of a coach, but rather replies in kind to his distracted players. For example, with regard to the question of wedding presents, he observes in part, "Well, ah, candlesticks always make a nice gift, and maybe you could find out where she's registered, maybe a place setting or silverware is good. Okay, let's get two [outs]!"

Ironically, while the movie was an immediate hit with both the press and the public, some film critics found this mound scene unrealistic. Yet, Shelton was later entertainingly expansive in the *New York Times* (May 4, 2003) on how this was probably the most realistic segment in the movie. (This would also explain the casual nature of Wuhl's coach.)

Shelton confessed, "In those timeouts around the pitcher's mound, we'd take time to argue about who was going to win the welterweight championship fight, or what was the best steakhouse in the town we were playing in, or what to get somebody for a wedding present. Sometimes it was to see if anyone had a line on some girl sitting in the stands. I mean, we talked baseball all the time, but that was during the baseball bus rides, which lasted forever."

The easygoing nature of this mound meeting might also be taken as a metaphor for the evolution of Crash Davis as the team's quasi-father. He comes to mentor several players besides Nuke. Moreover, he doubles as the squad's mischievous favorite uncle, such as the night he guarantees the tired players a much needed "rainout" by playing with the stadium's sprinkling system the night before a scheduled game. Never has the description of baseball as "a boy's game" been better showcased as Crash leads them in a game of running (and sliding) the bases in the mud.

Moreover, Davis also seems to be a substitute figure for Shelton, since he, too, seems to have played about twelve years in the minors with only one brief "cup of coffee" (a call-up to the majors near the end of season when rosters are allowed to expand). In addition, maybe the monologue he gives at another moment in the movie, which takes away the breath of the leading lady Annie (Susan Sarandon), is the best sign that he might be a better athlete of the mind, capable of starring in another "big show": "I believe in the soul, the cock, the pussy, the small of a woman's back, the hangin' curve ball, high fiber, good scotch, that the novels of Susan Sontag are self-indulgent overrated crap. I believe Lee Harvey Oswald acted alone. I believe there ought to be a constitutional amendment outlawing astro turf and the designated hitter. I believe in the sweet spot, soft core pornography, opening your presents Christmas morning rather than Christmas Eve. And I believe in long, slow, deep, wet kisses that last three days."

Consequently, while there are always exceptions, it is best not to question the total reality of a master work. However, as an interesting addendum, late in his life, my childhood baseball hero, Mickey Mantle, actually was most poignant in addressing the reality of *Bull Durham*. Appearing on *Letterman*, he saw this comedy along more tragic lines, since there were so many deserving Crash Davises who did not make the majors. (Mantle had made it to the "Big Show" as a teenager, and it was hardly limited to a "cup of coffee!")

Without really wandering off the reservation, this *it's too outlandish to be true* essay merits two more examples on the commonality of the phenomenon. The first is a variation of the *Bull Durham* scenario. In Richard Curtis' classic ensemble romantic comedy *Love Actually* (2003), ten relationships (often interlocked) are followed during the Christmas season. The only one which some critics felt stretched credibility involved Colin Firth and Lúcia Moniz.

Firth is an English author who had gone to his French cottage earlier in the year to write, after being romantically jilted. An agency had hired a Portuguese housekeeper (Moniz), but neither Firth nor Moniz knows the other's language. Still, a special platonic bond builds between them. This is accented through periodic comic voice over of their thoughts. Back in England he realizes the extent of his feelings for her, and starts to take classes in Portuguese, just as she is doing in English. By Christmas he decides he must track her down and propose. Firth finds Moniz at work as a waitress, and publicly proposes in amusingly broken Portuguese. She accepts to the joy of all the patrons.

It does sound over-the-top romantic. However, when Curtis wrote the *Love Actually* script, like Shelton's *Bull Durham*, the British writer/director drew upon as much reality as he could. Only in this case, Curtis badgered friends and colleagues for their love stories. This was one of them. Moreover, there are embellishments in it from Firth's own personal life. Thus, once again the critics are caught in a *Gottcha*!

The second example involves Barry Levinson's *Liberty Heights* (1999). One of the writer/director's celebrated autobiographical Baltimore tales. This film involves a friendship between two high school seniors, just after desegregation came to mid-1950s Baltimore. The youngsters are a Jewish boy (Ben Foster) and a black girl (Rebekah Johnson). Neither set of parents are pleased when it is revealed, especially Johnson's father. When he finds them combining afterschool homework with Red Foxx comedy albums, he forbids them from seeing each other.

Her prominent doctor father then drives the boy home. However, Foster's character has a thing about Frank Sinatra's mega-hit 1953-1954 song "Young at Heart." It happens to be playing on the radio as they reach the boy's house, but Foster's character can't leave the car until the song ends, otherwise it "would be disrespectful" to Sinatra. Just as *Bull Durham* is arguably the best baseball movie, *Liberty Heights* is in the conversation as a best coming-of-age film. However, while popular with my college students, the reality of this scene is sometimes questioned by them.

The pushback I give them is politely personal, except it is back in Ron Shelton sports territory. I am in a car with two fellow high school football teammates driving to practice, with no time to spare.

The year is 1968 and the Beatles' "Hey Jude" is on the radio as we arrive at the field. But even though we had a Woody Hayes-like coach (*read walk the plank scary*), which meant countless extra laps for lateness, none of us remotely considered exiting that car until "Hey Jude" ended. Keep in mind "Hey Jude" was over seven minutes long in an era of songs normally less than half that length. Plus, its slowly fading lengthy close of "Nah, nah nah, nah nah, nah, nah, nah nah, Hey Jude" could also be lengthened by constantly turning up the car radio volume. What can I say? It charted a then record nine weeks at number one. So I completely bought into respecting Sinatra's "Young at Heart" on the car radio.

Fittingly, as John Lennon once said, "Reality leaves a lot to the imagination."

Carol Reed's *THE THIRD MAN* —

Which the British Film Institute (BFI)

Ranked As Their Greatest Film of the 20th Century

Orson Welles attempts to escape through *The Third Man* (1949) sewers of Vienna.

The Third Man (1949) takes place in Vienna immediately after World War II (1945). It was largely shot on location in the city's bombed out ruins. The German term for such pictures are "Trümmerfilm" or rubble films. Given the period, it was obviously influenced by *the* movie movement of the time, "Italian Neo-Realism."

As with Berlin, Vienna had been divided into four sectors, each controlled by the budding Cold War players: the United States, Britain, France and the Soviet Union. The action is largely limited to the British and Soviet areas. The time period, the setting, and the nefarious activities are also most conducive to components which characterize film noir, a genre birthed, in part, by the war's ugly legacy. How fitting, therefore, to plop a picture down amidst its wreckage of buildings and people. Other pivotal noir elements include an existentialistic philosophy (often with dark comedy overtones), cynical heroes, intricate storylines, which, like life, end without all the answers. Plus, most strikingly, noir showcases a visual style combining German Expressionism's stark nighttime lighting effects and unusual distorted camera angles with on location disturbingly real documentaries. At its core noir embraces Expressionism's fatalism. That is, to become involved, even with the best intentions, is only to make matters worse for everyone. Ironically, one's altruism then embraces Jean Paul-Sartre's axiom, "Hell is other people."

The classic noir is normally built upon what literature calls "tough guy's fiction." Pivotal works would start with the writings of Raymond Chandler and his alter ego detective Philip Marlowe, and Dashiell Hammett's private eye, Sam Spade. Like German Expressionism, the best of Chandler and Hammett actually predate World War II, with Hammett's central Spade novel, *The Maltese Falcon* appearing in 1930, and Marlowe first surfacing in the 1939 novel *The Big Sleep*. Chandler likens these detectives to "tarnished knights" — not perfect, but doing the best they can in a dirty world.

However, noir need not have a professional detective. Often it is an amateur that falls into the task of attempting to solve an ugly mystery. Such is the *The Third Man* scenario, in which an American author of pulp Western novels, Holly Martin (Joseph Cotton) has come to Vienna with a job offer from an idolized old college friend. However, he has not seen this title figure, Harry Lime (Orson Welles), in some time.

Before further sketching out *The Third Man* scenario, one must underline its cinema significance. In 1999 the British Film Institute (BFI) declared it their country's greatest picture. Moreover, it invariably continues to appear on lists of unparalleled pictures. Indeed, a *London Guardian* article (August 2, 2015) revisiting the film was entitled " 'The Third Man' Review — a Near Perfect Work."

The film also has attracted attention for breaking the old maxim of "too many chefs spoil the broth." However, the talent involved on and off the screen has fueled an ongoing question of who was the true auteur. This question most involves director/co-producer Carol Reed, screenwriter Graham Greene (from a novel written in preparation for the film, and later published in book form), actor/director Orson Welles, and dueling producers — Britain's high profile Alexander Korda and America's David *Gone With the Wind* Selznick.

Most questions of authorship begin with Orson Welles, creator of the legendary noirish *Citizen Kane*. Moreover, while his charismatic Lime is only on the screen for 10 minutes, he walks away with the picture, despite being a black marketeer causing death by selling inferior penicillin. His anchoring of the film might best be described by Greene biographer Richard Greene (no relation) in *The Unquiet Englishman*:

There was something miraculous about Welles. From the moment a cat toys with his shoelace and the [sudden] light from an open window catches his face, he dominates the film. Martin Scorsese thinks this scene "might be the best revelation — or best reveal — in all of cinema." [Also] Some words Orson Welles contributed were among the most memorable in ... [Film History].

The latter mention of Welles' words is a reference to the fact that the actor was often allowed to write his own dialogue. Consequently, despite a brilliant script, the film's piece de resistance observation occurs after Lime has failed to persuade Martin to join forces with him, satirically observing:

> After all, it's not that awful. You know what the fellow says — in Italy, for thirty years under the Borgias, they had warfare, terror, murder, and bloodshed, but they produced Michelangelo, Leonardo da Vinci, and the Renaissance. In Switzerland, they had brotherly love, they had five hundred years of democracy and peace — and what did they produce? The cuckoo clock.

In the documentary *Shadowing The Third Man* (2005), undated archival footage has a sheepish Welles admitting to once claiming too much influence on the film. Welles' only assertion regarded authorship are his scenes. Comically, also appearing after his 1985 death, Welles has to tone down the ardor of sycophant interviewer friend Peter Bogdanovich in *This Is Orson Welles*. When Bogdanovich seemingly attempts to credit everything to him, Welles affectionally admonishes him, "It was Carol's picture, Peter — and Korda's." One might say Bogdanovich's "ringmaster" (Welles) has been reduced to being one of the acts ... though *the* most central.

As the years passed, all parties agreed that Korda's greatest contribution was just letting Reed and Greene make their own picture. Plus, despite the inspired screenplay, Greene's later preface to the 1950 publication of the film's novella blueprint, gave the lion's share of the picture's success to Reed. Still, there were interesting differences among the aforementioned key creative players. These will be addressed as the essay now returns to *The Third Man* narrative.

Cotton's character has just arrived in Vienna only to find that his friend Lime has seemingly been accidently killed by a car when crossing the street. Ironically, Holly's first act will be going to the cemetery service. At the funeral he meets British military policeman Major Calloway (Trevor Howard), who is less than positive about Lime. Between besmirching his friend and several inconsistencies about just what happened to Lime, Holly decides to stay. More irregularities surface. Welles' character had been hit by his own driver, and Lime's doctor just happened to be passing by. Moreover, the only multiple accident story constant included an unknown "Third Man."

Cotton's Holly is also much taken with Selznick's protégé Anna Schmidt (Alida Valli). The producer hoped he had discovered another Ingrid Bergman. Unlike noir's normal femme fatale, Anna is a world weary victim, inadvertently playing up Holly's out-of-his-depth innocence. That is, Cotton's character is like his no gray area pulp Westerns. Regardless, Holly and Harry eventually are allowed one extended scene together — *high up* in Vienna's giant Ferris wheel, the Wiener Riesenrad. Naïve or not, Holly has figured out Lime is alive and has already informed the Major, though at this point, the "B" Western novelist cannot turn in his long lionized friend.

The film's aforementioned signature dialogue involving the cuckoo clock ends this sequence, back on the ground. However, as entertaining as it is in bolstering the villain's charm, arguably another Welles observation from the highest point of the Ferris wheel is the film's (or any noir's) most telling line. It is a succinct tutorial on evil, or temptations:

Look down there [Holly]. Would you really feel any pity for one of these dots [people] to stop moving — forever? If I said you can have twenty thousand pounds [\$72,000 then, nearly \$900,000 today] for every dot that stops, would you really, old man, tell me to keep my money — without hesitation? Or would you calculate how many dots you could afford to spare? Free of income tax old man...

This bit of dialogue generates the most discussion among my college students ... if I can get them past their own deadly silent consideration of the sudden proposition before them.

Regardless, as a sidebar to Welles having gone all humble pie about his contributions to *The Third Man*, this temptation speech was authored by Greene — it is in his pre-film novella. Moreover, when it was later published in book form, Greene neither includes the cuckoo salvo, nor what he considers Reed's superior cinema ending. Indeed, this is a fitting time to address the finale.

Since *The Third Man* was made during the censorship era, naturally Lime must ultimately pay for his crimes. However, that does not mean the picture must end on an upbeat note. The film comes full circle, beginning with Lime's phony funeral, and ending with his actual burial. At the time, Greene felt the audience merited the closing suggestion that Holly and Anna would become a couple, which is how he ends the novella. However, Reed would have none of it, and one of the few contributions made by Selznick was strongly backing the director's decision.

Reed's widely noted reason was pure noir, "A picture should end as it has to. I don't think anything in life ends right." While one might question the statement's broader philosophy, it is spot on noir. Moreover, Reed wonderfully milks it. Holly and Anna are not together at the funeral's conclusion, and Cotton's character waits for her at the end of a long road straight from the cemetery. It is a lengthy long shot, long take (à la neo-realism) towards him, and when Anna reaches Holly she walks right by him, without even a turn of her face.

Intriguingly, it anticipates a similar situation at the finale of arguably the greatest postmodern noir/dark comedy, *Chinatown* (1974). Once again a great director, Roman Polanski, has worked closely with a gifted screenwriter, Robert Towne, on a tour de force Oscar winning script. However, Polanski also refuses to accept its quasi-hopeful ending. John Tiska's *The Detective in Hollywood* captures Polanski's comment, "When people leave the theatre, they shouldn't be allowed to think that everything is all right with the world. It isn't. And very little in life has a happy ending." Years later at a *Chinatown* tribute, Polanski even added, that without his downer *noir* ending, "We wouldn't be sitting around talking about it [the film] today."

So why was Korda so wise to let Carol and Greene run with it? Greene had discovered Vienna and it's amazing underground labyrinth of a sewer system river. (Tours are available today.) It is here that Carol orchestrates his extraordinary Lime chase scene, the tunnels being how Welles traveled between Vienna zones. Regardless, Carol has been gifted with the most obvious noir metaphor (a sewer). Naturally he pressed for shooting on location, as well as coming up with Welles' celebrated doorway entrance. Carol also pushed for a soundtrack entirely tied to a single musical instrument called a zither — a flat wooden sound box with numerous strings stretched across it. Unknown to most of the world, it was yet another tie to that specific region.

Most movie people felt Carol was taking a huge risk by keying on the zither — yet it became a global phenomenon. Indeed, Vienna musician Anton Karas' "The Third Man Theme" later became a number one United States hit song. Moreover, while zither music is mesmerizing, as Roger Ebert's online (December 8, 1996) revisiting of the movie suggests, the sound has a perfect coupling with noir, "jaunty but without joy, like whistling in the dark" — call it a nerve-tinkling dance of death ditty for Harry and Holly. Ironically, two decades later Beatles documentary footage even has them warming up with the song during a recording session that foreshadows the group's breakup.

Despite Greene giving Carol the most credit, between the novelist's longer more celebrated career, and the ongoing mystique of Welles, who also most praised Carol in Bogdanovich's book, the British director is the one most often neglected when credit is assigned for *The Third Man*. Yet, it would appear that Carol was *the* chef among many.

Carol had seemed incapable of doing wrong in the 1940s, including *Night Train to Munich* (1940) and *The Fallen Idol* (1948, for which he won the New York Film Critics Circle Award for Best Director, and Best Picture from the British Academy of Film and Television Arts, BAFTA). However, after this era his career had fallen off. Yet, if one has only seen the touchingly tormenting *Odd Man Out* (1947), what might be called an Irish film noir and the first recipient of the BAFTA Award for Best Picture, there is a strong case for calling Reed the true *Third Man* auteur. Indeed, he had to fight everyone to get Welles (over Noel Coward) for the Lime character ... without which the picture would have lost the rogue's charming allure.

Polanski is repeatedly on record as calling *Odd Man Out* his favorite film, with a gut wrenching finale that is capable of precipitating heaving sobs even with repeated viewings. In fact, Polanski's *Chinatown* noir-related comments are no doubt born here. Moreover, this makes for the perfect segway to the poignant Reed arranged near *Third Man* close in the Vienna sewer. A wounded Welles is dying in the sewer, with only his fingers ephemerally reaching through a street grating he cannot lift. His Lime turns to Holly and his eyes beg for a mercy killing. Finally, the narrative puzzle pieces magically fit for a Western writer whose novels always get their man, and an off-camera Holly obliges his friend.

This is Reed's picture.

(Reprinted with permission from *USA Today Magazine*, November 2021. Copyright © 2021 by "The Society for the Advancement of Education, Inc. All Rights Reserved.")

PLAY IT AGAIN, SAM:

Bogey as a Fairy *Godfather*

The Epitome of Film Noir Cool — Bogart.

> "I don't tan — I stroke!" — Woody Allen's wannabee
> Bogart discussing tanning in his tribute to *Casablanca*
> (1942).

Fantasy has always been associated with the comedy world of Woody Allen. The pervasiveness of his comic anti-hero stance, what Maurice Yacowar focuses on in *Loser Take All* (see closing works cited) as the comic outsider — in Allen's films, short stories, and stand-up comedy albums—has come to represent a pivotal view of the frustrations of modern society. Fantasy has been crucial in these presentations, be it the short sketches from *Everything You Always Wanted to Know About Sex But Were Afraid to Ask* (1972, where anti-hero consistency is maintained even when he appears as a sperm), or that moment of supreme self-satisfaction in *Annie Hall* (1977), when Allen suddenly pulls Marshall McLuhan out of nowhere to put down a pompous intellectual. Director Allen even underlines the fantasy magic of this moment by then giving his comedy character the direct address line, "Boy, if life were only like this."

For the student of comedy, it is quite natural to link the frustrations and fantasies of Allen's world with an earlier author who helped bring the comic anti-hero to center stage in American humor—James Thurber. In fact, if one's sense of a comedy chronology were a bit shaky, it would seem logical to note the Woody Allen-like nature of James Thurber's classic December 1939 *New Yorker* fantasy, "The Secret Life of Walter Mitty":

> Captain Mitty stood up and strapped on his huge Webley-Vickers automatic. "It's forty kilometers through hell, sir," said the sergeant. Mitty finished one last brandy. "After all," he said softly, "What isn't?" The pounding of the cannon increased. There was the rat-tat-tatting of machine guns …
> Something struck his shoulder. "I've been looking all over this hotel for you," said Mrs. Mitty. "Why do you have to hide in this old chair?"

It is important to keep in mind, however, that the Allen fantasy does not always represent the escape from frustration associated with Walter Mitty's secret life. For example, in *Bananas* (1971) Allen dreams that the monks carrying him on a cross are beaten out of a parking place by a second cross-toting group of monks; one fantasy in *Play It Again, Sam* (1972) even had *the* Bogey getting shot by Allen's ex-wife.

Frustration in comedy fantasy is, of course, nothing new. Charlie Chaplin was shot in the heaven scene from *The Kid* (1921, after he has succumbed to sin); and in the more modern variation on this in *The Seven Year Itch* (1955), Tom Ewell gets conflicting fantasy messages from heaven and hell about what to do when upstairs neighbor Marilyn Monroe comes visiting … but goodness wins, if you can call that a victory.

What is so unique about Allen's depiction of frustration in the fantasy world is that it occurs so often. In fact, in a film like *Sleeper* (1973), where Allen is defrosted in a Big-Brother-like world two hundred years in the future, the whole movie might be termed a science fiction fantasy of frustration—a comic nightmare. As John Brosnan has suggested in *Future Tense*, Allen actually had done science fiction trial runs for *Sleeper* the previous year (1972) with some of the episodes from *Everything You Wanted to Know About Sex But Were Afraid to Ask,* particularly one involving a giant, mobile killer breast.

But except for underlining the deep-seated nature of his comedy persona's frustration (which can cause real-world problems to show up in his fantasies), this aspect of Allen's imaginary world does not offer the viewer much new insight. However, when examined in tandem with more truly escapist fantasy elements in his work (also the more dominant), some rather interesting insights are revealed.

This is best exemplified in *Play It Again, Sam,* which Allen himself described in Eric Lax's *On Being Funny,* as "fun to write because it dwelt on fantasies and I could write all these romantic things you could not live out in real life." By casting Bogart (played by Jerry Lacy) in several of the fantasy scenes, Allen raised viewer identification to the nth degree. And without discarding occasional fantasy frustration, he was able to construct a story around such traditional Woody Allen requirements as his relationship with women, movie history, and personal identity. The film has no fewer than eighteen often lengthy fantasy scenes (his longest and most consistently integrated use of film fantasy at the time) and is his most effective balancing of the fantastic and the real for both comic effect and maximum viewer identification.

The film opens with Allen in a theatre watching the close of *Casablanca* (1942). As the film cuts back and forth between Bogart on screen and its antihero audience member, it is clear that Allen has momentarily become Bogart. He underlines this after the close of *Casablanca* (and his first fantasy) by saying "Who'm I kidding? I'm not like that. I never was, I never will be. Strictly movies."

For the next several minutes the film avoids fantasy, allowing the viewer to become acquainted with the "real-world" situation of Allen's character. It is familiar ground: Allen is a film journalist who is feeling especially frustrated sexually because his wife has recently divorced him. Most of this information is provided through two flashback scenes with his ex-wife (Susan Anspach), which help prepare the viewer for the next bit of fantasizing.

When Allen asks himself "What's the secret to being cool?" Bogart appears and essentially tells Allen to toughen up. (Bogart is about to become Allen's romantic Swiss army knife.) The "naturalness" of Bogart's appearance is helped by the fact that Allen's apartment is like a Bogart museum, with posters from *Casablanca* and *Across the Pacific* (another Bogart film, 1942) dominating everything, while smaller bits of Bogart memorabilia, like stills and books, lie scattered about. Allen tries Bogart's "prescription" of bourbon and soda and passes out; the result—his depression continues.

Next enter his supportive friends (Diane Keaton and Tony Roberts), who make it a point to play matchmaker. But Allen is so depressed now that his third fantasy occurs. It is a short vision of his ex-wife on a wild date with a Hell's Angel type, while she knocks Allen, "He fell off a scooter once. And broke his collar bone." (Just to look at Allen and Susan Anspach is to know their happy wouldn't be ever after.)

His friends manage to get him a date, and as Allen dresses, Bogart again appears. His message is be more earthy: tone down the mouthwash, deodorant, after-shave, and baby powder, or "you're gonna smell like a French cat house." Encouraged by Bogart, mimicking Bogart's mannerisms and inflections, and with a reflection of a Bogart poster in the mirror before him, he fantasizes the seduction of his blind date—curing her of frigidity.

As might be expected, however, the blind date is a horrible failure, as are his next several interactions with different women, from a suicidal girl who is interested in Jackson Pollock, to a drug user who nearly gets Allen's face redesigned by taking him into a biker's night spot (more Hell's Angel types). This series of failures is reminiscent of the comment by Shelley Duvall's character in *Annie Hall* (1977), "Sex with you is really a Kafkaesque experience," and is the longest passage of the film without a fantasy break. Fantasies will, however, occur regularly for the rest of the film, appropriately starting with an appearance by his ex-wife, who tells him, "You're not the romantic type." As in the Thurber world, Allen experiences few vanilla meetings between the sexes.

After she goes, Allen does not exactly negate her message when he ponders: "I wonder if she actually had an orgasm in the two years we were married—or did she fake it that night." In fact, there is more of the same in the very next scene, when Allen calls the home of a girl he took out in high school eleven years ago and finds that she has *still* left explicit directions with her parents not to give Allen her number.

By this point in the film the viewer has started to realize, though it has not yet become apparent to Allen's character, that this frustrated outsider just happens to have a lovely rapport with Diane Keaton. Since she is married to his best friend, she is the only girl he has not been trying to impress—a classic example of the success of being yourself. And since her nonstop businessman husband is also a "phone man" (a continuing gag finds him constantly calling his answering service to leave new numbers where he can be reached), Keaton and Allen have lots of time together. (The phone fixation makes it even more topical today.)

To top off the logical nature of their budding "relationship" is the fact that, despite her beauty, Keaton is as insecure as Allen: this is compounded by her husband's marital neglect. That all of this should culminate naturally in an innocent affair has been foreshadowed in the comically touching scene in which he gives her a plastic skunk for her birthday, the skunk being her favorite animal.

It is not long, therefore, before his next fantasy (number seven), finds him briefly imagining the seduction of Keaton. Appropriately enough, this fantasy is immediately followed by feelings of guilt, which just as logically brings Jerry Lacy's fantasy Bogart to the rescue, trying to downplay the guilt. This soon becomes the most important sequence since the *Casablanca* opening, because Allen's ex-wife then appears and proceeds to argue with Bogart about what Allen should do. It is a pivotal fantasy because it brings together for the first time the two poles of Allen's make-believe world—the castrating ex-wife and the macho legend, who will eventually do battle for control of Allen's real world. The scene is given an added comic touch by taking place in a supermarket (something Allen comically accents at the fantasy's close by saying, "Fellas, we're in a supermarket!"). From this point on, his imagination will become much more active. The market meeting is also a homage to a grocery setting between Barbara Stanwyck and Fred MacMurray in a pioneering film noir, 1944's *Double Indemnity*.)

On the way home Allen imagines how much easier it would be if his friends were getting divorced, and Roberts had asked him to take care of Keaton. The fantasy, though very brief, maintains an otherwise beautiful consistency with the rest of the movie by having Roberts leave by plane (echoing the *Casablanca* opening airport scene and anticipating its return at the close), and also by topping all previous telephone numbers at which he could be reached—he is meeting an Eskimo lover at "Frozen Tundra six, nine two nine oh."

At home now, preparing for a dinner date with Keaton (Roberts is again out of town on business), Allen imagines all his advances being misunderstood, with the cry of rape quickly dispatching this nightmare fantasy. Understandably sobered, he plays it very detached upon Keaton's real arrival. Allen's nanosecond of fear over things going romantically wrong is a tweaking of a comparable *Seven Year Itch* (1955) sequence in which Tom Ewell briefly gets nervous while planning a visit from Marilyn Monroe.

Bogart soon appears as sort of an on-the-job date counselor. It will represent his longest scene thus far in the film, as well as his funniest. Allen, like Buster Keaton in *Sherlock Jr.* (1924), effectively uses this example of a "real" screen lover to guide his own love life. And once again the mise-en-scène of Allen's apartment enhances the effectiveness and believability of Bogart stepping out of the shadows to coach Allen. That is, the Bogart posters seem to turn up in every shot, and bits of room décor ape the Moroccan set design of the original *Casablanca,* from a beaded curtain entrance in the kitchen, to the living room's rattan chair and shutters. But just as Allen is about to become Bogart's "A" student, the ex-wife appears and guns the teacher down. Needless to say this is a bit disconcerting to Allen, especially since the fantasy assassination takes place right over the living room couch on which he is courting Keaton. However, Bogart's pointers are not wasted, because everything comes to pass; thus, a long take of one very passionate Allen-Keaton kiss is intercut (once again courtesy of Allen's imagination) with a similar Bogart-Bergman kiss from *Casablanca.*

The next scene finds Allen and Keaton in bed the morning after, and though we seem to have returned to total reality (that is, if you can accept Allen in bed with anyone), the cue still seems to be taken from Bogart—a huge film poster of *Across the Pacific* appears over the bed, completely dominating the couple. In fact, this morning-after scene actually opens on a close-up of the poster, in which Bogart is "scoring" a one-two punch, as if suggesting a sexual pun on what has occurred the night before.

Allen and Keaton decide they have found something good and that Roberts must be told. Since Keaton insists she will tell him, Allen ends up with time alone to imagine how his best friend will respond. Thus, Allen's next three fantasies represent different possible reactions from the cuckolded husband. The first (number thirteen overall) is a monocle and pipe parody of two English gentlemen discussing things ever so rationally. Allen defuses any further possible hostility by giving Roberts a terminal disease anyway, and closes the scene with proper British civility—a toast and "cheers."

Cuckolded-husband fantasies two and three are both movie parodies, and do not run quite so pleasantly for interloper Allen. The first plays upon Allen's guilt and finds Roberts walking into the sea à la the first two versions of *A Star Is Born* (interestingly enough, director Allen will use the scene again, this time seriously, in his later *Interiors*, 1978). In *Play It Again, Sam*, however, even any lingering chance of melancholy is undercut by Roberts' parting soliloquy on the beach: "Why didn't I see it coming? Me, who had the foresight to buy Polaroid at eight and a half."

In the final fantasy of this trilogy it is Allen, however, who bites the dust. Passing a theater playing the often surreal Italian film *Le Coppie* (with a large display poster acting as a backdrop for the fantasy opening, and Woody thinking what an Italian would do?), Allen imagines Roberts as humiliated, hot-tempered and out for revenge. The knife-wielding husband corners Allen, who is a most unlikely baker attempting to defend himself with some of the limpest dough ever to put in a movie appearance. The little baker never has a chance.

Allen, however, is suddenly and comically jarred back to reality when, outside his apartment, he runs into Roberts. Though Allen fears the worst, Roberts only senses trouble, but does not suspect his friend. He pours out his love for Keaton to Allen, and then leaves our comic anti-hero Romeo with even more guilt. Not surprisingly, Allen decides he cannot breakup the marriage. Thus, his number-one anxiety becomes how to let Keaton down easily; this will not be simple, since "I was incredible last night in bed. I never once had to sit up and consult the manual."

The next two fantasies occur as Allen rushes to the airport to tell Keaton he has reconsidered, while Keaton is rushing to the airport to tell Roberts she has reconsidered (Roberts of course, is just rushing .... off on more business). In the first fantasy Keaton takes Allen's decision poorly, and it quickly turns into a melodrama parody, with Keaton asking for a mysterious letter (*Casablanca's* letters of transit?), and then pulling a gun. The fantasy closes just in time as Allen screams, "Don't pull the trigger, I'm a bleeder."

This near miss then cuts directly to Allen's second fantasy on the ride to the airport—Bogart is his cab driver, ready to give him more pointers, as well as settle him down. Bogart actually stops the car and shows Allen how to break it off with a "dame" (appropriately, again played by a gun-toting Keaton). This, along with Bogart's praise of Allen's sacrifice "for a pal," prepares Allen for the big romantic finish with Keaton.

This final fantasy brings us full circle to the film's opening, only this time instead of cutting back and forth between fantasizing audience member Allen and the projected image of *Casablanca*, both the situation (romantic triangle preparing for airport farewell) and the mise-en-scène (incoming fog and the separate starting of the plane's propellers) *Play It Again, Sam* actually recreates *Casablanca*. Then when the plane is safely away, Bogart assumes the original Claude Rains role by joining Allen in his walk into the enveloping mist.

Unlike earlier fantasies, however, in which Allen blindly tried to ape the complete Bogart persona, the closing scene uses the Bogart legend as a point of reference to aid Allen in the final liberation and acceptance of his own identity. Bogart is not even giving him cues from the wings, as he did earlier in the apartment. And though Allen does restate part of Bogart's farewell speech from *Casablanca*, it is the act of a mature person merely using past experience, rather than the alienated incompetent in search of a style that opened the movie.

Allen's own character capsulizes it quite nicely when he says, "I guess the secret's not being you (Bogart); it's being me." Moreover, as if to keynote this, even Bogart and Allen break up their stroll at the close; after the former's "here's looking at *you*, kid," Allen walks off into the darkness of the night (and into his future?) alone, but not quite so lonely.

These then have been the eighteen fantasies in *Play It Again, Sam*. As the fellow anti-hero Walter Mitty, the fantasies have, at times, provided Allen with unique adventure (hobnobbing with Bogart) in what is normally a rather banal life. At the same time, as already noted, there have been balancing fantasy frustrations. Yet, the key difference between Allen's fantasy life and Mitty's lies not so much in the latter point (important as it is may be) but rather in the fact that Allen's comedy persona (unlike Thurber's) is allowed to take his fantasy beyond mere distraction, using it to learn both to be himself and to accept himself. (At the close of *Manhattan*, 1979, his girlfriend will echo that same message when she tells him, "You have to have a little faith in people.")

In achieving this level of maturity, the Allen film persona no doubt needed both poles of fantasy, from the confidence Bogart could provide, to the occasional fantasy frustration keeping his values in perspective—which eventually steered him away from being just a Bogart clone. This final maturation has become the norm for much of his later work, be it the eventual touching acceptance of Annie (Keaton) as friend instead of lover in *Annie*

Hall, the realization late in *Stardust Memories* (1980) that the real joys of life can be locked in the most simple moments, the message of *A Midsummer Night's Sex Comedy* (1982) to seize the opportunities of life, finding the capacity to forgive at the close of *Broadway Danny Rose* (1984), and the touchingly upbeat conclusion of *Hannah and Her Sisters* (1986), which celebrates the most fundamental element of comedy, rebirth via marriage and an approaching birth. None of these situations, of course, leave him with any real answers to a man's eternal questions (the same might be said of the Chaplin-like exit of Woody in *Play It Again, Sam*). However, they do leave his character in a much healthier state of mind for coping with the darker side of existence.

In terms of comedy theory, the dominant element in *Play It Again, Sam* is the fantasy identification with Bogart and a situation in which the viewer could comically relate to having a Bogey tutor. The actions of this film fall under what theorist Northrop Frye's *Anatomy of Criticism* calls the "drama of the green world," representing the ideal romance of another place, such as our imagination. More specifically this type of comedy:

> begins in a world represented as a normal world, moves into the green world, goes into a metamorphosis there in which the comic resolution is achieved, and returns to the normal world.

In *Play It Again, Sam*, Allen's character has moved from a frustrated normal existence to a fantasy "green world" apprenticeship with Bogart (certainly a key romantic ideal to anyone immersed in film culture). A metamorphosis takes place (Allen learns to accept himself), and he then returns to the normal world after Bogart has tendered to Allen something of a "graduation" toast by way of his "Here's looking at you, kid." Through this interaction with one of the legends of cinema history, director Allen has tapped a seemingly universal romantic fantasy among the viewing public.

Allen, moreover, accents the universality of the Bogart figure by the realistic manner in which this macho symbol appears and interacts with today's most prominent example of the comic anti-hero. There is nothing like the white ball of light that heralds the arrival of the good witch Glinda in *The Wizard of Oz* (1939), nor even the special glossy environment one associates with the goddess of death in *All That Jazz* (1979). No, Bogey just drops in at Allen's apartment, appears at your typical A & P, and turns up behind the wheel of a cab.

This "realistic" tone in the fantasy scenes is consistent with the majority of other such excursions in Woody Allen's films. It also might help explain the tendency for Allen's more exotic fantasies never to reach the final film print stage, from his playing a spider caught in Louise Lasser's "black widow" web shot for *Everything* ... to the giant chess game using real people shot for *Sleep*, with Allen appropriately playing a white pawn about to be sacrificed but not without comically keeping the bargaining argument: "Hey fellas, it's only a game. We'll all be together later in the box." (See Ralph Rosemblum and Robert Karen's *When the Shooting Stops ... the Cutting Begins*.)

The generally natural tone of these fantasies, particularly the Bogart scenes in question, might be best classed under what Siegfried Kracause's *Theory of Film* labels "fantasy established in terms of physical reality." That is, the plot of *Play It Again, Sam* takes:

> the existence of the supernatural [in this case Bogart] more or less for granted, its presence does not simply follow from these visuals ... the spectator must from the outset conceive of them as tokens of the supernatural.

Thus, even to relate to the fact that a fantasy is in progress whenever Bogart appears, one must already be a practicing member of the modern world's biggest fantasy club—the film going public. And by getting the joke (a mixture of Allen's inadequacies and

Bogart giving home lessons in self-assertiveness), we go a long way toward becoming a part of it—for who has not felt similar inadequacies, at least in comparison to our favorite cinema superhero be it Bogart or 007?

Allen shares his own best example of such a fantasy world (daydreams peopled with cinema heroes) in Lax's text:

> I remember [as a child] seeing *Tom, Dick and Harry* advertised and saying "I can't wait to see that." It was one of those things that became a part of my conscious, because I lived in the movies and identified with that.

His comedy persona in *Play It Again, Sam* actually restructures part of his life to use the "experience" of his film fantasy existence, slipping in and out of this nether world as someone else might do with an old pair of shoes. Interestingly, all this activity tends to flirt with the tongue-in-cheek message of Oscar Wilde's delightful "critical" essay, "The Decay of Lying" —"Paradox though it may seem … life imitates art far more than art imitates life." That is, by so immersing himself in Bogart (with posters, movies, books, other assorted memorabilia, and an almost total Bogart mind set), Allen's screen persona both consciously and subconsciously tries to imitate film art—namely, the world of Bogey. Allen stops trying to be Bogart only when he inadvertently achieves romantic success by simply being himself. His closing walk off symbolizes a literal as well as physical break with Bogart. His posture changes from trying to ape art to constructively applying it to a less-than-perfect lifestyle.

This "be yourself" lesson parallels the closing message of America's favorite fantasy, *The Wizard of Oz*; there too the viewer is reminded (by way of Dorothy's refrain—"There's no place like home") that individual happiness can only be found within oneself. For this same reason, Allen's *Purple Rose of Cairo* (1985) has the saddest of conclusions. Overworked Depression waitress Mia

Farrow does not live happily ever after with movie idol Jeff Daniels—who had literally stepped off the screen at her local theater. The heartbreaking close comes about because Farrow cannot move beyond the mere fantasy escape level of the movies, just as Daniel's AWOL screen shadow does not know how to act in real life. Fittingly, the film's last image of Farrow is alone again—at the movies.

Fantasy for the Allen comedy persona has a continuing duality that he struggles with in each film (will he use fantasy as mere escape, or as a step toward maturity?), and much of this article has examined the struggle in the light of an opening reference to Thurber's most celebrated short story—the escapist "Secret Life of Walter Mitty." To come full circle, however, an apt closing observation on this duality might best be drawn from Allen's own most celebrated print story, "The Kugelmass Episode," which won the O. Henry Award as best short story of 1977 (the same year *Annie Hall* won an Academy Award as best picture).

"The Kugelmass Episode," initially reminiscent of the Mitty story, examines the life of an unhappily married professor (Kugelmass) out to put some excitement back in his life, preferably on a sexual level. His adventure, or escape, will come in the form of a fantasy-like invention that can transport a subject into the world of the written word. For Kugelmass, this means an opportunity to date any woman from literature. Walter Mitty could not have gone for it any faster. Thus, Kugelmass ends up having an affair with Emma Bovary. However, there are complications when the invention breaks down, causing the frustrated professor no end of grief, mentally and financially. Therefore, when the crisis is over, he maturely swears off these fantasyland time trips, happy in the fact that at least his wife has not found out.

However, Kugelmass's maturity is short-lived, and he tries another "trip" (this time into sexy *Portnoy's Complaint*), but the fantasy quickly becomes an eternal comic nightmare. The machine shorts out and is destroyed, the operator-inventor dies of a heart attack on the spot, and the essay ends with poor Kugelmass, instead of finding himself projected into *Portnoy's Complaint*, turning up in:

an old textbook, *Remedial Spanish*,...running for his life over a barren, rocky terrain as the word tener ("to have") —a large and fairly irregular verb—raced after him on its spindly legs.

Quite clearly, Allen is warning us that total fantasy escape can be dangerous (as it is later in *Purple Rose*) if it is not directed toward the character growth of a *Play It Again, Sam*. Otherwise, we might end up like poor Kugelmass—forever running away.

(This essay was originally presented at *The Second International Conference on the Fantastic*, Florida Atlantic University, Boca Raton, March 18-21, 1981. It was later published in Ball State University's *FORUM*, Summer 1987, Wes D. Gehring Copyright.)

Works Cited

Allen, Woody. "The Kugelmass Episode." In *Side Effects*. New York: Random House, 1980.

Brosnan, John. *Future Tense: The Cinema of Science Fiction*. New York: St. Martin's Press, 1978.

Frye, Northrop. *Anatomy of Criticism*. 1957. Princeton, New Jersey: Princeton University Press, 1973.

Jacobs, Diane. *But We Need the Eggs: The Magic of Woody Allen*. New York: St. Martin's Press, 1982.

Kracauer, Siegfried. *Theory of Film: The Redemption of Physical Reality*. New York: Oxford University Press, 1960.

Lax, Eric. *On Being Funny: Woody Allen and Comedy*. New York: Manor Books, 1975.

Rosemblum, Ralph, and Robert Karen. *When the Shooting Stops… the Cutting Begins: A Film Editor's Story*. New York: Penguin, 1979.

Thurber, James. "The Secret Life of Walter Mitty." In *The Thurber Carnival*. New York: Harper and Brothers, 1945.

Wilde, Oscar. "The Decay of Living." In *Critical Theory Since Plato*. Ed. Hazard Adams. Chicago: Harcourt Brace Jovanovich, 1971.

Yacowar, Maurice. *Loser Take All: The Comic Art of Woody Allen*. New York: Frederick Ungar, 1979.

THE BEATLES': *GET BACK*

"A Documentary About a Documentary"

The Beatles in a *Hard Days Night* (1964), left to right: Paul McCartney, George Harrison, Ringo Starr, and John Lennon.

The Beatles: Get Back (2021) is a documentary miniseries directed by Peter *Lord of the Rings* Jackson, with a running time approaching eight hours. It was originally released in three installments on Disney + in late 2021, with the much shorter "Rooftop Concert" edition given a limited IMAX theatre release in January 2022. Disney then began streaming it in February 2022. However, after a major delay, it only became generally available as a DVD in mid-July 2022.

Jackson has called it "a documentary about a documentary," because he constructed it from 60-plus hours of footage shot by filmmaker/artist Michael Lindsay-Hogg for his own 1970 documentary of the same name. The former film ran well under two hours and has been unavailable for decades. Each document three early 1969 weeks of Beatles studio sessions towards producing the album *Let It Be* (which had the working title *Get Back*). The *Let It Be* album's delayed release did not occur until May 1970, almost a month after the group's break-up.

The Beatles write and rehearse 14 songs while planning for their first live performance in years during this recording session. The ideas for the live event topper to their work is progressively scaled back. What starts as a quasi-epic showcase in sone ancient ruins outside England eventually becomes the modest but unforgettable London rooftop concert above their studio. The catalyst for revisiting this production, beyond all things Beatles being of interest, was to challenge the longtime belief that the original documentary was badly marred by the tension between the Beatles. The first documentary came to be seen as more the chronicling of a band going south than the creation of an album. So how does Jackson's miniseries compare?

First, I would concur overall with the almost universal critical praise given the miniseries. (Full disclosure — I am a major Beatles fan.) *However*, some important points are missed and/or marginalized in coverage of Jackson's *Get Back*. Most importantly, it still plays like a band breaking up. It's extreme length simply makes Paul McCartney come across as less of a taskmaster. To Jackson's credit he keeps the most painful sequence from Lindsay-Hoggs' picture, in which Paul repeatedly corrects George on how he wants a musical sequence played. The broken George is reduced to saying, "I will play it this way or that way or however you want." Nonetheless, George briefly quits the band, and must be implored (unfilmed) back.

While John Lennon was the founder and leader of the Beatles, by this point (1969) Paul had become the group's driving force for some time. For example, *Sgt. Pepper's Lonely Hearts Club Band* (1967), which was masterminded by Paul, is still seen by many as the most important album of all-time. The other Beatles were now either not as motivated, or in George's case, equally anxious to get some recognition for reaching the Lennon-McCartney song writing gold standard. (Harrison's "Something" is now the second most covered Beatles song, after McCartney's "Yesterday.")

Also, keep in mind the Beatles did essentially breakup in 1969, though the official dissolution is dated April 1970. Jackson's long take on "the end" does a great deal to soften it, given that there is also much joy shared in these sessions, yet there are also numerous other fissures revealed. To illustrate, periodically a seemingly biting-his-tongue Paul will mumble a mantra which might come down to "We need direction."

Second, while the Beatles fan in me loves every moment, Jackson's largely warm and fuzzy revisionism runs long. We get it after four or five hours; the boys could still have fun in the studio. To justify the length, one needs another reason. The real sales pitch should be Jackson's chronicling of the ephemeral nature of creating art. Along those lines, it ranks with the Martin Scorsese portion of *New York Stories* (1989). To illustrate, at different points in Jackson's picture, Harrison is struggling to create "Something," which will eventually end-up on the Beatles' *Abbey Road* album (September 1969). A nurturing Lennon sympathetically explains to George a variation on *the* basic writing symposium suggestion — "just get black on white as quickly as possible." One can sort everything out on the second pass.

Third, the added length actually brings one full circle back to the 1960s documentary movement "cinema verité" (observational direct cinema), the ever present camera steals a pure reality from subjects forgetting they are subjects. Yoko Ono has never come across so warmly, as she interacts with the group, or Paul's soon to be bride, photographer Linda Eastman. Paul as a loving father figure is entertainingly on display as he plays with Linda's six-year-old daughter, Heather. Indeed, Heather steals all her scenes, especially an affectionate impersonation of Yoko.

Sometimes, these direct cinema riffs leave one bowled over with questions, such as the Beatles at one moment warming up to the "Harry Lime Theme" song from *The Third Man* (1949), considered by the British Film Institute (BFI) as the country's greatest film. Fittingly, given it is a thriller starring Orson Welles, the Beatles' loosening up stops with a shock when George's mike shorts out.

Regardless, playing on an old actor's axiom, when a performer forgets his lines, it's called "going up the elevator." Jackson's film will keep you well-grounded.

(Reprinted with permission from *USA Today Magazine*, September, 2022. Copyright © 2022 by "The Society for the Advance of Education, Inc. All Rights Reserved.")

PART TWO:

LITERATURE & FILM

Ring Lardner *Pounding* the Kaiser for a Homer.

[Adapted from the author's award-winning book
*MR. DEEDS GOES TO YANKEE STADIUM:
Baseball Films in the Capra Tradition*]

Celebrated film director Frank Capra (1897-1991) was a pivotal architect of the feel good movie genre known as populism, which cherishes *the people*, families, second chances, and traditional American icons like small town pastoral life and baseball. But populism's beginnings are tied to the birth of the United States and the country's seminal comedy type — the crackerbarrel hero, a father figure of benevolent *common sense*. (Yet, in the chaotic modern world the phrase is often a misnomer: "It should be called 'rare sense.'") Regardless, the crackerbarrel populist lives in a methodical, one-thing-at-a-time linear world where conflict will eventually be worked out, because life is still perceived to be rational. This old-fashioned American mindset is equally applicable to baseball. As political columnist and baseball author George Will has noted:

> Baseball suits the character of this democratic nation. Democracy is government by persuasion. That means it requires patience. That means it involves a lot of compromise.... Baseball is the game of the long season, where small incremental differences decide who wins and who loses....

More recently, baseball historian Michael Shapiro has said that the "long season" is central to understanding why baseball (as compared to other sports) is more integral to the fabric of American-life: "Almost every day brings another game for the home team, week after week, month after month, all with the power to approximate painlessly the sensation of life—anticipation, joy, sadness, uncertainty."

This pervasiveness was undoubtedly a factor in why references to baseball turn up so frequently in the writing of Will Rogers (1879-1935), the most celebrated of the crackerbarrel populists. His multi-faceted persona (encompassing books and syndicated daily columnist as well as star of stage, screen, and radio) made him the genre's most beloved single character and a leading influence on Capra. After Rogers' untimely death, Capra began to focus on his own unique blend of populism—interweaving traditional values of the genre with a younger, more vulnerable hero, starting with *Mr. Deeds Goes to Town* (1936). The resulting phenomenon, *Caspraesque populism*, has had an ongoing and unique impact upon both American pop culture in general, and a smaller but no less important variety of baseball movie, such as the director's own *Meet John Doe* (1941), with Gary Cooper as a washed-up pitcher ultimately fighting fascism.

Be that as it may, Rogers merits a brief pause, as a populist most taken with baseball, as well as an articulate spokesperson. For instance, at the heart of populism is the belief in the underdog common man (symbolic of *the people*). Thus, during the 1929 World Series, Will Rogers observed in his syndicated daily newspaper column that "twenty million baseball fans ... still don't know whether Harvard is a town or a mouthwash [and], whether Yale is a yell or a lock.... So viva baseball. It's for us unfortunate ones who have no alumni." Populism is also about equality, granting no one special privileges. Consequently, in another 1929 column, Rogers kidded football's tendencies along these lines, in contrast to baseball's egalitarian set lineup: "Imagine baseball if every time you wanted a hit you could send in [Babe] Ruth. Every time you wanted a fly ball caught you could send in [Tris] Speaker.... Football don't need referees, they need United States census takers."

One could further embellish baseball's egalitarian nature by discussing what former Negro League All-Star Buck O'Neil called "that wonderful competition" of the batter versus the pitcher. Unlike football, where a halfback has blockers, or basketball, where an outside shooter expects a screen from a teammate, a baseball hitter faces the pitcher all alone. Not surprisingly, baseball is a more humbling, everyman sport. Even a great hitter batting .300 fails seven out of ten trips to the plate. In comparison, a gifted basketball player is expected to make at least half of his shots, while a star running back had best average five yards a carry — halfway to the first down. And, of course, baseball is the only major sport with complete *freedom* from the clock. As long as outs are avoided, a team is never handicapped or arbitrarily stopped by time running out. As former Baltimore Orioles manager Earl Weaver once observed, "You can't run a few plays into the line and kill the clock [as in football]. This is why this [baseball] is the greatest game of them all. You've got to give the other man his time at bat." Today one might add professional baseball, in marked contrast to football and basketball, is still largely populated by average-sized players — yet another variation on the game's egalitarian nature.

Both American populism and baseball share another date – the 1830s. Democracy's first popularly–priced penny newspaper and the serious study of crackerbarrel populist often begins with humorist Seba Smith's 1830s newspaper chronicling of the lanky New Englander Jack Downing. Plus, baseball legend credits the game's official beginning as the 1839 brainchild of American patriot Abner Doubleday.

Purists, however, have every right to quibble with this 1839 birthdate. Earlier precedents exist for both phenomena. For example, Robert Thomas' 18th century *Old Farmer's Almanac* is almost a paint-by-number homage to what we now know as populism, and Washington's troops were said to have played an early form of baseball at Valley Forge. In truth, baseball evolved over a long period, with probably no connection to Abner Doubleday. However, since codification often represents merely documenting what has evolved for an unspecified time, the year 1839 might just have some credence after all.

Regardless, this is the time when *the* American populist poet Walt Whitman (1819-1892) first embraced the sport as a participant and ultimately came to see baseball as personifying America. By the 1840s he was the editor and chief baseball reporter for the *Brooklyn Daily Eagle* – one of those popularly-priced people papers. Appropriately, Whitman went on to cite the game in his acclaimed *Leaves of Grass* (1855), when he noted several patently *American* activities – "enjoying pic-nics or jigs or a good game of base-ball...." Moreover, baseball peppers his prose. Indeed, Susan Sarandon's character even quotes him in the classic *Bull Durham* (1988), "Walt Whitman once said, 'I see great things in baseball. It's our game, the American game. It will repair our losses and be a blessing to us."

If American poetry begins with Whitman, Ernest Hemingway claims American prose starts with Mark Twain. Once again, Twain is a seminal writer with baseball on his mind. I am reminded of the central character of Twain's most provocative excursion into populism – the 1889 novel *A Connecticut Yankee in King Arthur's Court*. Twain quite literally transports his title character back to the Middle Ages and the Court of King Arthur. Of course, Twain's comic take on *diamond* diplomacy was often broader. For example, his baseball participants insisted on wearing their suits of armor. Thus, "when a man was running, and threw himself on his stomach to slide to his base, it was like an iron-clad [ship] coming into port." Still, Twain used baseball language in more serious moments of *A Connecticut Yankee* to underline the populist natures of the title character. For instance, the Yankee encouraged vigilance by saying a person should be forever "on deck." (Fittingly, Will Rogers would also play the Yankee in a 1931 adaptation of Twain's novel.)

Populism forever suggest baseball is the most American of enterprises, something Whitman noted in verse prior to the Civil War. However, probably the most famous nineteenth century linkage of the sport to literature, and populism occurred in a comically patriotic speech given by Mark Twain at a Delmonico dinner in New

York City on April 8, 1889. The banquet honored the return of Albert G. Spalding's baseball all-stars from an around-the-world tour to promote the sport. Several hundred were in attendance, including future president Theodore Roosevelt and comic De Wolf Hopper (already known as the voice of Ernest Lawrence Thayer's "Casey at the Bat"). Twain enthusiastically honored this new American export of baseball, which he likened to the country's late nineteenth century ambition: "[Baseball] is the very symbol, the outward and visible expression of the drive, and push, and rush and struggle of the ... booming nineteenth century!" Like Whitman, Twain thought of both America and baseball as untamed yet ingeniously improvisational (the proverbial "Yankee ingenuity"), and hell-bent on a progressive tomorrow. Regardless, Twain's over-the-top performance was also of a nature to suggest that a good share of the globe was mere backwater compared to baseball-loving America.

Of course, in mentioning Hemingway, one cannot help but think of arguably his most signature work, *The Old Man and the Sea* (1952). His title Cuban fisherman is painted with the brush strokes of a populist, à la Yankee baseball star Joe DiMaggio, "I must have confidence worthy of the great DiMaggio who does all things perfectly even with the pain of the bone spur in his heel." Conversely, when the literary giant F. Scott Fitzgerald wanted a catalyst for catastrophe (the decadent 1920s) in his watershed novel *The Great Gatsby*, what better blasphemy to tap into than cheating at the national pastime. Fitzgerald immediately turned to the Black Sox scandal of 1919: "It never occurred to me that one man [gambler] could start to play with the faith of fifty million ...." As Barbara Hershey's femme fatale convincingly suggests in the screen adaptation of *The Natural* (1984), if ancient Greece's legendary poet Homer were then alive (1920s) he would have written about baseball, since his subject matter consisted of "heroes and gods."

As it was, more modern literary lights from outside America immediately recognized the correlation between the country and heroic baseball, too. For example, of all the prominent people introduced to George Bernard Shaw (1856-1950) during a late 1890s visit to the United States, the celebrated Irish dramatist felt that the fiery third baseman for the Baltimore Orioles, John McGraw (later famous as the longtime manager for the New York Giants), was the "one true American" he encountered.

English stream-of-consciousness novelist Virginia Woolf (1882-1941) was fascinated by the early baseball stories of reporter and humorist Ring Lardner (1885-1933), feeling that this sport was especially suited for artistically channeling the American experience:

> It is no coincidence that the best of Mr. Lardner's stories about [baseball] games, for one may guess that Mr. Lardner's interest in games has solved one of the most difficult problems of the American writer; it has given him a clue, a center, a meeting place for the diverse activities of people.

Comically, Lardner's son John later expressed amazement over Woolf's ability to make this pivotal connection between American letters and baseball, given that the novelist "didn't know an infielder from a fungo bat." (Fittingly, with the country's involvement in World War I, Ring Lardner would further intertwine baseball and America for patriotic purposes – he sent his fictional ballplayer, Jack, off to fight in the popular humor book *Treat 'Em Rough: Letters from Jack the Kaiser Killer*. The darkly comic cover for the text even featured the title character in uniform batting a baseball-sized head of the Kaiser!)

Lardner's inspired ear for colloquial language was what had really attracted Woolf, as well it should, since it was liberally peppered with baseball terms ripe for metaphorical application. This vernacular was one of the things which attracted Frank Capra to the baseball-obsessed Will Rogers, what the director called a "democratic working language." Consequently, Capra's *Meet John Doe* is long on basic baseball phrases which double as populist calls to action, such as "We've all got to get in there and pitch," or "Don't wait until the game is called on account of darkness." Indeed, as a college student I remember being impressed that the pervasiveness of American baseball jargon even included the mindset of my favorite "tough guy fiction" author Raymond Chandler (of Philip Marlowe fame), who likened writing to being a populist pitcher:

The champ may have lost his stuff temporarily or permanently, he can't be sure. But when he can no longer throw his hard high one, he throws his heart instead. He throws something. He just doesn't walk off the mound and weep.

Maybe the hard news of approaching wars, or Chandler's film noir writing in general makes populist baseball all the more attractive to both crackerbarrel figures (like Rogers) and the public in general. As contemporary sports columnist Sandy Grady observed, "No matter how tough life may be ... [baseball] gives a fan a separate universe of heroics and drama ... it's like being engrossed in a season-long movie ... with the World Series as the last chapter; it may be fiction, but you gotta believe it matters." This is the same spirit filmmaker Ken Burns opens the fifth installment of his epic documentary *Baseball* (1994) with — New York governor Mario Cuomo observing, "You need all nine people [players] to work ... giving yourself up for the good of the whole [team]." Cuomo even makes the Christian caretaker connection Capra found so important to populism. He said, "I love the idea of the bunt, the sacrifice ... that's Jeremiah. The *Bible* tried to do that and didn't teach you. Baseball did."

Comically, Ken Burns makes another strong link between baseball as America in the opening of the fourth installment of *Baseball*; sportscaster and baseball author Bob Costas relates a famous crackerbarrel yarn about an escalating argument between an American and an Englishman on a subject unrelated to baseball. Ultimately, their differences turn ugly, and the exasperated American blurts out, "Screw the King!" Not to be outdone, the

Englishman thinks a moment, and then retaliates by saying, "Screw Babe Ruth!" In contrast to English royalty, the most universally *American* target the Englishman could think of was a ballplayer. As Barbara Stanwyck's character observes in Capra's *Meet John Doe*, "... a baseball player—what could be more American?"

Of all the writers so far quoted on the populist spirit of baseball, George Will holds the distinction of providing me with the two most decidedly different, but much appreciated perspectives on the game. The first comes in the form of a comic jab at baseball's current greatest usurper, "Football combines the two most worst features of modern American life – it's violence punctuated by committee meetings." The second is the seriously insightful observation that acknowledges the diversity that is supposed to be at the heart of American populism. Will places Jackie Robinson a close second to Martin Luther King Jr., as the "most important black person in American history." In fact, Will credits Robinson's integration of major league baseball as "not just one of the great achievements in the annals of sports, but one of the great achievements of the human drama anytime."

Author Gerald Early adds, "You can almost divide American history in the twentieth century [as] before Robinson and after Robinson. America was defined by baseball; this was our national game. So the drama of the moment was enormous." Coupled with this event, one must close with at least a portion of James Earl Jones' nearly closing speech from *Field of Dreams* (1989, the most populist of titles):

People will come Ray [Kevin Costner]. The one constant through all the years Ray, has been baseball. America has rolled by like on army of streamrollers. It's been erased like a blackboard, rebuilt and erased again. But baseball has marked this time. This field, this game, is a part of our past, Ray. It reminds of all that was once was, and that could be again. Oh people will come, Ray. People will most definitely come.

For fans of American populist baseball, these diamonds in the dark are like going home, too.

For as Robert Frost once said, "Some baseball is the fate of us all."

(Reprinted with permission from *USA Today Magazine*, March 2020. Copyright © 2020 by "The Society for the Advancement of Education, Inc. All Rights Reserved.")

CAPRAESQUE CURTIS

Upgrading Two Countries

Frank Capra flanked by Jean Arthur and Gary Cooper on the *Mr. Deeds Goes to Town* set.

One of my favorite movies last year was the Richard Curtis-scripted *Yesterday* (2019, directed by Danny Boyle). I should now say "spoiler alert." However, if a year has passed without you seeing it I ignore my conscience. Himesh Patel plays a struggling contemporary musician, Jack Malik, involved in a biking accident during a storm-producing power surge. After a brief hospital stay he slowly realizes no one in the world seems to have heard of the Beatles. Needless to say, the "Fab Four" jump start his music career.

Before long, he is the opening act for the ever-so-thoughtful contemporary (in real life Beatles influenced) British music star Ed Sheeran (as himself), and Jack is off to world fame and growing guilt over being credited for his songwriting magic. Plus, he ever so much misses his childhood friend and former manager Ellie (Lily James), who graciously steps aside as fame drags him off to Hollywood. Only then does it come out that she has always loved him, and he finally realizes that he feels the same way about her. *Yesterday* indeed.

Of course, what would a Curtis script be without love? This is the writer who brought us such films as *Four Weddings and a Funeral* (1994, the top grossing picture in British history up until that time), *Notting Hill* (1999, in which Curtis uses his personal London locale to out-gross *Four Weddings*), and a Christmas staple in my home, *Love Actually* (2003, also his directing debut).

Besides love, and the ever presence of at least a Beatle reference, there is a very high degree of civility in these films. A *New York Times* Curtis article (November 2, 2003) described the writer's world as a "rosy-eyed version of a loved up England." These components drive this normally cynical critic to Curtis films. Of course, if truth be told, we are both aging Baby boomers, and I must confess the Beatles and all things British once drew me to a college backpacking trip around England.

Yes, all this sounds rather corny which brings one to the essay's Frank "Capra-corn" connection with Curtis. The tie-in for me is a personal extrapolation of a comment made by the "Father" of

American independent filmmaking, John Cassavetes (1929-1989): "Maybe there really wasn't an America. Maybe it was only Frank Capra." If a viewer only superficially knows Cassavetes' work, such as *Faces* (1968), about a marriage coming apart, or *A Woman Under the Influence* (1974), in which Gena Rowland's good mother and wife is gradually cracking up, one might think this iconic filmmaker was being sarcastic about Capra. However, he really identified with Capra's idealistic cinema of hope, and felt he was the greatest director ever.

In the 1930s, the Motion Picture Academy of Arts of Sciences would seem to have also bought into Cassavetes' view of Capra films like *It Happened One Night* (1934, arguably Hollywood's most romantic title), *Mr. Deeds Goes to Town* (1936), *You Can't Take It With You* (1938), and *Mr. Smith Goes to Washington* (1939), which were all huge critical and commercial hits. Plus, the first three brought Capra Best Director Oscars. Moreover, *One Night* was the first of still only three pictures to win the five main Academy Awards: Best Picture, Director, Screenwriter, Leading Actor, and Actress. (It has since been joined by *One Flew Over the Cuckoo's Nest*, 1975, and *The Silence of the Lambs*, 1991.) With this Capra-Curtis-Cassavetes connection in mind, one might arguably scramble Cassavetes' claim to say, "Maybe there really wasn't an England. Maybe it was only Richard Curtis."

I do not own a working crystal ball. However, I am a great believer that life is a giant puzzle which you will never live to complete ... yet it behooves you to give it a shot. The effort helps one to better understand oneself and others. Think of art as "Hello, diversity." It is always time for everyone to find a universal right. Because if you have noticed, life seems to have once again lost its guard rails. How does this all tie in with Capra and Curtis? At different difficult points in history, both filmmakers have provided fleeting formulas on people getting along with each other.

The Capra and Curtis movie milieu has successfully provided examples of another movie which did not quite live up to its title

– *Play It Forward* (2000). You are what you do every day. It is a line I use when doing writing workshops. If you want to be an author, you write every day. This ancient eclectic axiom has recently been codified as the "10,000 Hour Rule," the time it takes to master a skill, which should include civility and love – like *Yesterday*'s Jack and Ellie growing up together. However, at times it does not seem the world has 10,000 hours left. Yet, it could begin with civility, and yes, love. Thus, how about taking some Capra and Curtis cues and maybe even beating that time requirement?

Now before readers think I am recommending flirting with diabetes, let me at least provide some backgrounds about the heydays of Capra and Curtis, not to mention the Beatles. Indeed, since the essay begins with "Yesterday," why not start with the Beatles song from which the title is taken. It is the most covered (recorded by others) number in music history. What does it deal with? Pain – a love that has suddenly gone away.

Moreover, even the Beatles' "All You Need Is Love" was composed at the request of the BBC to be part of the "first live global television link ... broadcast to 26 countries ... when the war in Vietnam [had] reached its height ...." (*A Hard Day's Write*, 1994). Written by John Lennon, the most cynical of the Beatles, he never shied away from creating artistic propaganda. The group's perspective anticipates the opening Hugh Grant voiceover to *Love Actually*, which suggests that despite September 11th, "love is all around us," if we will only take the time to look. Movingly, *Love Actually* begins and ends with real people joyfully greeting loved ones upon arrival at London's Heathrow Airport. (Curtis got the idea from a lengthy delay at Los Angeles' LAX Airport.)

Be that as it may, the Beatles always tended to write the most honest and often painful love songs. For instance, my favorite example is George Harrison's composition, "Something," the second most covered Beatles song after *Yesterday. The* tellingly truthful lyric answers the question, "You ask me will my love grow?" with the most sincere, "I don't know. I don't know."

Appropriately, Curtis uses "Something" at a crucial point on the soundtrack of his *Yesterday* film, with an even more poignant rendition of the number in the picture's DVD "Bonus Features," inexplicably not making the final-cut.

However, let us pump the brakes and focus on Capra and Curtis. Capra's greatest creative years occurred during the great depression of the 1930s and in 1940s' shadow of World War II. Love provided hope and/or a distraction when the world had metaphorically jumped the tracks. Capra addressed everything from corrupt and/or questionable Wall Street tactics, to fraud in the United States Senate. Curtis was at his most consistent during the 1990s start of the Gulf War years, to the proliferation of global terrorism in the first decade of this century.

Fittingly, the breakout pictures for both Capra and Curtis were screwball comedies – the aforementioned *One Night* and *Four Weddings*. Screwball comedies are first cousins to romantic comedy, except the former enjoys spoofing the ephemeral "L" phenomenon until the conclusion. In fact, both films demonstrate a closing element to the genre – near film-ending wedding breakups with the wrong people. While the Capra-Curtis links will periodically provide a framework, from this point on the focus will be on the aforementioned Curtis pictures.

Four Weddings launched a frequent early star of Curtis pictures, Hugh Grant. Critic Roger Ebert would later link him to screwball's ultimate 1930s leading man: "He has that Cary Grantish ability to seem bemused by his own charm ...." (Universal Press Syndicate, November 7, 2003). This picture, as with several early Curtis outings, has Grant (as Charles) leading a diverse group of friends, including the gay couple Garreth and Matthew (Simon Callow and John Hannah), Grant's zany red-haired forever job-hunting flatmate Scarlet (Charlotte Coleman), and the ever so wealthy aristocratic brother and sister duo – the beautifully chilly Fiona (Kristin Scott Thomas) and the endearingly Charlie Brown-like Tom (James Fleet).

Curtis' actual catalyst for *Four Weddings* was attending too many such ceremonies and deciding to spoof them (à la screwball parodying love), with a funeral thrown in to underline he really did embrace romance. Thus, the movie is a series of weddings to which Grant's Charles and Scarlet are forever comically late, with this tight dissimilar group often having fun with Grant's many comically disastrous girlfriends.

As in many screwball comedies, *Four Weddings* leading lady, in this case American Andie MacDowell's Carrie, has a stalking-like quality, such as Katharine Hepburn's response to Cary Grant in *Bringing Up Baby* (1938). While it might not seem that intense, there she is at all the weddings, and forever gravitating towards Hugh Grant, both when she is engaged, and at her own ceremony. Also, since it is the 1990s, she gives herself sexually to Grant, even when she is otherwise spoken for. In fact, Carrie seems to enjoy torturing him, as Barbara Stanwyck does to the *The Lady Eve*'s (1941) Henry Fonda, by sharing the dozens of past men before him. However, Stanwyck is not serious; MacDowell is.

It should be noted that one component of Curtis' English coming off as more sensitive and/or thoughtful is when they are contrasted with such driven Americans, including Julia Roberts *in Notting Hill*, *Love Actually*'s Billy Bob Thornton, and Kate McKinnen (*Saturday Night Live*) in *Yesterday*. One is reminded of that Eddie Izzard comedy routine in which he [now she] plays a school counselor that tells each youngster with a high career goal, "To scale it back a bit; you're British."

Regardless, screwball leading men are invariably antiheroically sympathetic. Moreover, when one takes the stereotypical British male as a bit stiff at romance, Hugh Grant is the genre's perfect male, and Curtis' alter ego in so many of the writer's early films. Then, given that his diverse British group of tightly knit loyal friends are forever around him, it adds to their symbolic likability. For example, the ever so sweet and wealthy putz Tom comes up with a delaying tactic when Grant's Charles wants to get out of his own wedding, observing, "The great advantage of people thinking you're stupid is that people are less suspicious of you when you lie."

Moreover, previously, Charles and Tom discussed the state of marriage, with Hugh's character suggesting that a thunderbolt of love is just not going to hit these two single men. However, James Fleet's Tom goes poignant with Grant and says he never really expected a thunderbolt, but rather a nice person who could put up with him.

Curtis' characters are also so affable because he shares a wealth of wit with everyone, such as little Charlotte Coleman's wonderfully eccentric Scarlet. Named after *Gone With the Wind*'s central figure, she likes to introduce herself as "I'm Scarlet, like Scarlet [of *Wind*] but not as much trouble." Indeed, an additional pleasing element of Curtis' figures is that they frequently talk in a shorthand movie language. For instance, Callow's Garreth, who owns any scene he is in, accompanies the Grant group to Carrie's Scottish marriage services, and goes on and on about "It's a *Brigadoon* [ceremony]." Plus, Grant, who so loves Carrie, describes this particular wedding as having double the impact of the "Shower Sequence in *Psycho*."

This loving support society showcases an adult example of what one thinks s/he might have had in bygone school days. For instance, it never comes out until near the picture's close that lovely Kristin Scott Thomas has always loved Grant, but has never revealed it because of the gang's special spirit de corps. That is love squared in the most touching way.

In fact, this example anticipates *Love Actually*'s biracial wedding ceremony of Juliet (Keira Knightly) to Peter (Chiwetel Ejiofor), in which the reception is taped by his best friend/best man Mark (Andrew Lincoln). It is casually revealed that the couple believe Mark dislikes her. Later when she drops by his flat to request a look at the reception tapes he shot, since the official ones have turned out poorly, she discovers all Mark's footage are enchanting close-ups of her. He then exits awkwardly and suggests his coolish behavior was about "self-preservation." Later, on Christmas Eve, she answers the door to Mark and a boom box cover of holiday songs, as if he is a caroler. He then silently reveals, via a series of touching cue cards, with no thought of reciprocation, he loves her but is moving on.

Not to pinball back and forth through movies, but this silent wedding-related sequence takes one back to Hugh Grant's *Four Weddings* inability to marry a Carry substitute. When the minister states the traditional, "If there is any man here ... [with objections]," the groom's deaf brother David (David Bower) makes a pounding sound and has Grant translate his sibling's doubts. Again it is awkward but loving and demonstrates the range of Curtis' affectionate concerned collection of friends and family in which he surrounds his central antihero.

Such endearing groups are a given in Curtis' films, and both equal the hopeful love stories he writes, and are arguably the pivotal characteristic which elevate his "rosy-eyed version ... of England." Moreover, these devotedly fond friends and family cut across class, sexual preferences, physical handicaps, ethnic groups and any other foolish differences that cause pain in life's "cockeyed caravan."

In fact, a Curtis film would suggest that true love should be the hardest thing that life (such as it is) gives you to tackle. Plus, for every happy ending Curtis romance, there are the struggling ones, such as Emma Thompson's straying husband (Alan Rickman) in *Love Actually*. Moreover, if the Beatles are the go-to musical support group, Curtis might be said to also suggest bittersweet comforting music is all around us, too. For instance, Thompson movingly finds some solace in Joni Mitchell's "Both Sides Now," and wondering "if one ever really knows love." In addition, as already suggested, a credit must be given to all those friends catching us when we fall.

Thus, to come full circle back to this essay's *Yesterday* beginning (the fate of writing professors), what about the troubled biracial couple Jack and Ellie, teetering apart because of his guilty fame and fortune (the Beatles foundation), and outsider Ellie – the happy elementary education teacher? At this point Curtis again employs a Capra chord – a bit of a fantasy, à la *It's a Wonderful Life*. One needs help from another world.

To properly set this up, one must note that throughout Jack's Beatles-inspired touring, viewers are given ever so brief shots of a perplexed looking couple. Eventually they get an audience with him, via a toy "yellow submarine" calling card. It turns out the duo also remember the Beatles. But as Curtis Brits, the two *thank* Jack for what he has been doing. That is, neither one of them is musical, and they are just happy he has brought the songs back – because it is a better world with the Beatles. However, when Jack still expresses his guilt and confusion, the couple give him an address of a home at an exquisite sea side setting. The owner is an age-appropriate John Lennon (an uncredited Robert Carlyle). When an overjoyed to see him Jack asks if he has had a successful life, John replies it has been a happy one with his wife. John then suggests that Jack go to the one he loves and always tell the truth.

With this advice, Jack performs one last concert arranged by his label. He confesses his plagiarism to a most forgiving British crowd and simultaneously has his roadie funny friend Rocky (Joel Fry) upload the music for free to the internet. Next, he reconnects with Ellie. This then morphs into them having a family and Jack teaching youngsters music.

Fittingly, the movie ends with Jack and his students singing the Beatles' "OB-LA-DI OB-LA-DA," an expression from the Nigerian Yoruba tribe meaning, "Life goes on." Lovely. Nonetheless, audiences should not need artists like Curtis and Capra to remind us what should just be a "play nice" norm. However, until that happens, one must cherish this duo, who, to paraphrase Robert Frost, "act as our awakeners."

AFI & BFI's Greatest Western:

THE SEARCHERS...

And its Neglected Novelist:

Alan Le May

John Wayne flanked by real life son Patrick Wayne (right) and Ward Bond in *The Searchers* (1956).

In 2007 the American Film Institute (AFI) designated legendary director John Ford's (1894-1973) *The Searchers* the 12th greatest American film ever made. The following year the organization upped the ante by selecting it as the greatest Western. Both the British Film Institute (BFI) and France's arbitrator of all things cinema, the historically celebrated publication, *Cahiers du*

Cinéma, rank *The Searchers* as one of the 10 best films ever made. The Writers Guild of America ranks the Frank Nugent screenplay as among the top 101 scripts ever composed. And in 1989 the United States Library of Congress judged *The Searchers* "culturally, historically, or aesthetically significant" and designated for preservation in its *National Film Registry* ---- one of the first 25 so honored.

Though *The Searchers* was well-received in 1956, it was not then embraced as a groundbreaking picture. The story is that of a young frontier girl, Debbie Jorgenson (Lana Wood) abducted by Indians, and the almost six-year Homer-like odyssey made by her uncle Ethan Edwards (John Wayne) and a quasi-stepbrother Martin Pauley (Jeffrey Hunter) to find her. The girl's family had been brutally murdered by Comanches. For Edwards, the search becomes a possible killing mission, because by the time Debbie (now played by Lana's older sister Natalie Wood) has been found, she is married to Indian Chief Scar (Henry Brandon). Frontier racism equated her with thus having been contaminated by savages.

In the context of the time, post-Civil War 1868 America, *The Searchers*' quest of hatred can be off-putting, yet as Tag Gallagher 1985 *John Ford* biography notes, "Ethan's conflict mirrors ideally the racism of society." Plus, one must add, it also reflects its complexity, since Wayne's character ultimately embraces his niece. Moreover, art is not created in a vacuum, and the movie appeared a mere two years after the Supreme Court's Brown vs. Board of Education ruling desegregating schools. Add to that today's political climate, and the picture is arguably even more topical now.

What else is there about *The Searchers* which makes it such a pop culture phenomenon? At the time Natalie Wood was fresh from the unique counterculture *Rebel Without a Cause* (1955, starring James Dean), making her a perfect fit for an angst-ridden youth caught between two cultures. Add to this a wannabe Texas rock 'n roll musician, Buddy Holly, being so taken with Wayne's mantra from the film, "That'll Be the Day," that it inspires him to write and record his first hit single, also called "That'll Be the Day."

A few years later this now "rock" standard was one of the first songs the Beatles ever play in a studio setting to prove they might have a future in music. However, it gets even more amazing. Flash forward further and one discovers that *The Searchers* inspired two of cinema's seminal pictures, Martin Scorsese's *Taxi Driver* (1976) and George Lucas' *Star Wars* (1977), a movie franchise onto itself. There are still other pop culture connections, but one gets the idea. This is a movie, as Hollywood would say, "with legs."

So who is this Alan Le May (1899-1965)? He wrote the 1954 novel from which *The Searchers* is adapted. Moreover, this is not a case in which an extraordinary movie is made from a mediocre book, à la Orson Welles' *Touch of Evil* (1958), or Mike Nichols' *The Graduate* (1967). No, *The Searchers* merits a scenario in which one studies it like the director's adaptation of *Grapes of Wrath* (1940) ---- with Ford in one hand, and John Steinbeck in the other. One is not saying Le May is Steinbeck, but he blows Owen Wister's *The Virginian* (1903) out of the water, or should one say "off the prairie?" And Wister's novel has forever been noted as *the* first significant Western novel ---- a template for the genre.

With regard to *The Searchers*, Le May has not been completely neglected. Glenn Frankel's 2013 book *THE SEARCHERS: The Making of an American Legend* throws a few oats his way. However, in no way is the Indianapolis–born Le May's novel given credit for how closely Ford's film follows his narrative, the nuanced characters, the complexity of the racial situation, the large number of memorable quotes taken directly from the text, and the book's greater attention paid to both Native American details, and a more realistic ending. Indeed, the novel fills in specifics not in the film, which otherwise sometimes makes the movie feel it is peppered with "jump-cut" (missing transitions).

Fittingly, however, there are certain parallels between Le May and Ford, besides being approximately the same age. Both men drew upon family for their Western work. Le May's paternal grandparents had been Kansas homesteaders, while his maternal grandfather was a Civil War veteran. The future writer ate up their stories, learning that there was nothing romantic about the West, with men *and women* both having to persevere. Ford, though born in Maine the son of immigrants, strongly embraced America's Western legacy. He also had a loving but strong-willed mother, so both men populated their stories with hardy women. And when the future director's beloved older brother, Francis, left for Hollywood to make Westerns, he soon had a dedicated shadow. Plus, keep in mind, this was a time when many real cowboys were working in the early industry, including Western film adviser *Wyatt Earp*!

Both Le May and Ford also profited from a 1920s America obsessed with horse operas, even neglected sources like *The Ladies Home Journal*, often serialized Western novels. Thus, with both artists anchored in this genre, each was frequently singled out. For instance, Le May's first novel was called *Painted Ponies* (1926) and featured a central character appropriately nicknamed "Slide," since he went back and forth between cowboy and Cheyenne cultures. At the time it was considered a more liberal look at the West, as it portrayed an increased sensitivity between two cultures. Almost a decade later yet another Le May Western novel, *The Smokey Years* (1936), was praised as "a completely literate Western" by the *New York Herald Tribune*

Though most of Ford's silent Westerns are now lost, his much-praised epic *The Iron Horse* (1924), about Lincoln's dream of a transcontinental railroad, has survived. Moreover, like his Westerns with cowboy star Harry Carey (whose oldest son and wife both appear in *The Searchers*), this was also a significant realistic Ford learning experience. But his perspective on the depiction of Native Americans was an ongoing work in progress, responsive in some pictures, like *She Wore a Yellow Ribbon* (1949), then harsh in *Rio Grande* (1950). However, by the time of *Cheyenne Autumn* (1964), in which he metaphorically links America's treatment of Native

Americans to the Jewish Holocaust, Ford confessed in Peter Bogdanovich's 1968 *John Ford*:

> Let's face it, we've treated them [Native Americans] very badly ---- it's a blot on our shield; we've cheated and robbed, killed, murdered, massacred and everything else, but they kill one white man, and, God, outcome the troops.

In addition, Le May and Ford were hard working artists who always denied they were artists. Moreover, each one was also talented enough to work in other genres when the Western periodically went out of favor. And despite none of Ford's four directing Oscars (still a record) being for a Western, both men found their greatest success and happiness in the post-World War II resurgence of interest in horse operas. Indeed, Le May even worked in Hollywood for a time and directed one of his own sagebrush scripts.

Regardless, let's compare Le May's novel and Ford's adaptation. The tales are almost identical, except for the opening and closings ---- the two most difficult things in the storytelling process. Indeed, I tell my college students to not sweat story openings. By the time one has completed the creative process, no matter how detailed the yarn's outline, the artistic process has a mind of its own, and your opening will need a rewrite. The differences between the openings *and* the closings of both takes on *The Searchers* are star driven. Le May begins with the killer Indian raid in which Debbie is taken about to happen. Ford first introduces the viewer to her family, and more importantly, to the arrival of John Wayne's Ethan (Amos in the book). He has been gone since the Civil War. However, more importantly, film fans get to see their troubled hero immediately. No waiting.

A variation of the same cinema demand makes Ford's close, like his opening of *The Searchers*, the only real bookend difference between the two presentations. Otherwise, almost the exact templates of recovering Debbie unfold. That is, in Le May's close Pauley rescues the girl, and Ethan *dies*. But John Wayne does not die. Okay, we won't quibble. He died maybe four times in over 200-plus pictures. However, you get the idea. Ironically, Ethan's death in Le May's book creates a more redeeming, poignantly changed man than Wayne's random swooping up of Wood in the movie. Ford's film provides no reason on why Ethan does not kill her. In the book there is a delayed reaction in his grasping of a young girl, as if to imply his thought process just cannot kill her. But paradoxically, his moment of paused redemption allows the Indian girl he has mistaken for Debbie to shoot and kill him at point blank range.

The novel's conclusion is also realistic as a substantial societal bellwether. It ends with Pauley (who has often thought he might also have some Indian ancestry) and Debbie as outcasts from both cultures. Throughout the novel and film Pauley has had the most patient of love interests, Laurie Jorgenson (Vera Miles). In neither narrative account of *The Searchers* has she fully understood the unyielding search for Debbie. Her thought process, as with most of the settlers, is that after such a long time Debbie should be forgotten and/or killed.

However, in the film when the kidnapped girl is finally brought back to "civilization" (so called) by Nathan and Pauley, all is forgotten and/or forgiven. It is implied that Pauley and Laurie will marry and Debbie will be embraced by the white community. Only Nathan will continue to wander, the mythological cowboy whose search for Debbie was merely a variation on the fate of all Western loners ---- to forever wander, the essentially existentialistic figure.

In contrast, Le May's novel has Laurie giving up on waiting for Pauley before the close. Indeed, she marries someone she and her family had previously never admired. However, he was always available. Plus, the novel's closing rescue of Debbie finds her and Pauley in the middle of the wilderness, suggesting there will never be any kind of white homecoming.

Le May based this conclusion on a composite of several 19th century Indian kidnappings of white girls, including the famous pre-Civil War case of Cynthia Ann Parker. None of the reunifications worked. Consciously or not, it suggests the immediate period Jim Crow resistance to the Brown vs Board of Education case, a situation with which contemporary events suggest the country is still struggling. Hollywood happy endings are always to be questioned, though at least here Ford seemed to be nudging America towards a higher (though altered) ideal, both then, and by implication, in the 1950s.

However, when all is said and done how does Le May's novel compete with Ford's staggering big screen gift for showcasing the "canvas" of his signature Monument Valley, arguably Wayne's greatest performance, and the director's ability to mix broad humor into the most troubling of stories? First, Le May's writing is often more poetically true in its authenticity. Though Ford was increasingly sympathetic to Native American culture, he was not overly concerned with details. Le May was fascinatingly precise. For example, Le May anticipates the ironic metaphorical designation of the Native Americans in Arthur Penn's later *Little Big Man* (1970) as "Human Beings":

They never used the name "Comanche" among themselves. That name was like the word "squaw" ---- a sound some early white man thought he heard an Indian make once back in Massachusetts ... Comanches called themselves "Nemmenna," which meant "The People." Many tribes, such as the Navajo and Cheyenne, had names meaning the same thing.

At another point a saloon girl movingly describes Pauley with a snippet of some long forgotten Spanish song: "I see a stranger passing, his heart is dark with sorrows, another such as I am, behind him his tomorrows." Like all great writing it simultaneously feels distinctive yet universal. To illustrate, during Pauley's seemingly endless trek with Ethan he has nightmares about Debbie, which always ended with "the redness you see through your lids when you look at the sun with closed eyes." In comic contrast, after a long fist fight, Pauley's opponent went down "as if all strings were cut at once." Finally, when the young man goes into his first mounted conflict, Le May again shows a flair for compressed comedy, "all hell coming at him personally."

Le May also has the ability to capture a cowboy's philosophy in either lyrical rifts of fatalism ---- "Like most prairie men, they had great belief in their abilities but a total faith in their bad luck" ---- or an earthy crackerbarrel axiom for poker and battles, which could be paraphrased as, "What you want is a simple, stupid plan. The reason you hear about the old flim-flams so much is they work. Never try no deep, tricky plan. The other feller can't follow it; it throws him back on his common sense ---- which is the last thing you want."

However, the most remarkable thing about Le May's novel is that every *Searchers'* line worth noting in either a quote and/or a paraphrasing from the book. This needs to be underlined, because Ford was still a silent director at heart, and his motto might have been that of director Leo McCarey, "Do it visually." Thus, Ford told Bogdanovich, "There's no such thing as a good script really. Scripts are dialogue, and I don't like all that talk." That being said, this is not an admonishment of Ford. To paraphrase *New Yorker* critic Anthony Lane in a review (January 14, 2019) of another adapted film, "[To] pluck morsels of dialogue or narration from the [original] text and drop them, barely altered [if at all], into the film [is] a sensible procedure, not the least at those moments of intensity which pierce the placid surface of the action." Moreover, such skeleton keys to clarity could even be a starting point for an argument on the superiority of Le May's novel.

Regardless, the narrative power of Ford's film would have been greatly hamstrung without Le May's inspired lines. For example, here is Ethan on persistence: "An Indian will chase a thing until he thinks he's chased it enough. Then he quits. So the same when he runs ... He never learns there's such a thing as a critter that might just keep coming on." And the story ballast from the film's pivotal strong pioneer woman, Mrs. Jorgensen (Olive Carey), is all Le May: "A Texan is nothing but a human man way out on a limb. This year, and next year, and maybe for a hundred more. But I don't think it'll be forever. Someday this country will be a fine, good place to be. Maybe it needs our bones in the ground before that can come."

Moreover, while Ford is entertaining with slapstick humor, such as the fist fight between Pauley and Charlie McCorry (Ken Curtis) over Laurie, much of Ford's comedy comes from what I would call "sputtering threats." And again, it is all essentially Le May material. To illustrate, early in the film Ethan does not like how Pauley is addressing him: "Drop this 'uncle' foolishness ... You don't have to call me 'Sir,' neither. Nor 'Grampaw,' neither. Nor 'Methuselah,' neither. I can whup you to a frazzle."

No one is better at Ford's "sputtering threats" humor than a member of the director's ongoing cast of players ---- Ward Bond. In *The Searchers* Bond is both a minister and head of the local Texas Rangers, with *no* psychological angst clouding this contradictory combination. Regardless, before the story's final battle Bond's composite character does not seem to be getting through to his men on just how he wants things done. Again, Ford owes a thank you to Le May for easily the best of these "sputtering threats" from Bond: "Don't pay them Comanches no mind, neither ---- just keep your eyes on me. I'm the hard case you're up against around here ---- not them childish savages. If you don't hear me first time I holler, you better by God read my mind ---- I don't aim to raise no two hollers on any one subject on hand." (For a verbally pared-down script, the total number of Le May lines is astonishing.)

Ford's film would also have been more cohesive at times if he had included some brief Le May narrative links, as mentioned before, to help make sense of some plot points. (Maybe Ford needed just a little more dialogue then he would admit.) The best example of several Le May links involves Debbie secretly coming to her trackers twice near the close of both the novel and film, once "the searchers" have finally located her tribe. At the first brief visit she discourages them, parroting a combination of the Stockholm syndrome and a Cheyenne lie about how they really rescued her from another killer tribe.

However, the second time in the film she unconvincingly comes to Pauley and Nathan after she simply seems to have changed her mind. In contrast, during the first visit in the novel, Nathan tells her to look at the back side of a golden buckle owned by a member of her new "family," Scar. It had belonged to her murdered mother and has a scratched inscription on the back to prove it. Thus, she comes to them the second time in the novel because she has somehow managed to substantiate the comment and now has a troubled but eye-opening reason to leave.

All in all, the test of time, Ford's visual forte, the fact that film is now the new "literature" for the masses, would suggest that his adaptation is arguably the greater work of art. However, history has truly dealt the novelist an unfair hand in his seminal influence on this "greatest" of all Westerns. This artistic reconfiguration must be addressed. However, the recent over-the-top phenomenon of being PC about all art threatens the ongoing legacy of both dark versions of America in *The Searchers*, Ford's ending notwithstanding. Therefore, the problem merits a brief addendum.

So many classic works of art are now being downgraded or dumped by contemporary readers and viewers who have discovered controversial elements of sexism or racism in the lives and/or works of many major artists. While I in no way condone such "isms," especially as in this case pertaining to racism in *The Searchers*, a caveat merits noting. It is best described through a *New York Times* essay (January 13, 2019) by Brian Morton. His provocative wrinkle in time article addresses old classics via a time machine metaphor.

Morton reminds us that the viewer or reader is the time traveler. We are journeying into some artist's masterpiece world and "taking a look around." In our journey back into this generally momentous creation, once we have had all our shots and proper attire taken care of (hopefully one's luggage has not gone to another classic), we might find some opinions abhorrent. Yet, if it is truly a quintessential work, such as *The Searchers*, there will be much more to learn and savor. Despite the past master's blind spots to your now more elevated perspective, appreciate and enjoy how generally ahead of her or his time the virtuoso was.

Now let us flip the equation, suggests Morton, and you have created a magical work that makes a casual reference to your cell phone, or the inexpensive garments you are wearing. Are you not aware that the cobalt mineral dug for that phone, or the stitching in your clothing, was probably done by a child in a 12-hour shift in some crawl space of life location? Would not a future cultured time traveler be put off by a flippant disregard for global interconnectedness in this otherwise wonderful work you have created?

Regardless, *if* the past gem you are now reading or viewing is really inspired, despite some PC blind spots, their creators had the same agenda we have today ---- attempting in humanity's flawed ways to make the world better. Be that as it may, check out Le May's novel. It really deserves a second read, or more than likely, a first one.

(Currently awaiting publication in *TRACES of Indiana and Midwestern History*, after a series of unprecedented delays going back to the 2020 beginnings of Covid; Wes D. Gehring Copyright.)

THE COMIC ANTI-HERO IN AMERICAN FICTION:

Its First Full Articulation

Pivotal antiheroic writer Robert Benchley reading the magazine most responsible for its importance (1936).

The comic anti-hero, who tries to create order in a world where order is impossible, is the dominant type in American humor today. Terms associated with anti-hero frustrations have entered our vocabulary, from Joseph Heller's "Catch-22," from the book by the same name, to Kurt Vonnegut's "and so it goes," from *Slaughterhouse-Five*.

America's favorite cinema clown—Woody Allen—is based on the anti-hero mold, just as is America's favorite cartoon character—Charlie Brown. In today's American literature, the important comedy artists also draw equally from this mold, from Philip Roth and John Barth to the aforementioned Vonnegut and Heller. In fact, a Nobel Prize in literature has recently been given to one of the most distinguished creators of anti-heroes, Saul Bellow.

Credit for the full blossoming of the anti-hero in American humor is usually given to the early *New Yorker* magazine (1925-30s): "The magazine which was more responsible than any other medium for the rise of a new type of humor …"[1] More specifically, this meant four writers— Clarence Day, Robert Benchley, James Thurber, and S. D. Perelman. Walter Blair has noted:

> …though they did not entirely break with the past—no humorist is likely to do so —they wrote humor based upon assumptions quite different from those of older humorists and employed techniques contrasting with older techniques.[2]

The real significance of the *New Yorker* was that it allowed the American comic-hero to come to center stage. Though he was not new to American humor, few comedy figures ever are, he had generally played a secondary role (when he appeared at all) to the more capable figure of the 19th century American humor, such as the practical New England Yankee or the crafty frontiersman of the Southwest (both capable crackerbarrel figures). A sustained articulation of the contrast between the two types of heroes is to be found in the *Biglow Papers* of James Russell Lowell. These letters juxtapose Yankee Hosea Biglow against anti-heroic Birdofredum Sawin. The complete stupidity of Birdofredum underlines the capabilities of the Yankee Hosea Biglow.

It should also be noted that even the capable 19th century figure—the crackerbarrel type—could sometimes display anti-heroic characteristics. Norris Yates has labeled such case examples of the "wise fool":

> …the humorous writers frequently made the country-store philosopher expound unwelcome truths behind a protective mask of character deficiency or of linguistic, logical or factual error … Thus, Huck Finn notices that the hogs have the run of a certain country church, and he says, "Most folks don't go to church only when they've got to; but a hog is different."[3]

Secondary characters like Birdofredum Sawin or "wise fools," such as Huck Finn, mark 19th century predecessors for the 20th century anti-hero. However, these anti-hero ancestors existed in a comedy world still considered to be rational. Thus, the dominant comedy type continued to be capable, reasoning crackerbarrel philosopher. Yates implied just that when he noted that "… one important difference between them [the crackerbarrel philosopher] and the Little Man [the comic anti-hero] is that the latter is not certain of his identity."[4]

As American comedy tastes began to find an increased affinity with the anti-hero, early in the 20th century, the anti-hero as well as anti-heroic traits became more visible in our comedy culture, from the cartoon strips of George Herriman (*Krazy Kat*) and George McManus (*Bringing Up Father*) to vaudeville comics like Joe Cook and Ed Wynn. Yet it still remained for the aforementioned *New Yorker* writers to create the first full articulation of the anti-hero.

A close analysis of the *New Yorker* work reveals five distinctive characteristics of the comic anti-hero. Each characteristic also constitutes a break with what was then still the dominant character type in American humor—the capable figure. Particular attention will be paid to the work of Benchley and Thurber, because it best exemplified the anti-hero and because they were most productive during this period.

First, the comic anti-hero of these *New Yorker* writers generally tends to have time on his hands. The use made of this leisure time is probably most often associated with Thurber (thanks to his "The Secret Life of Walter Mitty") and his protagonist's fantasy daydreams of bravery and high adventure. It is the free time fate of this figure to be a "hero" only in dreams:

> … Captain Mitty stood up and strapped on his huge Webley-Vickers automatic. "It's forty kilometers through hell, sir." said the sergeant. Mitty finished one last brandy. "After all," he said softly, "what isn't?" The pounding of the cannon increased; there was the rat-tat-tatting of machine guns …
>
> Something struck his shoulder. "I've been looking all over this hotel for you," said Mrs. Mitty. "Why do you have to hide in this old chair?"[5]

Secondly, the *New Yorker* anti-hero virtually never seems to have the opportunity, or the inclination to foster an interest in politics. His is a non-political but frustrating domestic lie, occasionally punctured by an equally frustrating sortie to the store, or a small social gathering. These minor domestic chores must take first priority for him to maintain some hold on reality. This hold, which is slipshod at best, is put at a precarious imbalance by world events and political figures. Thus, when a comic anti-hero makes one of his very rare excursions into the political arena, reality begins to swirl down the drain. Benchley wrote:

> Mussolini seemed to be a good man to interview; so I got an interview with him. "Mr. Mussolini," I said, "as I understand your theory of government, while it is not without its Greek foundations, it dates even further back, in its essence to the Assyrian system."
>
> "What?" asked Mussolini.

"I said, as I understand your theory of government, while it is not without its Greek foundations, it dates even further back to the ancient Assyrian system. Am I right?"

"Assyrian here seen Kelly? K-E-double-L-Y.

That was a good song, too," said ll Duce.

"A good song is right," I replied. "And now might I ask, how did you come by that beard?"

"That is not a beard," replied the Great Man.

That is my forehead. I am smooth-shaven, as a matter of fact."

"So you are, so you are." I apologized. "I was forgetting."

We both sat silent for a while, thinking of the old days in SyracuseHigh.[6]

The third characteristic of the *New Yorker* comic anti-hero is constant frustration. Any attempt to lead a rational life is destined to fail; it is an irrational world for him, and any attempt to bring order to its results in total frustration. The frustrations themselves, however, can be lumped into two main danger areas.

Women represent the first category of these potentially severe frustration spots for the man. The secret to this female power can be found in Thurber's "Destructive Forces in Life."[7] Near the beginning of the story he pens a drawing of an unhappy man and a smiling wife, entitling it "A Mentally Disciplined Husband with Mentally Undisciplined Wife." This domestic mugshot leads to the sad story of one more frustrated male. But the key point is the conclusion of the tale: "… the undisciplined mind [that of the woman] runs far less chance of having its purposes thwarted, its plans distorted, its whole scheme and system wrenched out of line. The undisciplined mind, in short, is far better adapted to the confused world in which we live today than the streamlined mind [the disciplined mind—that of the man]. This is, I am afraid, no place for the streamlined mind."[8]

To have an "undisciplined mind" merely means that one can cope with life, make decisions, and proceed with living. This often invites eccentricity in the anti-hero woman. In a sense, this is a slick offensive maneuver—what better way is there to deal with an irrational world than by being irrational? Probably Thurber's best example of such a woman is his grandma:

> who ... lived the latter years of her life in the horrible suspicion that electricity was dripping invisibly all over the house. It leaked ... out of empty sockets if the wall switch had been left on. She would go around screwing in bulbs, and if they lighted up she would hastily and fearfully turn off the wall switch ... happy in the satisfaction that she had stopped not only a costly but a dangerous leak.[9]

But the point remains that, as eccentric as Grandma Thurber may be, she makes decisions and does things—and then gets on with living. Meanwhile, the male attempts to make sense of it (both women and the world) and goes near crazy in the process of trying. Moreover, one cannot proceed without understanding and since there is no understanding ...

Machinery represents the other category of these potentially severe frustration spots for the comic anti-hero—something Thurber captures quite nicely in a story whose title says it all: "The Car We Had to Push." Yet, for the best capsule definitive of the dangers of mechanization, one must turn to Perelman's attempt to put together a mothproof closet known as Jiffy-Cloz—"The shortest, cheapest method of inducing a nervous breakdown ever perfected."[10]

It should be kept in mind, moreover, that the frustrations of the anti-hero, be they precipitated by females, machines, or other irritants, are often seen in physical terms. As has been the case with earlier American schools of comedy, what is generally funny about the *New Yorker* anti-hero's predicament are descriptions of physical frustrations, frequently displayed through bodily discomfort. A glance at some typically anti-heroic titles underlines this: "The Dog that Bit People," "The Night the Bed Fell," "The Calf in the Closet," and "How to Break 90 in Croquet." Moreover, this visual sense is accented by the celebrated drawings of Thurber, the delightful caricatures by Gluyas Williams that grace the Benchley stories, and the cartoons of Day.

The fourth characteristic of the *New Yorker's* anti-hero is the fact that he is portrayed as a childlike figure. This is most effectively shown in eight stores comprising "Part One: Mr. and Mrs. Monroe" of Thurber's *The Owl in the Attic*—especially in "Mr. Monroe and the Moving Men." In this story, once the wife leaves, the husband is helpless. This helplessness occurs despite the fact that before she left "… little Mrs. Monroe had led her husband from room to room, pointing out what was to go into storage and what was to be sent to the summer place …"[11] But now, "little Mrs. Monroe was away, unavoidably away, terrifyingly away," and he cannot remember where things should go and what she said.[12] And he certainly has no ready answers for the moving men's questions. The names they use to address him progressively indicate a loss of respect for him, and range from "chief" and "mister," to "buddy" and "pardner," to the child nickname of "sonny." By the end of the story, he is reduced to tears.

The fifth and final characteristic is that the anti-hero is an urban dwelling animal. In fact, the *New Yorker* was founded literally as an attack against the old value system—as a "magazine which is not edited for the old lady in Dubuque … a magazine avowedly published for a large metropolitan audience …" Thus, the *New Yorker* focuses on the city. Yet, what is written about metropolitan living hardly constitutes a love letter.

The trials of city living are nicely sketched by Benchley. He has a poor sense of direction and the complex modern city only compounds this—in "Spying on the Vehicular Tunnel," he becomes lost on a walking tour of the Holland Tunnel.[13] When he attempts to leave the driving to someone else (especially on formal dress occasions) by taking a taxicab, he invariably enters a musty vehicle that more closely resembles "… the old sleigh which used to stand up in the attic at Grandpa's barn in Mulberry" than an automobile.[14] Moreover, there are so many people squeezed into the city that he must stand in long lines for everything. For Benchley, this is best exemplified by the post office —"It has been estimated that six-tenths of the population of the United States spend their entire lives standing in line in the post office."[15]

Ironically, despite the fact that the *New Yorker* anti-hero is based in the city, he is a loner, either playing by himself or hiding. The city is full of eccentric people and he wants to avoid them. Yet, despite the fact that he avoids them, and possibly *because* he avoids them, his behavior also takes on something of an eccentric nature. For Benchley's hero, this eccentricity might be diagnosed as seeing little animals, while Thurber's has a tendency to hide in boxes or let his mind wander a bit too far. Despite the fact that these visions become plausible when explained as merely momentary harmless regressions to childhood or as typical fleeting daydreams, they are dangerous if too much time is spent in these *nether* conditions, for they might lead the hero to be institutionalized. Thus, like Thurber's "A Unicorn in the Garden" (where a wife tries to get her husband committed for seeing this mythical animal, but is committed herself), the anti-hero must be careful to whom he relates these phobias.

These, then, are the five main characteristics of the *New Yorker* comic anti-hero. Though each one was not necessarily new to American humor, as a group they represented a distinct break with the more traditional (and capable) figure of American humor, such as the Yankee crackerbarrel philosopher. There is no easy explanation as to why the transition, from capable hero to incompetent, has taken place. Yet, if a consensus were necessary, it would no doubt focus on Wylie Sypher's statement: "The comic now is more relevant, or at least more accessible, than tragic."[16]

In a world that seems every day more irrational, the anti-hero is fated to be forever frustrated. He is frustrated because he tries to create order (as his 19th century comedy counterparts did) in a world where order is impossible. But the scope of today's crises goes beyond the common-sense platitudes of any updated crackerbarrel philosopher. The anti-hero is "… incapable of inventing homespun maxims about hundred-megaton bombs, or a feeling any native self-confidence in the face of uncontrollable fallout."[17] He eventually deals with this frightening outside world by not dealing with it at all. Instead, he focuses: "microscopically upon the individual unit … that interior reality—or hysteria … In consequence, modern humor deals significantly with frustrating trivia."[18] Thus, the non-political, domestically frustrated anti-hero comes to represent that old cartoon of the ostrich with his head in the sand. Initially the audience laughs at him (instead of with him, as was the case with the capable hero) both with a feeling of *superiority* and with *surprise* (that anyone could be so incompetent) —embracing two classic comedy axioms. Yet, at heart, it is an audience that is only too aware of the closeness, even parallels, existing between the anti-hero's frustrations and their own lives—frustrations that are often mere microcosms of greater fears.

Anti-heroes help us cope (through laughter) with this absurd modern world, where our only good defense seems to be a humor founded in absurdity.

(Originally appeared in Canada's *THALIA: Studies in Literary Humor*, University of Ottawa,
Volume II, No. 3 Winter 1979-1980; Wes D. Gehring Copyright.)

NOTES

1. Walter Blair, *Native American Humor* (1937); rpt. San Francisco: Chandler Publishing Company, Inc., 1969), p. 168. (In my Ph.D dissertation, "Leo McCarey and the Comic Anti-Hero in American Film," to be published by Arno Press in the Spring of 1980, I demonstrated that the developments at the *New Yorker* were paralleled in film by McCarey's teaming and molding of Laurel & Hardy.)

2. Ibid., p. 169. (The comic anti-hero was preceded in American humor by various self-sufficient figures, best exemplified by the capable Yankee. In reading this essay it should be kept in mind that a figure such as the Yankee could be characterized as having a profession, being political, knowing only success, being a wise adult, and living in the country.)

3. Norris Yates. *The American Humorist: Conscience of the Twentieth Century* (Ames, Iowa: Iowa State University Press, 1964), p. 22.

4. Ibid., p. 257.

5. James Thurber. "The Secret Life of Walter Mitty," in *The Thurbers Carnival* (New York: Harper & Brothers, 1945), p. 51.

6. Robert Benchley. "An Interview with Mussolini," in *The Early Worm* (1927; rpt. Garden City, New York: Blue Ribbon Books, 1946). p. 29.

7. James Thurber. "Destructive Forces in Life," in *Let Your Mind Alone* and *Other More or Less Inspirational Pieces* (1937, rpt. New York: The Universal Library, 1973). p. 12.

8. Ibid., p. 18.

9. James Thurber. "The Car We Had to Push," in *My Life and Hard Times* (1933; rpt. New York Bantam Books, 1947), p. 41.

10. S. J. Perelman, "Insert Flap 'A' and Throw Away," in *Crazy Like a Fox* (1944; rpt. New York: Vintage Books, 1973). p. 285.

11. James Thurber. "Mr. Monroe and the Moving Men," in *The Owl in the Attic* (1931; rpt. New York: Harper & Row, 1965), pp. 125-126.

12. Ibid., p. 125.

13. Robert Benchley, "Spying on the Vehicular Tunnel," in *The Early Worm* (1927; rpt. Garden City, New York: Blue Ribbon Books, 1946), pp. 241-245.

14. Robert Benchley, "Here You Are—Taxi!," in *No Poems: Or Around the World Backwards & Sideways* (New York: Harper & Brothers, 1932), p. 121.

15. Benchley, "Back in Line," in *No Poems: Or Around the World Backwards & Sideways*, p. 158.

16. Wylie Sypher, "The Meaning of Comedy," in *Comedy,* ed. Wylie Sypher (Garden City, New York: Doubleday Anchor, 1956), p. 201.

17. Hamlin Hill. "Modern American Humor: The Janus Laugh," *College English* (December 1963), p. 174.

18. Ibid.

THE MANY SIDES OF W. C. FIELDS:

A Comedian Dodging "The Man

In the Bright Nightgown [Death]"

W. C. Fields in huckster mode on the set of *Poppy* (1936).

THE COMIC ASIDES AND DOUBLE-TAKES of W.C. Fields always were a welcomed fifth-column attack on the pestilence of day-to-day living during the Depression years. His entertaining cynicism seems even more pertinent today. In fascinating fashion Fields vacillated between two screen personas—the huckster and the henpecked husband.

Fields' trickster is in the literary tradition of the late 19th century, America's golden age of the confidence man. Like the classic pioneering diddlers who put a creative spin on Yankee ingenuity, the Fields manipulator kept on the move. The *London Times* said of his 1936 *Poppy* characterization: "Like all great showmen, he knows … the moment when the prudent man stops talking and makes hurriedly for open country—preferably on his accuser's horse." Movement protected his sneaky character from the law, creditors, and suckers who had wised up to the comedian's imaginative gambling skills. Being forever on the road offered opportunity as well as escape. As humorist Johnson J. Hooper has his notable huckster Simon Suggs observe, "It is good to be shifty in a new country." Like Suggs' old Southwest diddler, Fields' con artist engaged in small-time operations that did little, if any harm.

Huckster Fields could use either flowerily language, or the slight of hand for a funny fleecing. For example, he manages the outrageous verbal con of selling a "talking" dog at the opening of the sound film *Poppy* adaptation. And then he covers his tracks by telling the buyer the dog might now hold a grudge and never talk again. However, his typical scams remained in the world of everyday reality, such as the visual shell game featured so prominently in the silent version of *Poppy*—*Sally of the Sawdust* (1925). Regardless, his basic huckster axiom absolved him from a great deal—"You can't cheat an honest man." That is, the people he often swindled thought they were getting the best of him.

In contrast, Fields' antihero plays the most entertaining of contemporary victims, a browbeaten family man anchored to a going-nowhere position in a small-town America—though his best showcase of this world, *It's a Gift* (1934), eventually offers an 11th hour reprieve to a California paradise. (The turnaround is so extreme, even for a comedy, that one might best "read" it as a satire of happy endings.) While Fields is inspired in either comedic mode—huckster or antihero—his henpecked husband occasionally lets a bit of larceny come through. For instance, when his screen wife in *Gift* forces him to share a sandwich with their brat of a son, the comedian bends the meat onto his side before dividing the bread.

Ironically, the same year *Gift* opened, Fields also made what is arguably the comedian's best huckster picture, *The Old-Fashioned Way*. From its opening moments, *Way* is a case study of any-con-for-the-production. The movie begins with a sheriff at the train depot about to serve Fields' showman, "The Great McGonigle," with a legal writ to keep him and his theatre troupe in town because of unpaid bills. Yet, McGonigle manages to come up behind the sheriff and wastes no time in setting fire to the document, which the officer is holding behind his back. Fields allows himself to be seen just as the blazing writ is beyond rescue. The mistakenly confident sheriff then tells him, "I have something for you!" As the surprised constable produces a flaming document from behind him, Fields (with the timing of the comic juggler he was) uses this nonconventional blaze to light his cigar. McGonigle then tops the laugh by politely thanking the still stunned law enforcement officer. A little pop culture nihilism.

The manipulative McGonigle not only gets the best of adult establishment figures, he physically takes on oppressive youngsters like Baby LeRoy (Ronald LeRoy Overacker), managing to give him a kick in the backside. Comparing Fields' boot to the signature leg action of Charlie Chaplin's Tramp, a *New York World Telegram* critic went on to celebrate this kick as a comic catharsis, "[releasing] the suppressed desires of countless adults who have nearly been driven crazy by the abuses of some particularly noxious infant whose fond parents just beam on their offspring's antics and consider them cute." Yes, you can smile and be bad.

While Fields' alternate comedy personas were assisted greatly by the authors of two 1920s stage productions—Dorothy Donnelly's Broadway huckster play, *Poppy* (1923), with W.C. starring as the title character con man), and J.P. McEvoy's antiheroic musical comedy revue *The Comic Supplement* (1925, in which Fields starred as part of the "Ziegfeld Follies") —the comedian's own writing roots were tied to the world of the antihero. Between 1918-30, Fields registered 23 separate comedy documents on 16 subjects. This least known of his then-professional activities now looms as a fascinating look at the evolution of his antihero—his time usurped by dominating women, machines, and the urban setting in general. (He was most protective of his material. I played a hunch that the comedian might have copyrighted his sketches while preparing my book, *W. C. Fields: A Bio-Bibliography*, 1984. And like *Bewitched*'s Samantha twitching her nose, I suddenly found Fields neglected routines at the Library of Congress. I was reminded of the filing cabinet definition: "A place in which one loses things alphabetically.")

Regardless, that Fields was fond of showcasing his antiheroic screen comedy in a world of small town, mealy-mouth sanctimoniousness reflects his undoubted influence by what literature terms "the revolt from the village." This movement of the late 1910s and 1920s focused on the dead-end hypocrisy of small town life, but it was, according to literacy scholar Anthony Channell Hilfer, "an overall attack on middle-class American civilization." This new artistic wrinkle was precipitated by poet Edgar Lee Masters' *Spoon River Anthology* (1915), although it took several years for the influence of the book to permeate popular culture. The movement was a major influence on Fields and can even be seen as reflected in Charlie Chaplin's ironically titled small-town saga *Sunnyside* (1919).

Fields generally assumed this antihero persona when he wrote comic essays for assorted magazines. Fields the print humorist is sadly neglected today. However, the most ambitious undertaken along these lines resulted in the book *Fields for President* (1940). Originally serialized in the *New York Herald Tribune* Sunday magazine supplement *This Week*, the collection is invaluable for Fields study for two reasons. First, coming late in his career, the book is a compendium of Fields material gathered over a lifetime—a comedic well from which he would do some final drawing in his last films.

Second, *Fields for President* represents an excellent guide to the essentially comic antihero nature of his best work. Like contemporary humorists Robert Benchley and James Thurber, Fields' art is most often drawn from the little, yet irremediable, frustrations of life—so nicely exemplified by his book's Chapter 3, "How to Best the Federal Income Tax—and What to See and Do at Alcatraz." Of course, even here Fields could not resist inserting a bit of the huckster. While President Franklin Delanor Roosevelt and Republican challenger Wendell L. Wilkie did not seem worried over Fields' candidacy, the comedian certainly offered the public a punningly funny platform. For instance, "I shall my fellow citizens, offer no such empty panaceas as [FDR's] "New Deal," or an "Old Deal," or even a "Re-Deal." No, my friends, the reliable old False Shuffle was good enough for my father and it's good enough for me." (In real life the federal government frequently took him to court over eccentric tax write-offs. Still, he enjoyed dictating letters of complaint to them.)

Fields' huckster character also has ties to "the revolt from the village" movement, but it is hard not to be most drawn to his antihero figure because the poignant implications inherent to this small town (village) victim are more universal. *New York Times* critic Andre Sennwald best summed this up: "Not to be aware of the tragic overtones in the work of this middle-aged, whiskey-nosed, fumbling and wistfully incompetent gentleman is to be ignorant of the same tragic overtones in the comedy of Don Quixote." Moreover, he never kowtowed to societal norms in private either — as he led a self-destructive life dodging death, calling him "The Man in the Bright Nightgown."

(Reprinted with permission from *USA Today Magazine*, November 2006. Copyright© 2006 by "The Society for the Advancement of Education, Inc., All Rights Reserved.")

GENRES OF THE FANTASTIC

Horror, Science Fiction, and Fantasy:

With a Stephen King Foundation

Psycho (1960) director Alfred Hitchcock in an unnecessary chair.

The most popular college class I teach is film genres. Each week a different type of movie is examined. Sometimes these genres are best linked under a broader umbrella. Plus, it should come as no surprise that for the current university crowd the three favorites are horror, science fiction, and fantasy. These are the "genres of the fantastic."

The order is not random. Film genres are simply literacy retreads. Under this provocative parasol of genres of the fantastic, the most significant solemn literacy texts have come from horror. Do not shoot the proverbial messenger. Take it up with Stephen King's nonfiction text *Dance Macabre* (1979). He makes a convincing argument that horror gets to go first. He bases it on the literary trilogy of Mary Shelley's *Frankenstein* (1818), Robert Louis Stevenson's *The Strange Case of Dr. Jekyll and Mr. Hyde* (1886), and Bram Stoker's *Dracula* (1897). Moreover, are you *really* going to argue with Stephen King on the subject of horror? (You might pick a bone with him on trying to keep his novels under a thousand pages, but one best throw in the towel when debating horror.)

Within cinema horror, no image tops that of director James Whale's iconic creation of *Frankenstein* (1931), with Boris Karloff in the title role. Whale even manages to top himself with the 1935 sequel, *Bride of Frankenstein.* Karloff reprises his role, joined by Elsa Lanchester's title figure. She also plays Mary Shelley in a quasi-comic prologue. In James Curtis' *James Whale: A New World of Gods and Monsters* (1998), one sees the obvious physical links between the look of the creature and a Whale sketch of a demented character he had played on the London stage in 1928's *A Man with Red Hair.*

To comically demonstrate the prevalence and multi-faceted storylines in which Shelley's paragon of horror has been showcased one has only to turn to critic Leonard Maltin's yearly *Movie Guide* of nearly 16,000 pocket modern movie overviews. Besides those mentioned, what follows is a *modest* sampling of actual Frankenstein films: *Son of Frankenstein* (1939), *Ghost of Frankenstein* (1942), *Frankenstein Meets the Wolf Man* (1943), *House of Frankenstein* (1944, which also includes roommates Wolf Man and Dracula*)*, *Revenge of Frankenstein* (1958), *Frankenstein Conquers the World* (1965), *I Was a Teenage Frankenstein* (1957), *Abbott and Costello Meet Frankenstein* (1948), and *Jesse James Meets Frankenstein's Daughter* (1966). The comic numbers are nothing short of the Marx Brothers trying to climb Mount Dumont.

So what is so hypnotic about old flattop (for easier access to inserting a brain) Frankenstein? His nuts and bolts appearance seems the most magnetic of what is referenced as a "man-made monster." His closest rival would be the 16th century Jewish folktale figure called the Golem. In yet another time of Jewish persecution a rabbi created a clay figure to protect his people. However, as with Frankenstein, something went wrong, and a monster was the result. Before Shelley's book, Golem tales were much more prevalent. Indeed, the figure is often assumed to have been the inspiration for her creature.

Like all art and/or popular culture phenomena which does not go away, it speaks to different eras in different ways. However, the overriding message here is a religious one — man should not play God. Yet, because Shelley's mother died in childbirth, with the author almost suffering the same fate, feminist have often also interpreted the story as a commentary on the horrors of 18th century childbirth.

In later years, director Whale's ongoing influence as *the* interpreter of Shelley's story, and the architect of the creature's iconic look, has been drawn into another Frankenstein "angle of vision." Whale was one of the first openly gay Hollywood artists. In Bram Christopher's excellent Whale biography, *Father of Frankenstein* (1995), one can be persuaded that maybe the director's greater empathy for the creature was born of being an *outsider*, too. (This is further examined in the 1998 screen adaptation of Christopher's biography, *Gods and Monsters.*) Mel Brooks certainly acknowledged this perspective in his parody *Young Frankenstein* (1974).

Moreover, art is never created in a vacuum, and Whale was a World War I veteran. Medical advances of the time managed to allow many badly disfigured soldiers to survive the conflict, which horror historians generally credit for helping fuel the genre during the post-war era. Whale saw combat and would have been cognizant of this development. Also, the period between the two world wars were plagued with American Jim Crow lynchings, especially directed at returning black veterans. The mob mentality cornerstone of so many Frankenstein movies during the early sound era are also often linked subtextually to this sorry chapter in American history.

While the "don't play God" axiom can be seen as a strong reason to lead with Frankenstein, beyond his mesmerizing mug and Karloff's poignancy, I find Stevenson's *Jekyll and Hyde* a more riveting universal tale. I have never even had a thought of creating a lovely lady, à la John Hughes' tale of nerdy teens (Robert Downey Jr., and Robert Rustler) using computers for that purpose in *Weird Science* (1985). However, I believe it all-inclusive that everyone has a dark alter ego. Through some vague formula, Stevenson's Dr. Jekyll was able to unleash his Mr. Hyde.

Happily, most people do not act upon this impulse. However, even an underage Jesus killed a playmate, or two in the *Gospel of Thomas*, one of the *Gospels* that did not make the "final four." Naturally, he brings them back to life. Yet, it is ironic that this gospel did not make the *Bible* cut, if its goal was to show the human side of Jesus. Regardless, it made for some interesting discussion in my childhood Sunday school class.

Sadly, in poor little Alfred Hitchcock's youth it was not a topic in his religious studies, yet he certainly intuitively included such potential thoughts and/or actions in most of his films. As John Russell Taylor wrote in his *Hitch: The Life and Times of Hitchcock* (1978), though it might just as well come from Donald Spoto's *The Dark Side of Genius: The Life of Alfred Hitchcock* (1983):

> It is probably not stretching fantasy too far to guess at the
> first hint of how he [Hitchcock] latterly delighted to tread the
> cool, remote-seeming blond heroines of his films in the
> resentful dreams of a plain, pudgy fourteen-year-old
> watching some evidently unattainable blond girl near home
> thinking, "If only I had her in my power, just for a few
> moments …"

Regardless, most artists drawn to depictions of mankind's dark side have uttered some variation upon "humanity's thin veneer of civilization."

Indeed, in H. C. Wells' *War of the Worlds* (1898) he plays upon such fears in others. The catalyst for this novella was late 19th century Europe's fears about the ongoing Prussian war machine, which was just warming up for the 20th century. However, Wells wanted to break new scary ground. Thus, he projected such fears upon a life force from another world. In doing so Wells also embraced science fiction, too. This demonstrates how the "genres of the fantastic" are often intertwined.

For example, while the original *Alien* (1979) takes place on a commercial spacecraft, it is essentially just a haunted house in outer space. Plus, director Ridley Scott even borrows a fantasy writing rule from C. S. Lewis' *An Experiment in Criticism* (1961) by giving Sigourney Weaver that damn cat. That is, when wanting to engage a reader/viewer in an outlandish situation, one introduces a universal piece of realism, like a pet. Consequently, an audience member might "buy" the idea of Weaver putting herself at risk when her cat wanders off.

Despite the interweaving of the "genres of the fantastic," there are some basic differences to help separate them. For instance, horror generally keys upon fear of dying. Science fiction is more apt to be about fear of the future. Moreover, science fiction must have at least one foot in reality. In contrast, fantasy is just not going to happen. I love *The Wizard of Oz* (1939), but witches can only fly coach like the rest of us. The same thing applies to the original *Star Wars* (1977). It is wonderful mind candy forever mislabeled as science fiction. However, one cannot have World War II style "dog fights" in outer space — too fast, and there is no sound in a vacuum. Moreover, one cannot just hop out of the space vehicle of your choice without a suit.

Returning to *Jekyll and Hyde*, this is the foundation of most modern (post-1960) cinema horror creatures — the "human fiend," starting with *Psycho*'s (1960) Norman Bates. Fittingly, such a "monster" is often inspired by a real person, as was Bates. Indeed, *Psycho* and British director Michael Powell's *Peeping Tom* (both 1960) marked a transition in the horror film. Prior to this, the genre tended to be anchored in the European past, and often showcased creatures "back from the dead," à la Stoker's *Dracula*. This is not to say there had not been contemporary American horror films prior to 1960. Writer/producer Val Lewton did a number of classic "B" horror pictures at RKO during the early 1940s. Yet, after 1960 horror was more likely to involve that nice, quiet contemporary boy living next door.

Guillermo del Toro's Spanish-Mexican production *Pan's Labyrinth* (2006) is an enthralling merging of both realistic horror and a dark fantasy. While returning to the European past (Fascist 1944 Spain), the young girl caught in this sometime fairy tale is confronted by both a traditional fantasy monster and a modern fascist captain. The latter real figure easily proves to be the most frightening fiend.

Moving from King's pivotal literary horror trilogy, Wells essentially represents a one-man-band of quintessential novellas which mix horror and science fiction: *The Time Machine* (1895), *The Island of Doctor Moreau* (1896), *The Invisible Man* (1897), and *The War of the Worlds* (1898). Before examining these Wells texts, it must be stated that World War II impacted all genres, *but* especially the genres of the fantastic. Darwin had long before underlined the beastly nature of man's "survival of the fittest." However, concentration camps and the "Final Solution" chronicled just how horrific mankind could be. While I might be that rare liberal who believes dropping at least the first atomic bomb saved lives, nuclear war must also be added to the list of mankind's inhumanity to man.

Unlike horror's marriage to religion, with Jack the Ripper keying on London prostitutes, or the video store teen "professor" preaching that only promiscuous girls "buy the farm" in the original *Scream* (1996), *science* is part of "science fiction" marquee. Of course, Wells can be a wild card. In *The Island of Moreau* Wells' mad scientist mocks the Ten Commandments by creating his own list to keep his victims in control. Yet, in *War* the Martians initially defeat Earth, but suddenly the aliens start dropping from bacteria native to the planet. One could "read" this as God having created a protective "blanket" around Earth.

Of course, for decades a more insightful science fiction is to forget religion *and* Darwin and examine two basic plotlines. The first is that life on Earth was jumpstarted at various times by a superior alien life force. The second narrative is take some current contemporary activity and project it into the future. In both cases Stanley Kubrick provides *the* example. The former is best exemplified by *2001: A Space Odyssey* (1968). It draws upon Arthur C. Clark's 1948 short story "The Sentinel," which was the starting point for the film.

The second pivotal modern science fiction narrative is Kubrick's adaptation of Anthony Burgess' novel *A Clockwork Orange* (1971), which applies 1960s programs to correct anti-social behavior into the near future. The cost is the loss of free will. A variation of this occurs in the *Minority Report* (2002), in which potential harmful behavior can be anticipated and stopped even before it occurs. As with horror's failures over attempting to play God, these alternate plot lines tend to produce frightening failure, too.

Indeed, beyond these "what if?" dark attractions of science fiction, public intellectual Susan Sontag was more direct. In her influential essay "The Imagination of Disaster," she suggests the real attraction of the genre might be likened to the not to be denied attraction of staring at the cosmic car wreck: "…the aesthetics of destruction — the peculiar beauties to be found in wreaking havoc."

Yet recent science fiction has sometimes become problem film-like in addressing contemporary issues. These would include: recognizing tendencies sliding towards Nazi concentration camps and South African Apartheid in *District 9* (2009, shot in and co-produced by South African filmmakers), mismanagement of the planet in Christopher Nolan's epic *Interstellar* (2014), and Guillermo del Toro's galaxy sized look at romance and diversity in the science fiction fantasy *The Shape of Water* (2017).

As the latter film would suggest, fantasy has largely left *Oz* and *Wonderland* to attack many of the above issues without the restrictions of reality. Put another away, "we have entered Marvel Comic Movie Land. While frequently special effects get in the way of these stories, there are also notable poignant exceptions, such as the groundbreaking *Black Panther* (2018). This was the first Marvel film with both a predominantly black cast and black director (Ryan Coogler). It is also on its way towards becoming a fantasy franchise. The *Star Wars* juggernaut need not worry, but the general fantasy playing field is becoming overcrowded.

To paraphrase an old comic axiom, "You don't need to read the tea leaves. You just need to know how to read," to see the lines are increasingly blurring between the genres of the fantastic — especially with regard to science fiction and fantasy. At one time a basic guideline helped decide. It was a fantasy if a choice of worlds was provided at the end, be it Oz versus Kansas in *The Wizard of Oz* (1939), or Earth versus some distant planet in *Cocoon* (1985).

However, mankind's scientific and technological expertise is moving at such a pace that yesterday's fantasy is today's reality. For example, a *New York Times* piece well before Covid hit suggested *Eternal Sunshine of the Spotless Mind* (2004) clinics could be in your neighborhood soon. (This would be an outpatient medical center in which bad memories could be erased from one's mind.)

More disturbing, however, is that science fiction exists, in part, to help us avoid "future shock." Thus, if man's technological facility is moving at morph speed past our moral and emotional development is there going to be a *time to come*? Indeed, last century was the first time in which anti-utopian literature was in the forefront, such as C. S. Lewis' *Out of the Silent Planet* (1938). In fact, Wells' *Time Machine* anticipated the movement. Consequently, when Wells' less than optimistic time traveler goes back to attempt to change the darkest of futures, it behooves us to embrace the closing words of the novel's narrator: "If that is so [the end of mankind], it remains for us to live as though it were not so …"

(Reprinted with permission from *USA Today Magazine*, May 2021. Copyright © 2021 by "The Society for the Advancement of Education, Inc. All Rights Reserved.")

SIGNATURE SONGS:

The Power of Movies to

Redefine Popular Music

Ben Vereen (left) and Roy Scheider put a new spin on the Everly Brothers' "Bye Bye Love" in *All That Jazz* (1979).

I have always been fascinated by the power of movies to redefine popular music, including changing its signature status from one performer to another, or making it the background soundtrack of our lives, and sometimes even morphing it into entirely new imagery. I will explore seven variations on these themes, some of them touching upon multiple components.

First, and arguably the most broadly engaging illustration of these possibilities occurred with Dolly Parton's 1974 "I Will Always

Love You." She penned it as a musical exit to the mentor who had launched her career on his syndicated TV program, *The Porter Wagoner Variety Show.* So sweet you felt like you were being strangled by a rainbow, it quickly went to number one on the "Billboard Hot Country Songs" charts. It even made her country female vocalist of the year.

Yet it really garnered more attention when Parton reprised the song in the 1982 film adaptation of the Broadway hit *The Best Little Whorehouse in Texas,* co-starring Burt Reynolds. This was back when Reynolds was America's perennial favorite star, and the song again went to number one on the country charts, as well as doing major crossover business. This would certainty seem to have nailed her public ownership of the song. How can this not be a one and done?

However, then Whitney Houston recorded her version of the song for the film *The Bodyguard* (1992, in which she co-starred with Kevin Costner). When Houston's "I Will Always Love You" was released as a single it totally dwarfed Parton and any other female singer in recording history. It reduced everything before it to the color of collection plate pennies. Houston's version spent a record-breaking 14 weeks at number one on the "Billboard" Hot 100 chart. (The Beatles' "Hey Jude" had been number one nine weeks.)

Critics worked over *The Bodyguard* like someone on the production owed them money. Indeed, it was made from a script which had been bouncing around Hollywood twenty years. Originally written for Steve McQueen and Diana Ross, the story is an unlikely romance between a singing star and the head of her security. But Costner, then a major Hollywood player, was such a McQueen fan he not only got the green light, he even copied McQueen's closely cropped hair style. (It not did enhance the picture.)

Despite the movie being savaged by critics, the "I Will Always Love You" driven soundtrack went on to being the best-selling soundtrack of all-time and made the movie the second-highest-grossing film of 1992. Indeed, by the time the soundtrack had won the Album of the Year Grammy, the picture had become the 10th highest-grossing film through 1993 movie history.

As is her nature, Parton generously credited Houston's voice for the transition in signature status. (Indeed, after the latter singer's untimely (2012) death, "I Will Always Love You" almost went to number one yet again.) However, there were other factors involved, such as *Bodyguard* (despite the critics) being a much better melodramatic launching pad then the broad comedy of *The Best Little Whorehouse in Texas*.

Plus, while Parton is a pioneering country crossover artist, Houston made it mainstream. In addition, more than one music critic (see especially Curtis W. Ellison) suggested *The Bodyguard* matched the ephemeral changing nature of ambiguous 1990s relationships, not to mention the bi-racial couple card. Thus, like all great art, from deep dish to pop, the song could suddenly be a gateway to a place that was not visible to us before.

Second, despite the inspired writing of the Beatles, one of their most trademark numbers is John Lennon's raspy 1963 rock cover of the frequently recorded Isley Brothers' 1962 hit song "Twist and Shout." However, the Beatles took an upbeat number, increased the tempo, and with Lennon's almost desperate blues driven demand to have fun — "Twist and Shout" is intoxicating.

Film writer/director John Hughes later obtained the rights to use the Lennon rendition for his iconic coming-of-age picture *Ferris Bueller's Day Off* (1986). It chronicles the saga of a cheeky teenager (Matthew Broderick), in Lennon cocky swagger, cutting class with friends for an adventure around hometown Chicago. Broderick swashbuckles his way through a litany of "Windy City" escapades, from spoofing the "Impressionists" at the Art Institute, to a must stop at Wrigley Field. When he then manages to be on a float in a downtown parade perfectly lip syncing John's "Twist and Shout" as the whole city seems to provide a perfectly choreographed backdrop, suddenly it is an epic MTV video. Leonard Malten would later describe this Lennon song validation as "one of pop-culture's landmarks of its time."

Third, a young Willie Nelson writes and records the song "Crazy" (1961). Later that same year, Patsy Cline records it, and like the Parton scenario, Nelson ungrudgingly acknowledges it as a Cline song. Of course, here the situation is somewhat different. Nelson is nearly an unknown, and Cline's shooting star short life (1932-1963) is on a "Billboard" chart number one roll.

However, another movie type of validation quickly comes into play for Cline's "Crazy." Long before Jessica Lange lip synced her way to an Oscar nomination in the Cline biopic *Sweet Dreams* (1985), "Crazy" had become one of Hollywood's most go-to soundtrack songs. The singer's posthumous successes, fueled by the number's ambiguous title, put it on more movie soundtracks, with the possible exception of Dean Martin's "Ain't That [Love] a Kick in the Head," than one has time to count. However, if forced to play "Where's Waldo?" for Cline film soundtrack diversity, here are my three favorites, from three different genres — nearly 30 years after Cline recorded it.

As a baseball fan, I will start with my favorite. Shortly after novice farmer Kevin Costner starts hearing "The voice" in his populist *Field of Dreams* (1989) cornfield, he tries to discuss it in the local farm implement store. However, he quickly changes topics when an in-film radio plays "Crazy." Second, in the personality comedy, *Tommy Boy* (1995), David Spade and Chris Farley get lost somewhere on seemingly Planet Grim. (Their backroad location would still no doubt shut down any of today's GPS systems, short of a NASA intervention.) David and Chris stop at a gas station and Spade goes in to see how far they are from Davenport, Iowa. Given that the duo are not even in the right state, another nicely timed radio rendition of Cline's "Crazy" more than answers Spade's question. The third most notable and easily the most unexpected movie use of "Crazy" is the science fiction film *Assassin's Creed* (2016), a too strange to follow storyline to explain, unless you know the video game that inspired it. Yet, no worries, or need to pick that pivotal "Crazy" soundtrack placement. Why? "Crazy" is the "official song" for the *whole film*, a fact conspicuously matched in all title print size for its poster art. Who knows, "Crazy" might be in the grade Z science fiction picture number now lost to film history with the mind boggling title, *Truck Stop Women On the Moon*.

My fourth musical movie illustration has the audacity to take a Beatle song and give its signature status to someone else directly by way of a movie. "With a Little Help From My Friends" was written by Lennon and Paul McCartney for the groundbreaking 1967 album *Sgt. Pepper's Lonely Hearts Club Band*. It is an entertaining "B side" number written for the limited musical range of Ringo. However, given the iconic nature of that album, which *Rolling Stone* magazine still rates the greatest piece of vinyl ever, how does this particular song's identity become more linked with Joe Cocker?

Cocker's version underwent a slower arrangement, with a lengthy instrumental introduction, and his wailing voice takes a whimsical child-like song (other Ringo numbers include "Yellow Submarine" and "Octopus' Garden") into distressed blues territory. Cocker's cover was a 1968 European hit single. However, it did not crack the Top 50 American charts. Yet, then came 1969's *Woodstock*, with Cocker reprising the number. When released as *the* rock documentary concert film (1970), suddenly *Rolling Stone* was calling Cocker's variation the "Anthem of a Nation," and Paul told *Billboard* magazine, "It was just mind blowing, [it] totally turned the song into a soul anthem and I was forever grateful for him [Cocker] for doing it." *Cocker*'s take of the song eventually made it into the Grammy Hall of Fame.

Number five is the consummate follow-up to the previous *Woodstock* American discovery of Joe Cocker's "A Little Help from My Friends." *Monterey Pop* (1969) was the first major rock concert film. It was shot at the *1967* Monterey Pop Festival, with Janis Joplin's performance of the legendary Big Mama Thorton's "Ball and Chain" bringing down the proverbial house. It was written and recorded by Thornton (1926-1984) sometime in the mid-1960s (dates vary). Joplin was a huge fan of the then too often neglected black rhythm-and-blues artist.

In 1968 Joplin (1943-1970) asked Thornton for permission to record "Ball and Chain." It became a hit on Joplin's *Cheap Thrills* album (1968). However, it was not until the following year's *Monterey Pop* concert film was *finally* released that "Ball and Chain" became a Joplin signature song. Her almost tortured yet energized rock blues rendition of the number was as searing as Cocker's take on "A Little Help From My Friends." Kinsley Suer's much later *The Many Influences on Janis Joplin* (2019) chronicled Thornton's opinion, "That girl feels like I do." Though no concert documentary tops *Woodstock,* many rock critics place *Monterey Pop* a strong second, because of Joplin's mesmerizing "Ball and Chain," and Jimmy Hendrix (1942-1970) pyrotechnical "Wild Thing" — from two pivotal rockers who died much too young.

Besides these five film differentials of signature baton passers, two music/movie variations on a similar theme merit noting. The first involves Stanley Kubrick's film *A Clock Work Orange* (1971). This still provocative dark comedy involves several vicious young hoods set in an Orwellian near future. Led by a spellbinding monster, Malcolm McDowell, he enjoys committing the most horrific crimes while warbling Gene Kelly's title song from "Singin' in The Rain" (1952). This demonstrates a basic element of dark comedy. It is that rare genre in which the film's music is juxtaposed with the visual. Like an abstract and/or avant-garde picture, the goal is to disturb the audience by joining conflicting emotions. In this case, clashing the joyful charm produced by Kelly's number with extreme violence.

While unlike the earlier examples, the song "Singin' in the Rain" continues to "belong" to Kelly. However, if one knows Kubrick's high profile *A Clockwork Orange,* it is most difficult to fully enjoy the 1952 classic musical without thinking of what McDowell describes as his "ultraviolence" whenever the number is heard.

Kubrick enjoyed further meshing the two presentations of the number by playing Kelly's rendition over the closing credits of *A Clockwork Orange*.

The second similar example even goes more macabre by involving a darkly comic *musical* — Bob Fosse's *All That Jazz* (1979). The picture doubles as a thinly veiled biography of the brilliant workaholic and hedonistic Fosse (1927-1987). The only person to win an Oscar, Emmy, and Tony in the same year (1973), one can add an additional eight career total choreography Tony Awards and the Palm d' Or at the Cannes Film Festival for *All That Jazz*.

His script research for *Jazz* basically involved interviewing friends and co-workers about the period in which he had nearly died from a massive heart attack while simultaneously editing his latest film and rehearsing the next Broadway play — while maintaining a self-destructive lifestyle. It is essentially a dark comedy, or as the period *Playboy* critic Bruce Williamson engagingly put it, "When was the last time anyone made a big musical about a coronary seizure, especially one that proved fatal."

Among the film's many great numbers, the key one comes down to a signature closing song by the Everly Brothers, "Bye, Bye Love." While it forever remains in their canon, Fosse's modest tweaking makes sure you will never quite hear it in the same way again. During the finale there are several big production numbers, with the topper being Fosse's death take on "Bye, Bye Love."

It is the only number in the classy close in which Fosse's screen surrogate (Roy Scheider) takes part. He sings it in close harmony with Ben Vereen's character. While the Everly Brothers sing it as a sad lost love ballad, with the most modest of edits, Schneider and Vereen turn the number into an upbeat death dirge. Remember, dark comedy enjoys emotionally pulling you in opposite directions. What are the minimalist changes? "Bye Bye Love" becomes "Bye Bye Life," and "I think I'm gonna cry" segues to "I think I'm going to die." The Everly Brothers' original song even contributed to Fosse's dark revision with the line, "I feel like I could die."

The Everly Brothers' 1957 version went to number one on both the "Cash Box Pop" charts, and "Billboard Country Charts." *Rolling Stone* ranks it at 210 of the magazine's "500 Greatest Songs of All Time." It has been covered by countless artists, including George Harrison. Plus, it holds the unique distinction of being the first number Paul McCartney ever preformed on stage. The Beatle references are not casually added. From the beginning, the ongoing goal of John and Paul were to harmonize as well as the Everly Brothers. Yet, after all this, any fan of dark comedy and Fosse finds it difficult to hear this song and not think of *All That Jazz*.

So what does all this mean? It covers a lot of ground. Of course, Groucho said the same thing to Margaret Dumont in *Duck Soup* (1933). However, every article is panning for gold, or what is the point of writing? Moreover, one writes so as to not forget. Most obviously, the essay suggests (sans Parton) the power of not necessarily being the first recording on the calendar, but rather the first on film. It also implies an emotionally piercing performance by a short-lived artist sometimes gives an added nuance to a movie song, like Lennon being a James Dean of rock. Though movie and music genres are constantly morphing into something new, there is often a gauziness of the past still present. To accomplish a movie music metamorphosis, it must be done as lightly as critic Richard Corliss' description of an old gangster story (*Miller's Crossing,*) turning to neo-noir, "Floating on a breeze like the frisbee of a fedora sailing through the forest."

MY MAN GODFREY

And Filling in the Story From the

Original Novel, *1101 Parkway Avenue*

My Man Godfrey's Carole Lombard and William Powell (1936).

Before addressing the unique and often unexplored nature of the iconic screwball comedy *My Man Godfrey* (1936), several guidelines need to be established. First, the term "screwball" has often proven to be an unfortunate expression. Sadly, many equate it with the most baseless of personality comedians, à la *The Dumb & Dummer* franchise (starting in 1994). Nothing could be further from the truth. Screwball comedy is a form of American farce starting during the

1930s depression. The genre is an eccentric second cousin to romantic comedy, both in escapist La De Da settings.

The genre's origin date is approximately 1934, when the Hollywood censorship code was kicked off. Since screwball comedy is farce, it necessitated being the "sex comedy without sex." As far as the misleading "screwball" term, it first appeared in 1930s slang meaning an eccentric person, though in late 19th century colloquial expression it meant having a "screw loose" (being crazy), or becoming "screwy" (drunk) — given traits for this then new form of farce. For example, both conditions nicely match *My Man Godfrey*'s seemingly crazy post- debutante Carole Lombard, and her eternally blotto household, and sometimes soused butler Godfrey (William Powell).

By chance, period baseball stimulated the word "screwball" by the 1934 world champion St. Louis Cardinals, a team noted for its nutty behavior and nicknamed the "Gas House Gang." Their zany antics were highlighted by star pitcher "Dizzy" Dean. His madcap behavior even placed him on the cover of *Time* magazine (April 15, 1935), calling him a "legend... to every literate U.S. citizen and whose antics [were] ... gracious or absurd." This is the pocket definition of *Godfrey*'s Lombard. Indeed, *Variety*'s *My Man Godfrey* review (September 23, 1936) stated: "... she needs only a rosin bag to be a female Rube Waddell [a Dizzy Dean-type turn-of-the-century pitcher]." Fittingly, since the mid-1930 "screwball" has also been a baseball reference to a pitched ball suddenly moving in any unusual or unexpected way.

Second, through the years critics and historians have mistakenly used the designations "screwball comedy" and "romantic comedy" interchangeably. If one wanted the simplest distinction between the two it would mean that the former category accepts a partner as is, versus romantic comedy necessitating someone change — such as *As Good As It Get*'s (1997) tag line: "You make me want to be a better person." In other words, romantic comedy puts love on a pedestal and makes any negatives verboten. Indeed, in Rob Reiner's

When Harry Met Sally (1989) there are even narrative breaks when the viewer is exposed to random romantic testimonials from elderly married couples from a "love seat."

In contrast, to use a celebrated screwball comedy title, there is "nothing sacred" from laughter in this genre, including love. Consequently, screwball comedy mocks love right up until the focus couple unite. Moreover, supporting screen couples either mock marriage and/or find it dysfunctional. In fact, Lombard's *Godfrey* mother (Alice Brody) forever comically argues with her husband (Eugene Pallette) and has a live-in "protégé" — 1930s code for gigolo.

Third, an expanded comparison of screwball and romantic comedy centers upon two additional points, beyond screwball accenting laughter over love. Since romantic comedy is more reality based than its counterpart, screwball comedy has extra slapstick and eccentric people. *Godfrey* has a character inspiringly showcasing both traits — Mischa Auer's gigolo Carlos — whose talented technique for gorilla impressions merited an Oscar nomination for Best Supporting Actor. Additionally, screwball comedy's pace is constantly escalating, such as Lombard's orchestrating a blitzkrieg finale marriage to the charmingly puzzling title character butler. In comparison, romantic comedy's close at no time pumps the breaks over the genre's weighty commitment to love for a lifetime, without a thought of Oscar Wilde's axiom, "One should always be in love. That's the reason one should never marry."

Godfrey centers around a Fifth Avenue family named the Bullocks (Pallette and Brady), two grown daughters (Lombard's nutty egalitarian Irene, and Gail Patrick's elitist Cornelia), Auer's gigolo Carlos, witty maid Molly (Jean Dixon), and the mysterious new butler Godfrey (Powell). The tale is based upon Eric Hatch's novel, which was printed under *two* different titles: *1101 Park Avenue*, and the later *The Butler And the Debutante*. The simple period theme is a job provides purpose, without it one is the stereotypical bum, or a vacuous socialite. *Godfrey* is the rare screwball comedy that acknowledges the era's "forgotten man." The screenplay was co-scripted by the novelist, but director Gregory LaCava was the auteur powering the picture.

What is forgotten today is the movie's historical significance to screwball comedy. Unlike any of the genre's predecessors, including the madcap *Twentieth Century* (1934), *Godfrey* offered a full menu of screwballs. Thus, for many 1930s critics the latter film represented a more obvious starting point for the genre. For example, Kate Cameron's 1938 *New York Daily News* review of the memorable *Bringing Up Baby* placed it in the tradition of "the whole crazy variety of screen comedies that began with *My Man Godfrey*" (March 4, 1938). Moreover, the decade's most exceptional critic, the *New Republic*'s Otis Ferguson, stated in the international journal *Accent* (Autumn 1940): "With '*My Man Godfrey*,' in the middle of 1936, the discovery of the word screwball by those who had to have some words to say helped build the thesis of an absolutely new style in comedy."

Thanks to Lombard's former husband, William Powell, the actress was given the romantic lead. The actor best known today for the *Thin Man* franchise (with Myrna Loy), felt she would be perfect for the part, given her eccentric comic personality. This jelled with director LaCava, who told *Colliers Magazine* (March 26, 1938): "Give me real people to work with, people like Bill Powell and Carole Lombard, and we'll give you a picture ... When I direct them I tell them to use their own personalities, not to assume someone else's."

Moreover, LaCava started as a newspaper cartoonist and a silent film director, so he mixed a strong comic visual touch with an obsession for improvisation. No one topped former Mack Sennett comedian Lombard in spontaneity, so she repaid Powell's casting kindness by calming him when the more traditional performer was nervous about LaCava's casual style. Lombard had worked with LaCava before and knew his technique was perfect for the picture.

Of course, this free and easy set was enhanced by a devil-may-carefree flow of liquid fun. It fit the pickled world of screwball society, from the *Thin Man* series through the *Topper* pictures. LaCava was a close drinking buddy of W. C. Fields. The comedian's first biographer, Robert Lewis Taylor, *W. C. Fields: His Fortunes and His Follies* (1949), observed: "... the picture [Godfrey] was by no means made possible by liquor, but LaCava believes that his keen analysis of the causes and cures of scenario tension was much appreciated by the company [cast and crew]." Years later I interviewed LaCava's friend and sometimes producer Pandro S. Berman, and he said visiting the set was "like going to a cocktail party." (Berman is most famous now for teaming Fred Astaire and Ginger Rogers and producing their RKO pictures. He also shared with me that those musicals were "essentially screwball comedies set to song and dance.")

In a Lombard article for *Screenbook* magazine (February 1937), punningly entitled "My Man Gregory," the actress said that partying helped LaCava like everyone on a shoot and "... he MUST like the cast, the workers, the technicians, the cameraman [and] anyone else that has anything to do with the making of that particular picture." The creative party atmosphere was a circular phenomenon; LaCava dominated the improvisation. His tweaking of an original work could be extensive. For instance, when he later adapted the play *Stage Door* (1937) it become an even more popular film. The joke then circulating in Hollywood was the movie should have been retitled *Screen Door*. (LaCava was the Oscar nominated Best Director for *Godfrey and Stage Door*.)

Another neglected backstory is that *Godfrey* appeared in the early heyday of print humor's antiheroic *Little Man* period, initially most associated with the *New Yorker* magazine (founded in 1925). *Godfrey* and screwball comedy rode a seismic shift in the history of American comedy. Prior to this, crackerbarrel male humor, best symbolized by a rational world view of a Will Rogers-like figure dominated. However, the antiheroic character began to make major comedy inroads early in the increasingly absurd 20th century. With World War I, the birthing of the *New Yorker*, and then the depression, antiheroes obtained permanent ascendancy. Antiheroic writers from James Thurber, Robert Benchley, S. J. Perelman, Hatch, Thorne Smith (the *Topper* author), through Woody Allen, Steven Martin and others to follow all had *New Yorker* ties.

Yet, pop culture in general was also making the transition, including pioneering newspaper comic strips like *Bringing Up Father* and *Krazy Kat* (both 1913), to *Peanuts'* Charlie Brown forever befuddled by Lucy (1950). Like *Krazy Kat*, the movies often added that strip's existentialistic overtones, especially the silent films of Buster Keaton and Laurel & Hardy. Moreover, vaudeville had dozens of "Dumb Dora" couples, best symbolized now by George Burns & Gracie Allen. (LaCava started in film by reconfiguring early newspapers strips into cartoons.) The catalyst behind all these examples is a befuddled male trying to make sense in an irrational world ... dominated by women embracing the irrational. Thurber and others called this changing of the comic guard "The Battle of the Sexes," with the male usually limited to success only in his daydreams, á la "The Life of Walter Mitty." Screwball comedy merely placed this template in an upscale setting, populated by beautiful people, with only mildly more balanced screwball battles, yet with outcomes still going to the females — somehow naturally inoculated with an irrationality which matched modern life.

Godfrey's Hatch, like sometimes fellow *New Yorker* staff writer Benchley, divided his time between Gotham and Hollywood. This screwball comedy transition from print to film brings one to a key neglected backstory — comparing this novel to the film. I am *unaware* of anyone ever having made the effort. Why? Is this not done all the time? Did LaCava's reputation for massive improvisational changes make it seem pointless? Could Hatch's co-scripting credit have made it seem like an exercise in the period axiom — "a whole lot of nothing?" However, given the *Godfrey* glut of material printed about it, both then and now (no doubt negating many forests), it seems as if someone would have explored a topic otherwise addressed in every way.

In fact, even W. C. Fields wrote a comically blistering letter of complaint to the Academy of Motion Picture Arts and Sciences over Lombard *not* winning her *Godfrey* Best Actress Oscar nomination. Plus, one assumes his language was stronger than how Hollywood's "Hitler" Hays censorship code forced Fields into screen subterfuge, like using "Godfrey Danials" for "God Damn." (After Lombard's loss, it is said her companion and later husband Clark Gable gave her his 1934 *It Happened One Night* statuette.)

Regardless, in examining this strangely neglected backstory comparison of the *Godfrey* novel and film, Thurber represents the best antiheroic parallel, since he reigned supreme in the early male underdog battle of genders. For every rare Thurber antiheroic victory, such as his "The Unicorn in the Garden" short story, the author devoted whole books to defeat, including *Is Sex Necessary?* (1929, with fellow *New Yorker* writer E. B. White), and *The Owl in the Attic and other Perplexities* (1931).

First, Thurber normally had his women characters physically in charge. Thus, early in Hatch's novel Irene caught Godfrey with his arm around the upstairs maid. Lombard's character had already established her instant (squirrel!) attachment to Godfrey, though he had not yet been worn down by her persistence. The following Godfrey comments in print are Thurberesque:

" ... he knew that Irene would not take the logical view of this. She would take the wife-with-rolling-pin view of it. She wouldn't even realize that his arm had been around Molly friendly-wise and without amorous intent. She would take the worse possible view of it. She did."

Second, the Thurber male is sometimes caught off guard with women because he confuses feminine irrationality with lack of knowledge. What follows is just such a Hatch perspective — Godfrey's first thoughts about Irene: "Nature created her, it must have been late of a Saturday afternoon and that the office had been closed before she was quite completed." The fear/confusion that a Thurber male suddenly had after misreading a situation as just described by Hatch was compounded by the women's size. Thurber brilliantly visualized this in his minimalist drawings of dominating women which accompanied his stories. (LaCava often drew minimalist drawings of characters on the set, too.)

Regardless, Hatch actually did Thurber one better by making Irene a *giant* of sorts. However, the revelation also reveals a captivating non-Thurber tender hidden depth to Irene wrapped in a self-referential delivery, à la *New Yorker* women: "You [Mother] — you and Cornelia — have been apologizing for my being dumb — and Amazonian for so long now ... to explain why I didn't get married years ago ... [However,] Do you know what you are? You're the kind of woman we read jokes about in the *New Yorker*. You probably live as false a life as any woman who can get a table any place without reserving it."

Moreover, before Hatch returns to Irene as a Thurber-like woman steamroller capturing Godfrey at the close, the writer also saturates her with a reason for Powell's character to surrender happily. Godfrey often found her loyalty "gazing at him with that [large brown eyed] bowline, affectionate look that always both touched and frightened him. Thus, LaCava largely followed Hatch's softening of the Thurber woman. Engrossingly, however, LaCava's greatest impact on the adaptation was not what he changed but what he left out. Herein lies the most consequential of Godfrey backstories.

First, near the novel's close one discovers how an aristocratic-like title character bum began on a New York Hooverville ash heap at the story's beginning. He was the last item on a scavenger hunt list (a "forgotten man") competition. Lombard's Irene wins but feels badly about the whole concept of this idle rich game. She takes him home as her wannabee protégé butler. Both the book and the film have Powell's character's coming from Boston blueblood background. Later the seemingly wealthy Bullocks have financial problems, and Godfrey's once moneyed past saves the day, and Lombard and Powell end as a couple.

LaCava leaves it at that, with Godfrey's ash heap beginning seemingly being some sort of "deep-dish" depression dropout triggered by class guilt, or the "ism" of your choice. However, the ending of Hatch's novel has the metaphorical impact of a blindsided smack of a sockful of nickels. (It is harder to trace, unless one has included some buffalo head nickels.) The book reveals Godfrey's formerly unnoted society wife had cheated on him, and he had been jailed for two years for attempting to strangle her lover. Since he provided no defense and allowed her to keep his fortune, his prison time was kept to two years.

This is how Godfrey found himself upon an East River ash heap, with his whereabouts unknown to any extended family. He just did not care. However, by the instant compassion of Lombard's crazed character, and a job that allowed him to study his former upper-class life from a new perspective, he is quite literally a new man. LaCava was probably right to tighten it and keep Godfrey somewhat mysterious. However, Hatch's novel is actually the dark side of the Thurber battle of the sexes, since Powell's character was a validated Boston antihero done wrong by a woman.

Moreover, if the murder subplot had been retained, it would not be without keeping with many screwball comedies through the years, including all those *Thin Man* movies (six between 1934 and 1947) which always had a bothersome murder disrupting all that high society copious drinking and flirtatious banter between Nick (William Powell) and Nora (Myrna Loy) Charles, *His Girl Friday* (1940), *Arsenic and Old Lace* (1944), *Unfaithfully Yours* (1948, remade 1984), *Some Like It Hot* (1959), *A Fish Called Wanda* (1988), *America's Sweethearts* (2001) ....

In fact, screwball comedy's next closest second comedy genre is dark comedy, and herein there is no question that "nothing is sacred."

(Reprinted with permission from *USA Today Magazine*, May 2022. Copyright © 2022 by "The Society for the Advancement of Education, Inc. All Rights Reserved.")

PART THREE:

PROFILES AND/OR

CAREER MOMENTS

KARL MALDEN WAS THE REAL GOODS:

A Blue-Collar Oscar Winner

Malden nearly nabs a second Oscar for *On the Waterfront* (1984).

Born Mladen Sekulovich in Chicago on March 22, 1912, Malden's Serbian immigrant father moved the family to Gary when Karl was a preschooler. The oldest of three sons, Karl had to work for everything… even before the Great Depression of the 1930s. His father had initially toiled in the Gary steel mills before a job-related injury had him delivering milk in a horse-drawn wagon. Growing up, Malden would often assist his father in these well-before-dawn milk deliveries. After Karl's high school graduation (1931), he also risked injury for three years as a Gary steel foundry worker.

Malden later described his father's legacy as instilling in him a "fierce work ethic." Karl applied this blue-collar mindset to his acting. Indeed, throughout his long career Malden was fond of likening an actor's work to "digging ditches —— sometimes they're deep and sometimes they're shallow but we keep digging them." The actor's drive is also apparent in the title he selected for his autobiography, *When Do I Start?* (1997, written with his youngest daughter, Carla).

Another son-of-an-immigrant/school of hard knocks actor, Kirk Douglas (1916), shared in his memoir, *The Ragman's Son* (1975), how pleased he was that his son Michael would be working with Malden on what became the very popular hour-long ABC series *The Streets of San Francisco* (1972-1977): "Michael, you're going to learn a lot. You're never going to be able to keep up with the pace that Karl sets." Years later, Michael Douglas wrote *Time* magazine's Malden obituary (July 20, 2009):

> He taught me just how fortunate I was to be an actor … Karl was a habitual teacher who prided himself on making everyone around him understand how to make the whole piece work …. He was my mentor. And he topped all this off with a wonderful sense of humor and a great, maniacal, cackling laugh. Karl always made me feel like I was the son he never had. I loved him and will miss him so.

Modest Malden's often self-deprecating sense of humor might best be exemplified by how he referred to his Oscar turn as the shy, inept suitor of Blanche DuBois (Vivien Leigh) in *Streetcar Named Desire* (1951). Keep in mind, though Leigh's Blanche is an aging, neurotic former Southern Belle the actress is still remembered as one of film's signature beauties —— thanks to her Academy Award-winning Scarlet in *Gone with the Wind* (1939). Thus, Malden enjoyed referring to himself as probably "the only ex-milkman Vivien ever kissed in a movie."

Besides Malden's driven work ethic, and his comically entertaining ability to maintain an average hat size, the actor also owed his career longevity to realizing early a basic truism: "I was never going to be a leading man." Acidic cinema critic David Thomson once described Malden as "becoming increasingly indispensable as a good-natured but ugly support [ing player]." A W.C. Fields-like bulbous nose was his most distinguishing characteristic, especially synonymous with his popular television ads (1970s) for American Express travelers' checks, with his tag line, "Don't leave home without them," becoming a national catch phrase.

Still, Malden was determined "to be No. 1 in the No. 2 parts I was destined to get." But first he had to recognize acting was his ticket out of a steel mill existence. Ironically, his dangerous Gary work setting was a fixture in any movie about steel towns —— molten iron ore being poured into ingots like so much lava, while lethal sparks imitated incoming fireworks. In his memoir, Malden said, "It's a lot like working in hell."

At Gary's Emerson High School, Malden's twin passions had been sports and acting. Fittingly, for an Indiana youngster, he confessed, "I joined the ranks of all good Hoosier boys and basketball became my consuming passion." But more than a mere localized hard-court story, Malden's experience tapped into a typical child of immigrants' tale —— embrace an American sport and better fit into this new culture.

An old-world carryover, however, which impacted Malden more than American basketball, was his father's (Peter) interest in Serbian church theatre. The actor's dad was Gary's authority on the subject, and his staging of plays for his Eastern Orthodox Church always included parts for children. Neither Peter nor Karl was overly religious. But they enjoyed the theatricality of the setting … not unlike the pageantry of Catholicism contributing to Martin Scorsese becoming a director.

Yet, *the* mystery of mysteries to Malden, about his father, was the following contradiction: though "The theatre was like a church [to Peter] … acting was not a respectable profession." Moreover, and here the practicality of most parents kicks in, Peter did not see any career potential in acting. Theatre was an amateur church passion which helped keep/teach Serbian culture alive in the wilds of Gary.

Other than a brief aborted try at college, which failed because the impoverished youngster lost an athletic scholarship, it appeared Malden would never escape Gary's version of the boulevard of broken dreams. But his desire for a still undefined "something better" made him save his steel mill money. After three years (1934), he gambled upon himself and applied his meager nest egg to the first quarter tuition of Chicago's nearby Goodman Theatre Dramatic School. Malden was soon offered a full tuition scholarship and his life changed.

Still strapped for money, Malden initially commuted daily by train from his parents' home in Gary. Finding extra paying work as a Goodman stagehand on weekends, he joyfully threw himself into a theatre life which, to paraphrase Noel Coward's love of writing, "Was more fun than fun." But "fun" came with a grueling schedule —— morning classes, and afternoon/evenings spent rehearsing a play, building sets, and eventually performing. The Goodman presented one adult play a month during the school year, with each production running one to four weeks. The public's purchase of membership series tickets helped fund the school. The Goodman also showcased a full series of children-focused plays. Thus, at any one time a student would be simultaneously working on one production and prepping for another.

Malden's Goodman experience was invaluable to his acting career. The theatre's playbill archives (now in the "Special Collections" of Chicago's Herald Washington Library) credits him with parts in fifteen different productions, ranging from Shakespeare's *The Winter's Tale* (as King of Sicilia) and Mark Twain's *The Prince and the Pauper* (as the Chancellor), to *Jolly Robin Hood* (as Little John), *Jack and the Beanstalk* (as the Giant), and *Red Riding Hood* (Nicholas). With Malden being well over six feet tall, he was sometimes cast opposite the diminutive Goodman classmate Mildred (Mona) Greenberg in the school's plays for children. Thus, her *Little Red Riding Hood* title character is rescued by Malden's woodman, while she is the Giant's (Malden) wife in *Jack and the Beanstalk*. The couple's contrast in size heightened the drama and/or comedy for young audiences. And befitting fairy tale co-stars the two would eventually marry (1938) in real life, too. Their happy union would endure over seventy years and produce two daughters, Mila and the aforementioned Carla. Malden was fond of saying his wife "has always been and continues to be my luck." Loyalty and work were the constant measure of this man.

Graduation from the Goodman in 1937, Malden's next stop was …. Gary's Cloverleaf Dairy Company. Déjà vu! Until Broadway called, his father managed to get Malden hired as a milkman. Not surprisingly, the *possibility* of a stage role had the young actor in New York by that autumn. While this metaphorical Cracker Jack box escape plan produced no prize (part) for Malden, relocating to New York led to the most fortuitous of friendships. Elia Kazan, then a Group Theatre actor, was immediately impressed upon meeting the Hoosier rookie, though Malden would not be aware of this until much later. Kazan was established on Broadway via his earlier electric performance as the taxi driver in Clifford Odet's *Waiting for Lefty*. Kazan had a meaty role (the gangster Fuseli) in Odet's next play *Golden Boy*, about a doomed boxer. Through Kazan's influence, Malden would win a small part in this high-profile vehicle. This break, and Kazan's later move to directing, would significantly impact Malden's career.

Over the next twenty years, Malden would appear in "nineteen Broadway plays, seven of them chosen among the top ten productions of the season" (*Current Biography, 1957*). This time span also included a World War II stint in the Army, which gave him the opportunity to appear in Moss Hart's Broadway air corps production, *Winged Victory* —— which featured a men-in-uniform cast. But Malden's personal moon-shot year for the theatre occurred in 1947, courtesy of director Kazan. Malden was a standout in Arthur Miller's *All My Sons* and Tennessee Williams' *A Streetcar Named Desire* —— both directed by Kazan, with the latter making Marlon Brando a huge star.

Critic John Beaufort's take on Malden's performance in *Sons* was typical of the actor's notices for Miller's award-winning play: "Karl Malden gives one of his characteristically illuminated portrayals as the dismayed and tragically disillusioned son ...." (*Christian Science Monitor*, February 1, 1947). And Malden's awkward, naïve suitor to Blanche DuBois for *Streetcar* would win him a Donaldson Award (in honor of *Billboard* magazine founder W.H. Donaldson) for best supporting actor. (The Donaldson predated today's Tony, though the two awards competed for most prestigious honors from 1947-1955, when the former was discontinued.)

Sons and *Streetcar* represent a central theme in Kazan's post-war work —— "the politics of the family" (Richard Schickel, *Time*, March 8, 1999), ranging from the failure of patriarchal figures, to women pushed towards breakdowns by a crass modern society. This Kazan focus is pertinent to Malden, since their future film collaborations would continue in this vein. For example, Malden would reprise his *Streetcar* role in Kazan's later screen adaptation (1951) of Tennessee Williams' play. After winning an Academy Award for this part, Malden would next be Oscar-nominated for his passionately political priest in Kazan's *On the Waterfront* (1954, again co-starred with Brando). And the actor would receive a rare film lead in Kazan's production of the controversial Tennessee Williams script, *Baby Doll* (1956).

Kazan's friendship and influence over Malden also surfaced in a myriad of other ways. For instance, the actor-turned-director was the one who convinced Malden to change his Serbian name (Mladen Sekulovich) for Broadway. Kazan (whose full Greek surname was Kazanjoglou) argued that Sekulovich was both too long for a marquee, and sounded too Jewish. Kazan had seen how the liberal politics of his 1930's Group Theatre activities had suffered from anti-Semitism. Sadly, this was an era in which many real Jewish entertainers also felt the need to hide their ethnicity with an Anglicized name. Period examples would range from star Danny Kaye (David Kaminski), to Malden's struggling future bride, Mona Greenberg, who used the name Mona Graham for her New York auditions. Thus, Mladen Sekulovich dropped his surname, and replaced it with his given name ... after changing the order of the l and the a. Next, he appropriated a favorite uncle's given name (Karl) to finish, or more correctly, *start* the metamorphosis to Karl Malden.

Ironically, despite Kazan's gift for both theatre and screen directing, as well as molding a stable of method actors (from Marlon Brando to James Dean) through his later Actors studio (co-founded with Lee Strasberg), Kazan is now most famous/infamous for naming names (1952) to the House Un-American Activities Committee (HUAC) during the McCarthy Era. This Judas act, in the eyes of many liberals, added yet more victims to the list of blacklisted film artists during a dark period in the history of American civil liberties.

How does this pertain to Malden? Despite Kazan's own lack of loyalty to friends and colleagues whose names he gave up, the apolitical Malden still stood by his mentor. But Kazan's ties to many of their mutual friends, including Arthur Miller and Rod Steiger, were permanently shattered. Indeed, decades later Malden's co-star from *On the Waterfront*, Steiger, still had the most visceral emotions about Kazan's actions: "It was like I found out my father was sleeping with my sister. The passing of time can do nothing to ease the pain of those who suffered" (*Entertainment Weekly*, February 5, 1999).

Paradoxically, the catalyst for Steiger's painful reminiscence has a direct link to Malden. In 1989 Malden started his term as president of the Academy of Motion Picture Arts and Sciences. A decade later he effectively lobbied the board to award Kazan an honorary Oscar for lifetime achievement. Malden said of his decision, "If anyone deserved this honorary award because of his talent and body of work, it was Kazan" (*New York Times*, July 2, 2009).

This 1999 event remains the most controversial honorary Oscar ever bestowed. In fact, during the Kazan portion of the ceremony, while some audience members stood and applauded ... others turned their backs. Maybe nationally syndicated humorist Donald Kaul struck the best balance on the evening: "He [Kazan] deserves his award [on artistic achievement]. The fact that he's kind of a louse shouldn't make any difference. If you withheld Oscars from Hollywood people for being louses, you'd only get to give out about three a year" (*Des Moines Register*, March 21, 1999). Though Malden's efforts for Kazan represented payback from a loyal friend, making the award all about the work is pure Malden. Remember the title of his memoir —— *When Do I Start?*

Given Malden's long association with Kazan, one might assume the Hoosier was a Method actor, an approach sometimes also called the "total immersion system," since the performer is asked to completely draw upon personal experience. If the actor can embrace this total involvement, s/he is rewarded not only by a great performance but also by a sense of freedom. The intensity synonymous with Method, coupled with its proclivity for inarticulate realism, had some critics affectionately deriding it as the "itch-and-scratch" style. That playfulness is apparent in

Malden's memoir comment about *not* being a Method actor: "I do have a method, of course. That is, any method that works." Still, a sense of Method helped him get inside two of his most diverse characters. For *Streetcar*'s Mitch, Malden's epiphany was realizing how central this figure's mother was to everything he did —— despite the fact she never appears in the play/film. Thus, Malden kept his own mother's voice in his head when Mitch pondered questions like, "What would my mother think about Blanche?" Malden's Mitch is a gentle befuddled giant for much of *Streetcar*, completely out of his element as Blanche's suitor. It was also a character close to the real Malden, as Kazan later revealed in his book-length interview with Jeff Young (*Kazan*, 1999): "We didn't have to do much with Karl … [on *Streetcar*]. He was very well cast psychologically. He was very polite with women because he was very uncertain [romantically]." In contrast, Malden was equally memorable as the cruelly domineering father in the Jimmy Piersall baseball biography film *Fear Strikes Out* (1957). This stark profile of a diamond star (Anthony Perkins) pushed to a mental breakdown by a perfectionist parent resulted in Malden instinctually tapping into the Method. At first the actor felt he had found the character through his normal preparation —— repeated readings of the script and lengthy private reflections. But after viewing early rushes (the day-to-day film footage) of *Fear*, Malden realized he was essentially channeling the controlling voice of his own old world immigrant father.

This writer's favorite Malden performances are the positive leaders, such as the crusading priest of *On the Waterfront*, or his fatherly General Omar Bradley in Franklin Schaffner's *Patton* (1969, which is such a wonderful and necessary balance to the explosive personality of George C. Scott's Oscar-winning title character). But the villainy inherent to Malden's angry parent in *Fear* foreshadowed several later threatening characters. These parts would include the sadistic sheriff in Marlon Brando's *One-Eyed Jacks* (1961), the warden in *Birdman of Alcatraz* (1962, starring an

Oscar-winning Burt Lancaster), the Nazi-like cavalry officer in John Ford's *Cheyenne Autumn* (1964), and the Western killer in Henry Hathaway's *Nevada Smith* (1966, opposite Steve McQueen). Consequently, one could argue that Malden's brilliance as a character actor was tied to parts peppered with moral weight ... or entirely devoid of morality.

Inherently shy in real life, and being the perennial loner, born of childhood poverty and an immigrant-like status (growing up in Serbian neighborhoods), Malden also excelled at vulnerable antiheroic roles, from *Streetcar*'s Mitch, to the cuckolded crooked dealer in Norman Jewison's *The Cincinnati Kid* (1965, with McQueen), However, maybe his most multi-faceted figure was the agent/hustler of Mervyn LeRoy's *Gypsy* (1962, with Natalie Wood), which allowed him to play everything from musical comedy to romantic victim. The experience was also a plug for the studio system. Malden told Natalie Wood biographer Suzanne Finstad (*Natasha*, 2001) "[*Gypsy*] was challenging for *both* of us. I'm not a singer and dancer, she wasn't a singer and a dancer, and we both went at it. She wanted to do it badly, and so did I. It was something we never would have gotten a test for if we hadn't been under contract with Warners."

The most amusingly poignant tale of Malden's real world *everyman* nature is, ironically, tied to the night he won an Oscar. Initially, he had not planned to attend the Academy Awards. Malden's home and professional base was still New York (with Broadway then being his bread and butter); he was in Hollywood by mere coincidence at the time of the Oscar ceremony (shooting *Operation Secret*, 1952). But a Warner's executive encouraged him to borrow a tux from wardrobe and attend. Given that the pre-television Oscars were neither *the event* of today, nor feeling he had a chance against fellow nominees like Peter Ustinov for *Quo Vadis*, and Gig Young for *Come Fill the Cup* (both 1951), Malden at least felt little pressure when he drove his rented Chevy to the ceremony.

However, when Malden approached the limousine traffic and klieg lights near the Pantages Theatre entrance, he began to realize the magnitude of the event. To avoid attention, he parked several blocks away and inauspiciously walked to the theatre with a brown topper over his tux. Once inside, he found his seat near Humphrey Bogart, whom he vaguely knew from the Warner lot. Shortly, he was shocked to hear his name called as the Best Supporting Actor. Ever the practical one, he asked a bemused Bogart to watch his topper, before he went to collect his statuette.

After winning an Oscar, there is a backstage press conference which goes on forever. Malden was still answering reporters' questions when Bogart suddenly appeared, statuette in-hand, Best Actor winner for *The African Queen* (1951). Yet, Malden's first comment to the iconic actor was about the overcoat. Bogart responded, "Fuck the overcoat! You just won an Oscar!" Malden was never *Casablanca* (1942) cool… but few are.

In later years Malden was so stereotyped as a villain that he actually spoofed the phenomenon by playing an over-the-top terrorist in the parody picture *Murderers Row* (1966, with Dean Martin reprising his tongue-in-check James Bond-like Matt Helm character). Other notable Malden heavies would range from his slovenly cowboy in Delmer Daves' *The Hanging Tree* (1959, opposite Gary Cooper), to playing Barbara Streisand's stepfather in Martin Ritt's *Nuts* (1987, a character whose molesting of Streisand as a child had resulted in her figure's later prostitution). Though Malden's part was not large, the payoff revelation is pivotal to this screen adaptation of the play.

Malden's talents included directing, though he was such a consummate actor, that megaphoning was almost too overwhelming. His one credit as a director, *Time Limit* (1957), was done as a favor to the film's star, Richard Widmark, who also co-produced the picture. Malden's filming of this courtroom drama, about a former Army POW who might have collaborated with the enemy during the Korean War, is riveting. The film poses two intriguing questions:

"What would one do under torture?" and "Is it permissible to shift ethical guidelines under such circumstances?" The movie also has an added sub- textual resonance, given Malden's relationship with Kazan and other artists impacted by blacklisting and the HUAC "trials." Because of Malden's success with *Time Limit*, he was also asked to finish the direction of the equally acclaimed *Hanging Tree*, when illness kept Daves from finishing the picture. I am also of the belief that a factor in Marlon Brando's decision to ask Malden (a longtime friend since the Kazan days) to co-star in *One-Eyed Jacks* involved Brando's lack of experience as a director. Then, if any problems occurred, Malden represented a safety valve director in the cast. Many first-time directors have followed a similar plan, such as Clint Eastwood casting his megaphoning mentor (Don Siegel) as the bartender in *Play Misty for Me* (1971), in case Eastwood stumbled in his behind-the-camera debut.

As Malden's film career began to wind down in the 1970s, he found new professional challenges and recognition on television. The transition was, however, almost as psychologically difficult for Malden as his early 1960s decision to focus primarily on film, after over twenty years of defining himself as a stage actor. Regardless, his most enduring small screen legacy is the aforementioned *Streets of San Francisco*, in which his humanistic police detective arguably gave him more pop culture recognition than anything else in his long career. Once again he was the passionate good guy, not that far removed from his activist priest in *On the Waterfront*. His Lt. Stone was gruff(checkout that name), but there was a wonderful odd couple relationship with the young co-star, Michael Douglas.

Malden also won new TV fans by spoofing his all-business detective *Stone* on Johnny Carson's *Tonight Show*, much as Carson had had fun with Jack Webb's even more somber police Sgt. Joe Friday, from the *Dragnet* series (1952-59, 1967-70), Malden's comically self-deprecating appearances with American's favorite funnyman (sometimes wearing a Malden-like bulbous nose) subtextually announced to millions of viewers that Malden had fully arrived as a major player.

When not appearing on *Streets*, he frequently surfaced on television as the previously noted popular pitchman for American Express travelers' checks. Television also allowed him to "essay" a role he knew only too well from his Hoosier youth —— a hard bitten steel worker in *Skag* (a short-lived NBC series, 1980). And his Oscar received some statuette company in 1984, when Malden won an Emmy for NBC's drama *Fatal Vision*, in which he played a father who discovers his son-in-law is a murderer. Malden continued to appear sporadically on television as late as 2000, when he guested on *West Wing* during its inaugural season, playing a priest advising the president (Martin Sheen) on the death penalty. It had been nearly a half century since his Academy Awards nominated performance as a priest in *On the Waterfront*.

To paraphrase a Mark Twain quip from late in his life, "The older I get, the more clearly I recall events.... that never occurred." This was not the case with Malden. For me, a frequent biographer, Malden's crowning achievement was his aforementioned memoir. Like many of Malden's heroic characters, the text is direct, honest, and forever balanced, when checked against other sources. That is seldom the case in most autobiographies —— which might better be spelled alibiography. Malden was the real goods.

(Originally appeared in *TRACES of Midwestern History*, Winter 2012; Wes D. Gehring Copyright.)

RED SKELTON:
IT ALL STARTED WITH THE DONUTS

Red Skelton in the midst of his donut routine (circa 1938).

As often happens in life, the catalyst for a memorable moment came out of desperation — young vaudevillian Red Skelton needed new material. There are two variations, however, to the donut rescue. One story has the comedian tanking in a Montreal nightclub, the Lido, because on his initial mid-1930s visit to French Canada he overreached his talents, attempting to be a Hoosier Maurice Chevalier. But when Skelton fell back on his tired standard shtick, his exasperated wife/manager Edna Stillwell said, "'I could write stuff better than that.' Red's answer was, 'Why don't you?' also in sarcasm. But she did, and she has written his material ever since. [*Indianapolis Star*, August 31, 1941]."

The second take on how Stillwell came to create the sketches is born of triumph, not failure. Skelton is a smash success at the Lido club, and one night a representative for Montreal's top vaudeville house/film theater, Loew's Harry Anger, sees the act. Anger is bowled over and signs Skelton for an extended booking at Loew's. After a short exit to honor a prior Chicago commitment, the comedian is again headlining at Loew's, but Anger wanted all new material. Skelton noted: "That floored me, but again it was Edna to the rescue. She said she could write 'em. I said, Well, now was certainly the time for her to display her hidden talent, if any ... So Edna took over my writing, and she's been at it ever since. And there's no [one] better [*Milwaukee Journal*, December 12, 1941]."

These two 1941 comments were *both* credited to Skelton within a time span of three months. Such are the frustrations of a biographer. But as noted chronicler Paul Murray Kendall reminds fans of the genre, getting the "absolute truth" is nearly an impossible task. Instead, one must inspire for the "best truth." In this situation, the "best truth" would seem to be that in the mid-1930s (probably late 1935) Skelton elevated his performance skills to "major league" status. This soon led to vaudeville's "A" bookings, all of which was dependent upon Stillwell's observational humor. (Critiques of Skelton's performances at Loew's began to appear in the *Montreal Gazette* during 1936.) An additional "best truth" take occurs in yet another 1941 article that indicated Stillwell's initial writing "didn't seem funny to that experienced comedian, Red Skelton. 'But the customers laughed,' he said. 'Edna knew what she was doing. She kept on writing my material [*New York World Telegram*, August 14, 1941]." Fittingly, this later article was amusingly entitled, "Ex-Usherette [Wife] Leads Skelton to Success." And this title is hardly hyperbole. As a *Photoplay* essay from the following year stated. "There can be no story of Red Skelton without Edna [July 1942]."

So where does the aforementioned coffee shop donut man figure in these proceedings? Well, the young, desperate-for-new-material couple were sitting in a Montreal diner when the eureka moment arrived. Skelton recalled, "Edna noticed a man at the counter dunking donuts in coffee and Edna said, 'There's our first routine.' Darned if the gal wasn't right …[what followed was] probably the best thing I've ever done.'" Skelton's 1979 biographer Arthur Marx (son of Groucho Marx) even called this donut epiphany the "exact moment when [Red] quit being just another entertainer and crossed over to the ranks of the superstars."

The donut-dunking routine that evolved from "slightly exaggerating" reality had Skelton inventively demonstrating various types of dunkers, from the petite to the sloppy, with several sorts in between. The other varieties included both the flamboyant dunker and the timid one who tries to dunk on the sly. But my favorite Skelton donut dunker is the most antiheroic, the poor person who miscalculates his pastry submersion time and dissolves the donut!

Drawing from period reviews, which sometimes suggest as many as nine dunker types by 1937, Skelton also further embellished the routine through making a big deal of dragging onto the stage a table, a large cup of coffee, and a plate of donuts. After this comic setup, Skelton peppered his visual shtick with amusing verbal patter. One might label this a pioneering example of gross-out humor, since Skelton talked with his mouth full, occasionally "broadcasting" donut chunks in every direction. The comedian also became known for throwing several "sinkers" into the audience. Not quite gross-out Gallagher, the melon-smashing fanatic of fifty years later, but it was still groundbreaking comedy for the Great Depression. Appropriately, one critic praised the merry mess of a routine as the "donut-dunking massacre [*Milwaukee Journal*, June 20, 1937]."

Despite the realistic foundation of Skelton's sketch, the ultimate over-the-top "donut-dunking massacre" nature of the routine reminds me of pop culture critic John G. Cawelti's description of the comic-laden mystery prose of Dashiell Hammett, where "'realistic' detail [can take on] a surrealistic flavor." For film comedy guru Leo McCarey, a writer/director contemporary of Skelton and Hammett, starting with an anchor in reality is central to comic exaggeration: "Even in comedy of the most fantastic variety there has to be a could-be quality lurking around in every sequence. We may stretch the credulity of audiences to the breaking point one moment—but we have to snap right back into reality [for people to fully connect with the comedy"]— (*Hollywood Reporter*, October 28, 1939). Thus, Skelton's donut sketch realistically started with one type of dunker, only to have the comedian amusingly pervert the situation. Red would then "snap right back into reality" with another "could-be" dunker that he would then comically exaggerate, and so on.

Sixty years after the routine's creation Skelton confessed, "When I did the donut bit for the first time I had written on the tablecloth the next little piece of business I was going to do." And during the initial performance history of the sketch he sometimes changed his personal prompter, depending upon the audience's response. Skelton added, "The first time, it ran, like, fifteen minutes [he chuckled]. The stagehand said, 'Hey, that's a funny bit but it's awful long.' So then I started cutting things out that didn't get the big laughs [Oral History, New York Public Library of Lincoln Center, February 20, 1996]."

This routine defined him for years. For example, when Skelton's film career making movie *Whistling in the Dark* (1941) opened, it was not unusual for critics, such as the *New York Journal American's* G. E. Blackford, to footnote just who this new movie comic was by way of the sketch: "Many know Mr. Skelton from his efforts to educate the amusement-seeking public as to the correct and modern and most efficacious [provocative] manner of dunking a donut [August 28, 1941]."

Of course, for a vaudevillian such as Skelton, even in that medium's declining 1930s, a classic routine could fuel a career for years. Unlike the later "glass furnace" nature of television, where a nightly audience of millions metaphorically burned up countless material, a stage sketch played to just a fraction of those numbers. Moreover, with a vaudevillian only visiting a given city once or twice a year, positive word-of-mouth comments even gave legendary bits an added uniqueness, and a reason to repeat the sketch.

Skelton's donut shtick also represented an entertainingly amusing subject for a series of advertisement-like articles. For instance, in 1938 *New York Daily Mirror* writer Robert Coleman turned mathematician as he documented that the routine necessitated the comedian eat *nine* donuts a show and vaudeville had him doing *five* shows a day! Is it any wonder that Coleman observed, "Red is a doughnut consumer. He slaughters doughnuts in wholesale lots [November 10, 1938]." Earlier that year the *New York Daily Mirror* film critic Blaud Johaueson also went the merry math route with regard to Skelton's famous sketch. Though her numbers were somewhat inflated, the article was titled, "At 12,000 and Each Made 'em Roar [July 13, 1938]." Again, crediting Stillwell as Skelton's writer, Johaueson posited that the "American public always gives a doughnut a laugh." At the same time Skelton gave his own comic take on the subject to the *New York Daily News*, "Red Skelton, the doughnut-eating fool at Loew's State, says he has eaten so many doughnuts in the last few years that he swells when it rains [July 8, 1938]." Years later Skelton told me this avalanche of the Great Depression donuts resulted in a more than thirty-pound weight gain. When Hollywood eventually called to put the routine on film, in

Having Wonderful Time (1938), the producing studio (RKO) put the comedian on a strict diet.

Sometimes the donut-related problems had nothing to do with the added poundage. Often it was difficult just maintaining the pastry supply. Skelton needed five to six dozen donuts a day; four dozen were for the show, with the extras covering the random hungry fellow vaudevillian, who would eat the "props." But shortly before one late 1930s Milwaukee opening, Skelton and Stillwell arrived at the theatre to find empty donut boxes. At first they thought it was a prank or overly ravenous performers. It soon became apparent, however, that the Skelton's Boston bulldog, Jiggs, had eaten more than sixty donuts. While the various stage acts on the bill fanned out in the neighborhood in search of "sinkers" for Red's routine, the comedian took care of a very sick Jiggs. This was the same bulldog that figured in some later entertainingly hyperbolic Skelton stories. Skelton's daughter, Valentina, remembered how Jiggs would be somehow lowered out an upper story boarding house (where pets were not allowed) window for his late-night constitutional. One evening this allegedly caused a passing drunk to stumble back to a nearby bar and shout, "There's flying bulldogs out there." — [interview with the author, September 18, 1986.]

The thankfully preserved sinker sketch of *Having a Wonderful Time*, with a dieted thin Skelton, is a more streamlined look at the routine. Running right at three minutes, it features three dunker types: the cross-eyed variety, the society sort, and the sneaky dunker. Though not as outrageous as the review descriptions of the stage original, the movie take on donut dunking gives one a sense of the added business the comedian brought to the bit, from using a second tablecloth as a comic bib, to his ongoing patter: "Notice [coming out squeaky and high pitched] how I hold the little creature [the donut], with the index finger. The pinky [finger] should always be out, that's so if you slip you won't go to your elbow [into the coffee cup]."

Naturally, one need not be a psychology student to see a certain irony in an eating routine being so popular during the Great

Depression. Granted, funny films of all eras feature food sketches, from Charlie Chaplin stealing hot dog bites from a child in *The Circus* (1928), to John Belushi's instigation of the food fight in *National Lampoon's Animal House* (1978). Still, there are a plethora of eating-related sketches in Depression-era movie comedies. And the range is simply inspired, be it loopy Stan Laurel munching on wax fruit in *Sons of the Desert* (1933), or Chico and Harpo Marx pitting their combination peanut and hot dog stand against Edgar Kennedy's lemonade concession in *Duck Soup* (1933).

The proverbial golden spoon, however, for *the* Depression-era food-conscious clown would probably go to Joe E. "cavernous-mouthed" Brown. The comedian's first extended comedy scene in one of his definitive films, *Elmer the Great* (1933), is predicated upon his title character eating the largest breakfast on record — stacks of pancakes and ham, apple pie, gingerbread, donuts and jam, and assorted fruit (especially a comic favorite, the banana), while drinking coffee and a large glass of milk. But unlike a more typical comedy eating scene, such as when the Marx Brothers focus on pigging out in *Room Service* (1938), Brown's breakfast in *Elmer* has him talking away, too. He later amusingly confessed, this was no easy task, "even with my mouth."

I dwell on Brown for a special food-related comedy connection to Skelton. Upon the release of *Elmer,* a *New York World Telegram* article appeared titled "His Heavy (Eating) Role Fits Joe Brown Exactly [May 6, 1933]." The piece revealed that the comedian "attributes his propensity for eating parts to the time when he would have appreciated them because of the scarcity of good [eating] fare in his days of initiation into show business." This catalyst was equally applicable to Skelton. In fact, he told me as much on several different occasions when I was preparing my first [of three] books on the comedian. But for both Brown and Skelton, the lack of food factor predates their early apprenticeship as entertainers. Each of these funnymen had Dickensian childhoods, where a square meal was almost as rare as a new pair of shoes. Flash forward to the Great

Depression, and millions of fellow Americans were suffering through similar deprivation. Consequently, just as 1930s screwball comedies featured the escapism of watching the eccentric idle rich, the era's personality comedies often showcased another vicarious bit of voyeurism—a comic abundance of food. One could even liken the sweeping comprehensiveness of individual food phenomenon bits to Barbara W. Tuchman's definition of the biography, "The universal in the particular."

"Success," as the old axiom goes, "often has many parents." While Stillwell was the author of the donut sketch, she might have been inspired by director Frank Capra's hit film *It Happened One Night* (1934), a pioneering screwball comedy with Clark Gable and Claudette Colbert. Where's the donut connection? Capra's movie had an auto camp scene in which Gable's man-of-the-people type briefly demonstrates the appropriate way to dunk a donut to his debutante sidekick Colbert. It is a fleeting moment in a film that otherwise milks such scenes. But it might have planted an idea in Stillwell's mind.

What are the chances she even saw the film? Excellent. There is a period photograph of Skelton parodying another more famous *Night* scene — Gable's how to hitchhike routine. Paradoxically, for all the worldly wisdom of Gable's everyman, his tried and tested thumb is no match for Colbert's revealingly shapely leg. The aforementioned Skelton-spoof photograph has him exposing a less than lovely limb. But even without this *Night*-related picture of the comedian, it would have been hard to miss the influence of the Capra movie. *Night* is one of the seminal films in Hollywood history. And it was a box office smash that would not go away, getting extended 1935 playing dates after that year's Academy Awards made *Night* the first film to ever sweep all five main categories— Best Picture, Director, Actor, Actress, and Screenplay. (This is something that has still only happened twice since *Night*—*One Flew Over the Cuckoo's Nest* in 1975 and *Silence of the Lambs* in 1991.) The Oscar overdose that came *Night*'s way, followed by 1935 repeat business, approximates the genesis of the Skelton donut-dunking sketch.

Of course, one could argue that a whole "how to" mentality permeated 1930s comedy, from the hitchhiking and donut examples of *Night*, to Stillwell's proclivity for variations upon the signature donut sketch she created for Skelton. For example, another Stillwell routine for Skelton, which was also featured in *Having Wonderful Time*, had the comedian amusingly demonstrating the various ways people go up and down stairs. But the nominal 1930s comedy king of "how-to" humor was Robert Benchley. His first book-length collections of comic essays began to appear in the 1920s, something he complemented with drama reviews for the old humor magazine *Life* (before moving to the *New Yorker*) and the occasional comic lectures in vaudeville. One could argue that after the 1935 death of Will Rogers, Benchley soon assumed the mantle of America's favorite print humorist. He was certainly one of the most active. While the popular writing continued, he was increasingly active in film and on radio. Most germane to the Skeltons were Benchley's acclaimed short films, such as his Oscar-winning (Best Live Action Short Subject) *How to Sleep* (1935).

Benchley had pioneered the live-action sound short with such brilliant early outings as *The Treasurer's Report* (1928), which he originally made a hit in 1920s vaudeville) and *The Sex Life of the Polyp* (1928). However, the plaudits generated by *How to Sleep* had Benchley doing assorted "how-to" films for years. As with the 1935 awards and reissuing of *It Happened One Night*, *How to Sleep* was generating attention at approximately the same time Stillwell was creating the donut-dunking sketch for Skelton. Moreover, the numerous observational routines that Stillwell soon penned for her husband were often reminiscent of Benchley's lecture or professorial style. Indeed, this Skelton-Benchley link is given a historically casual connection in a July 3, 1937 *Detroit Free Press* rave review of Skelton's donut sketch. On the same page that critic James S.

Pooler praises the comedian's routine as a comic "lecture" is a review of Benchley's latest parody lecture, *How to Start the Day Right* (1937).

By 1938 Skelton himself was accenting the professorial slant. *Pic* magazine, drawing upon the comedian's material, stated, "Professor Red Skelton, B. D. (Bachelor of Dunking), is currently delivering his lecture on 'Dunking As Art and Science' in the Movies [August 23, 1938]." With a photo spread done at Maxwell House Coffee's "doughnuttery" on Broadway, Skelton had the comic last word. "'The field of dunking,' says the professor, 'has not yet been fully explored. And I for one think it's just as well.'"

None of the previous professorial parallels need take away from the comic creativity of Skelton's partner. One could simply liken this Depression-era tendency for "how to" humor to what the Germans call zeitgeist—the mood or spirit of a particular period of history. Regardless of the source of inspiration, this donut-dunking bit would lead the Skeltons to star status in 1930s America. The sketch also brought Skelton some early fame back home in Indiana when the *Indianapolis Star* ran a Sunday feature titled "Indiana Boy's Doughnut Dunking Hit on Stage [June 27, 1937]." Ultimately, the Stillwell routines brilliantly bring an audience a slice-of-life silliness that, to paraphrase the much later *New Yorker* critic Hilton Als, was "not her world but *the* world."

While Stillwell's writing made a unique contribution to Skelton's career, it is not unusual for celebrated comedians to be greatly assisted by creative women. For instance, today's most prominent Hoosier humorist, David Letterman, owes much of his success to his longtime companion and former *Late Night* head writer Merrill Markoe. Even her take on Letterman's style, what she labeled "perceived reality," is comparable to Stillwell making Skelton appreciate "slightly exaggerating" reality. To borrow an insight from art critic Holland Cotter, "Sometimes a revolution is just a matter of altered perspective, a changed position." Interestingly enough, a few years after Stillwell's writing and managing helped orchestrate

Skelton's stardom, one of his eventual celebrated comedy contemporaries, Danny Kaye, came to owe his success to another writing/manager wife, Sylvia Fine. The description of Fine's relationship to Kaye, by the comedian's definitive biographer, Martin Gottfried, might just as well be describing Skelton and Stillwell: "The most important thing in Danny's life was to succeed as an entertainer, and for that he lacked not just material but a performing identity. Sylvia, as a writer, needed a medium. In Danny, she found a purpose, almost a maternal one: to use her gift to conceive and nurture the man of her dreams; to give birth to Danny Kaye." Much the same could be said of the Skelton-Stillwell relationship.

Ironically, the obsessive drive of both Stillwell and Fine ultimately soured their personal relationships with the comedy legends they helped to create, though Stillwell continued to manage and write for Skelton well into his second marriage. But that is getting ahead of the couple's donut-changing beginnings.

(Originally appeared as the cover page article in *TRACES of Indiana and Midwestern History*, Winter, 2009; Wes D. Gehring Copyright.)

LOST IN PARADISE/CONDEMNED TO HELL:

Actress Frances Farmer and a

Comparison to Carole Lombard

Frances Farmer as the daughter in *Come and Get It* (1936).

As during Farmer's turbulent troubled life, when much of her story was grossly misrepresented, her profiles in death have been compounded by more lies. Even the celebrated film biography of the actress, *Frances* (1982), for which the striking look-alike Jessica Lange received a Best Actress Oscar nomination, is peppered with errors. The movie's white knight lover/protector (Sam Shepard) is pure Hollywood fabrication. Worse yet, William Arnold's biography, *Frances Farmer: Shadowland* (1978), is a pulp-fiction novelization of her life, which took a later court case to make the author admit.

Although Farmer's unnecessary mental institution incarcerations are an indictment of the troubled American health-care system of the 1940s, the actress did not have a lobotomy, nor was she the victim of alleged prostitution rings administered by orderlies at these various facilities. Nevertheless, Farmer passed many nights/ years in a metaphorical Gethsemane----and then some. Yet, both Arnold's book, and Farmer's own alleged memoir, *Will There Really Be a Morning?* (1972, largely ghost-written after her death by her friend Jean Ratcliffe), are studies in sensationalism, with the aforementioned lobotomy/prostitution claims merely the most inflammatory of the travesties noted.

To both tell the real story of Farmer, and to better place her in the context of the times, one might start by showcasing the numerous period parallels with Hoosier-born contemporary actress Carole Lombard. Each woman came from a dysfunctional family ruled by an eccentrically independent mother. Each of these parents committed, for a time, to what was then called a "Victorian divorce," by relocating to a separate city with her children in tow. In each case the city in question was Los Angeles. Although the Seattle-born Farmer and her siblings later returned, for a time, to their father's Seattle home, she never knew a strong male presence as a youngster.

Both Lombard and Farmer eventually became Paramount studio film stars during the 1930s. Also, each of these independent, salty talking, blonde beauties ("profane angels") had the same pivotal Hollywood mentor, legendary Hoosier-born director Howard

Hawks. His work with Lombard on *Twentieth Century* (1934) was instrumental in making her a headliner. Hawks's close collaboration with Farmer on *Come and Get It* (1936, co-directed with William Wyler) also made Farmer a star. The *New York Times* described Farmer's dual roles, "first as Lotta Morgan, the cabaret singer, and then as her daughter ... are not merely a delight to the masculine eye but an actress of more than usual merit."

Each actress' signature movie appeared in 1936----Lombard's *My Man Godfrey* (for which she received her only Best Actress Oscar nomination), and Farmer's *Come and Get It*. The latter picture was a particular triumph for the young performer, given she was a Hollywood newcomer asked to play such diverse types, essentially a prostitute and a virginal young woman. Because of these successes, both Lombard and Farmer received a great deal of in-print attention the following year. Finally, both actresses' screen careers ended in 1942; Lombard was killed in a plane crash shortly before the opening of *To Be Or Not to Be,* and Farmer's life started to spiral out of control after the release of *Son of Fury*.

There were differences, however, between the two actresses. Unlike the gregarious Lombard, Farmer was more of an intellectual loner, a wannabe writer craving what most writers want----solitude. Her early talent as an author contributed to further pushing people away. In a 1931 West Seattle High School creative writing class, Farmer penned an essay titled, "God Dies." Included in her sister's (Edith Farmer Elliot) self-published 1978 biography of the actress, *Look Back in Love* (a flawed but more honest attempt at a profile), Farmer's brief article stated, in part: "It wasn't a murder. I think God just died of old age. And when I realized that he wasn't any more, it didn't shock me. It seemed natural and right! [Things] happened whether he wanted them to or not ..... It seemed a waste of time to have him .... I felt rather proud to think that I had found the truth myself, without help from anyone. It puzzled me that other people hadn't found out, too. God was gone .... Why couldn't they [adults] see it? It still puzzles me." Her impressed teacher entered the essay in *Scholastic Magazine's* prestigious national writing competition. She won and received a hundred-dollar prize — the equivalent of nearly $2,000 today.

Not surprisingly, given the times and the topic, Farmer's joy turned to consternation when her winning essay became a catalyst for coast-to-coast conservatives bemoaning the increasing atheism and/or godless communism running rampant in the country's public schools. The hometown criticism was particularly severe. Years later, the actress confessed in a *Colliers* May 8, 1937, article, "It was all pretty sad, because for the first time I found out how stupid people could be. It sort of made me feel alone in the world. The more people pointed at me in scorn, the more stubborn I got, and when they began calling me the Bad Girl of West Seattle High, I tried to live up to it." This legitimately earned rebel attitude did not serve her well in the decades to come.

While Lombard and her mother were forever allies, Farmer and her mother, Lillian, had more of a love-hate relationship. For example, during the "God Dies" controversy, Lillian called press conferences and made the injustice more about an attack upon herself than her daughter. Frances just wanted the controversy to go away, but Lillian relished the secondhand attention.

Lombard always wanted to be in the movies and enjoyed every aspect of filmmaking. In contrast, when Farmer was bitten by the stage bug during her time at an avant-garde theater program at the University of Washington, she embraced the standard elitist perspective on motion pictures as a poor substitute for real acting. If anything from Farmer's memoir sounds like something she could have written, the following passage reflected her thoughts on the two media: "Working before a camera was uninspiring and consisted mainly of long waits with tedious consideration given to angles and shot dimensions. Sequences were not related or in sequence, and it was difficult to catch a feeling and hold it. A characterization was never given a chance to grow.... In comparison, the theatre was alive and orderly."

Given the right director, such as Hawks, Farmer was capable of cinema greatness. In Joseph McBride's book-length interview with the director, *Hawks on Hawks* (1982), the master filmmaker claimed, "I don't think there's any doubt that Frances Farmer was the best actress I ever worked with .... If it hadn't been for personal things that happened to her, she'd have gone on and been a very big star." Keep in mind that Hawks's leading ladies included Louise Brooks, Joan Crawford, Katharine Hepburn, Jean Arthur, Rita Hayworth, Rosalind Russell, Barbara Stanwyck, Lauren Bacall (his most famous discovery), Ann Sheridan, Ginger Rogers, Marilyn Monroe, Jane Russell, and Angie Dickenson.

One could even argue, as Todd McCarthy does in his definitive biography of the director, *Howard Hawks: The Grey Fox of Hollywood* (1997), that Farmer's *Come and Get It* cabaret singer was the first fully realized prototype of the legendary Hawksian woman, "the tough, assertive, sexy, comfortable in the company of men romantic lead." The director's nickname for Farmer's older figure in *Come and Get It* was "lusty wench." Farmer's naturally deep throaty voice was also something the director liked in his actresses. Hollywood legend has it that he even had the then novice Bacall leave the set and literally scream for a prolonged period of time to give her voice the husky provocative sound that became her trademark.

A fourth contrast between Lombard and Farmer was their approach to acting. Lombard excelled at playing a variation of herself. Hawks had been unimpressed with Lombard's early films, and only cast her in *Twentieth Century* after seeing the real free-spirited actress at a Hollywood party. This was the quality he wanted for his picture, and it would forever after be a basic component of the Lombard persona. In contrast, the Method-oriented Farmer wanted to lose herself in each part----becoming that character. Hawks also respected this position. The two went out one evening in search of a beer joint where they could find the type of "lusty wench" prostitute Farmer was to portray in *Come and Get It*. Once they found a Los Angeles red-light district, the *Hawks on Hawks* interview has the director telling her to come back every night for two weeks and play at being picked up: " 'Whoever ... [the guy], talk to him, be that woman, with her mannerisms and everything. And then we'll make a [screen] test.' She was just fabulous in the part."

Just as Farmer parallels with Lombard demonstrate what might have been (a successful movie start tied to one persona), the contrasts provide clues as to why Farmer unraveled in the 1940s. Farmer was an artistic loner disgusted by a medium (movies) little interested in producing meaningful art. Ironically, William Wellman, who often produced film classics, had an attitude about those who tried to find art in Hollywood that was typical of the times: "It's like calling canned goods caviar." Consistent with this observation, the Great Depression-era film capital was known as a "dream *factory*." Worse yet for Farmer, besides disliking the Hollywood assembly-line system, stars were then expected to always be on call for public relations campaigns. Farmer simply wanted to act. By 1937, as the *Photoplay* piece noted, Farmer had burned all her Hollywood bridges: "What you may hear is that she is another *enfant terrible*, out Hepburning [the independent Katharine] Hepburn [a Farmer favorite, and] out-sulking [the perfectionist Margaret] Sullavan ... [as] a cocky brat." When Farmer's instability escalated in the early 1940s, there was no safety net (the studio system) available to save her from a mental-institution nightmare, and many film folks just did not care.

So why did Farmer not walk away from what she saw as Hollywood hypocrisy? Her goal was to use cinema success as a catalyst for her own dream: appearing on Broadway. Indeed, the plan worked, at least briefly, when she starred in playwright Clifford Odet's left-wing Group Theatre New York hit production of *Golden Boy*. The *New York Times* called her "sufficient to the part and excellent in the romantic scenes." Once again, she found a mentor, Odets, who also became her lover. Unfortunately for Farmer, the Odets/*Golden Boy* collaboration ended badly for the actress. After touring with the production to even greater hosannas in the United States, Odets abruptly dropped her from both a European tour *and* his personal life. Biographers of the gifted playwright are universal in their criticism of his treatment of the actress.

Farmer was devastated and never got over this betrayal. She returned to Hollywood in 1938 as an even more distrustful loner. Ratcheting up her potential powder-keg instability was that few of the fourteen films she appeared in between 1936 and 1942 were either memorable or artistically challenging. Instead, they were often mind-candy entertainment. As a star, her two greatest box-office hits were *Rhythm on the Range* and *Come and Get It* (both 1936). While the latter is her cinematic tour de force, *Variety* perfectly summarized her *Range* part by noting, "Miss Farmer is just the ingénue in this one but a nice looking girl." Largely through the casual kindness of Bing Cosby, *Range* was a rare Hollywood production she remembered fondly, although newcomer Martha Ray stole the picture, which was a musical clone of the farce *It Happened One Night* (1934).

The *New York Times'* critique of the actress in *Range* was cryptically pertinent: "the decorative Frances Farmer," an apt phrase for much of the actress' Hollywood work. For example, she is breathtakingly beautiful in the big budget, but box-office disappointment, *Toast of New York* (1937, opposite Cary Grant), and even more lovely in the Technicolor *Ebb Tide* (1937, opposite Ray Milland). In these films she is only asked to be gorgeous----a frustrating dilemma for a talented and hardworking actress. Indeed, during the production of *Come and Get It*, besides the dangerous Method "research" of playing a prostitute, she also routinely took home her character's corseted 1880s gowns to practice feeling sexy in decidedly uncomfortable garb. She was never wired to be merely decorative.

Farmer's growing exasperation with Hollywood, which she found increasingly hard to keep under control without profane language and drinking, was further fueled by the film industry's habit of loaning stars out to other companies. The studio doing the borrowing paid the parent company (in Farmer's case, Paramount) a bonus fee, above her normal salary, of which she never received a penny. A performer did not have to be a leftist, which Farmer was, to cry foul. Of course, her breakout picture, *Come and Get It*, had been on loan to producer Samuel Goldwyn and released through United Artists. Still, the generally negative nature of the procedure was further compounded later in her career by the lesser "programmer" quality of the pictures she was getting.

Ironically, sometimes these modest films, such as Warner Brothers' *Flowing Gold* (1940, about oil wildcatters) allowed her to be more than just decoration. Paradoxically, *Frances* used an uncredited scene from this movie, with Lange/Farmer repeatedly falling in the mud, as an example of Hollywood punishing the rebellious actress. Yet, the *New York Times'* review said, "Miss Farmer is still a very striking lady who is also a good actress." Teamed with a New York Method actor with whom she was still on good terms, John Garfield, this remains one of my favorite Farmer films, even though Warners was trying to cash in on the much anticipated and simultaneously released MGM blockbuster oil industry picture *Boom Town* (with Clark Gable and Spencer Tracy).

Farmer's last A movie was a loan to Twentieth Century-Fox called *Son of Fury* (1942, with Tyrone Power starring in a lavish romantic adventure-drama). Farmer has been reduced to a supporting part as a sexy bad girl betrayer of Power. Yet, she is both beautifully showcased and compelling in a complicated role. She was well reviewed, although *Variety* was catty with its praise: "Frances Farmer suits her role well—and gives it as much warmth as could be permitted." Such a dig in the most widely read publication in the entertainment industry only contributed to her increasing instability and her negative view of Hollywood.

Farmer's acting career started to unwind on the night of October 19, 1942, when she was arrested by Santa Monica police for driving with her high beams on (during World War II a blackout zone affected much of the West Coast), possible drunk driving, and verbal abuse. She received a fine and a suspended sentence. In December 1942, according to a later Academy of Television Arts and Sciences interview with Ricardo Montalban, Farmer was unable to complete a quickie Mexican film, *Five Were Chosen* (1943), Montalban's debut picture), because of "mental problems."

In January 1943, Farmer was involved in two altercations----a Hollywood restaurant fight and an alleged assault on a studio hairdresser for the poverty-row studio Monogram. Farmer only completed one day's shooting on the ironically named *No Escape* (1943). She also still owed money on her driving fine and a bench warrant was issued that same month for her arrest. The nightmare escalated when the police came for Farmer in the middle of the night at her Knickerbocker Hotel residence; she did *not* go quietly. Purportedly wrapped in only a shower curtain, she was kicking and screaming as the police drug her out through the lobby of this then high profile hotel. The following morning Farmer's hearing was another disaster; the actress behaved erratically and belligerently, treating everything as a joke. At one point, she told Judge Marshall Hickson, "Listen, I put liquor in my milk. I put liquor in my coffee and in my orange juice. What do you want me to do, starve to death?" This resulted in her first admission to a psychiatric ward. For the rest of the 1940s, she was in and out of various mental institutions. In the fall of 1943, she walked away from the Kimball Sanitarium in protest over the insulin shock treatment she was receiving for a diagnosis of paranoid schizophrenia.

At this point Farmer's mother, Lillian, won a lengthy battle for guardianship of her daughter. Farmer moved back in with her controlling mother, but the relationship remained contentious. After threatening and/or attacking Lillian, Farmer was committed to the Western State Hospital in Steilacoom, Washington. At Western State she received convulsive shock treatment and was pronounced cured by 1944. Briefly spending time with her family, she soon disappeared and was arrested for vagrancy. Eventually returning to her mother's home, Farmer was again sent by Lillian to Western State. Other than one short visit home, Farmer spent the rest of the decade at the state hospital. Conditions were abysmal but nothing like the sensationalized reports that still circulate. Worse yet, much of this could have been avoided had Farmer not constantly rebelled against everyone and everything.

Most Farmer tales make her mother out to be the story's true villain. Yet, it was Farmer's sister-in-law who first suggested mental illness. The sometimes vindictive Lillian was certainly a player in the travesty, yet few tragedies are as simple as a single villain. While Farmer never merited being institutionalized, let alone for nearly a decade, she was not unlike her stubborn, often unstable mother. Throw in alcoholism, anger-management issues, and an understandable distrust of people, and she had plenty of excuses for self-destructing. Plus, as she often noted in later life, when the subject of mental illness came up, "You know, if you get treated like a patient, you're apt to act like one."

Thankfully, Farmer's life had an improved albeit bittersweet second act. At her parents' request she was paroled in 1950 from Western State in order to care for her aging mother. Although the former star's civil rights were essentially restored at this time, Farmer was not initially so informed. She cared for Lillian, ever fearful that any personal act of rebellion might send her back to the mental ward. Once Farmer became aware of the truth, she still petitioned to a local judge in 1953 to document her competency and full civil rights. Indeed, for increased peace of mind, and in order to protect herself against any further competency actions by her parents, she married Seattle city worker Alfred Lobley in 1954. (During her film career, Farmer had been married to actor Leif Erickson from 1936 to 1942). Then, like a character in a film noir, Farmer, in 1954, disappeared.

The actress had pawned all possessions and spent it all on a bus ticket to anywhere. Like a punchline in a bad joke, anywhere turned out to be the small town of Eureka, California. Finding work as a bookkeeper in a photography studio, Farmer was able to maintain her anonymity for more than two years. Then Lee Mikesell, a promoter/opportunist, recognized her in a bar and convinced the still hard-drinking actress to attempt a comeback. Moving Farmer to a larger media market, San Francisco, he staged a rediscovery of the actress *Photoplay* magazine had dubbed "Miss Sex Appeal of '37." For a time, she generated national attention, including two 1957 appearances on CBS's *The Ed Sullivan Show*, the most high-profile television variety hour of the medium's golden era. Of equal importance, she effectively sang her signature *Come and Get It* number "Aura Lee" there, which period phenomenon Elvis Presley had recently reprised as "Love Me Tender." Farmer was back. There was even one more movie for her old studio, Paramount's mediocre melodrama *The Party Crashers* (1958, though Farmer is respectable in a supporting role).

Other television work included the period's mandatory comeback appearance on NBC's *This Is Your Life* (1958), forever an awkward experience for guests, given its exploitive smarmy host Ralph Edwards. Farmer also performed admirably on CBS's prestigious drama *Playhouse 90* (1958), and on Lloyd Nolan's ABC series *Special Agent 7* (1958, Nolan had costarred in Farmer's *Ebb Tide*). This was decidedly a woman who had never been lobotomized. Despite her talent and tragic life, an always fickle national audience soon moved on to other sob stories, and Farmer found acting opportunities in regional theater and summer stock. While touring in a production of *The Chalk Garden*, she appeared in six performances at Indianapolis's Avondale Playhouse. When offered the security of hosting a matinee movie program on WFBM television, she jumped at the chance. Undoubtedly, Indianapolis native Mikesell, who was now her third husband, as well as her quasi-agent, helped influence her decision.

Frances Farmer Presents consistently won its time slot throughout a 1958 to 1964 run, and the period represents a time when the actress regained some measure of happiness and confidence. There were early tough spots, from learning to feel comfortable as a daily television host, to her 1959 separation from Mikesell. (They divorced in 1963). In addition to introducing classic movies, Farmer, because of her Hollywood ties, was also able to snag interviews with prominent entertainers passing through Indianapolis, including such stars as Ginger Rogers, Helen Hayes, and Shelly Winters. There were many other casually engaging offbeat interviews, ranging from a pleasant talk with first husband Erickson, to band-leader/composer Mitch Miller making her blush when he confessed to a still-harbored boyhood crush on her.

Sadly, the *Shadowland* biography, which so misleading sensationalized Farmer's earlier years, is just as mistaken about her time in Indiana. Biographer Arnold described her television hosting as "a depressing spectacle," made worse by showing "trashy movies" and interviewing mere "semi-celebrities." Of course, there was an irony in a pioneering Hollywood rebel becoming a television host. However, Farmer seemed to blossom, for a time, in her new admiringly friendly Indiana setting. She even made special appearances for the station, something she was loath to do for Paramount. Plus, both before and after her television job, she embraced several local creative opportunities in Indiana. The most meaningful was acting in Purdue University Theatre productions, including Anton Chekhov's *The Seagull* and Thomas Wolfe's *Look Homeward Angel*.

The many Indiana letters from Farmer that her sister, Edith, included in *Look Back in Love* frequently reflected a much happier Frances. One typical example, from January 16, 1963, read, in part, "There are so many other [positive] things I want to tell you but I've run fresh out of time. The Purdue play is set, and looks like it will be good for my TV standings as well as my artistic ambitions ... I can put you all up [for a visit] and I'd just love to share my Hoosier background with you. I enclose a descriptive brochure of the Brown County sections we were talking about ...

to give you an idea of the baked apple butter and fried biscuits famous hereabouts."

Unfortunately, Farmer brought many of her old demons to Indiana. In talking to some of her former WFBM colleagues, who wished to remain anonymous, she was described as sometimes difficult to work with, and on occasion she appeared at the station either drunk and/or acting erratically. These incidents resulted in her being fired, announced as a "resignation" in the April 30, 1964, *Indianapolis Star*, which was soon followed by the *Star* reporting on May 21: "Frances Farmer Back with WFBM Again," only to have the yo-yo scenario end with the newspaper documenting her WFBM "termination" on September 9, 1964. However, the people to whom I spoke also believed that an April 1964 Farmer appearance on NBC's *The Today Show*, in which the actress was questioned about her years of institutionalization before a national audience, might have been the reason for her increasingly self-destructive behavior. Regardless, the general consensus among my sources was that WFBM's "management had had enough."

Although Farmer's interest in the arts continued after leaving WFBM, including performing in a weeklong Purdue production of the tragic/comic Avant-garde play *The Visit* (October 1965), she now turned to various business ventures, including a line of cosmetics and the Frances Farmer Studio of Home Decoration, located on North College Avenue in Indianapolis. While invariably receiving excellent publicity for these enterprises, such as a full-page Sunday article touting the studio in the April 3, 1966, *Star*, all the businesses ended in failure. Farmer's aborted attempts at writing a memoir were equally unsuccessful, though the actress's constant companion in her final years, Radcliffe, fashioned a misleading tale after Farmer's death from cancer in 1970.

Ironically, where Farmer finally achieved success, the girl who first attained fame/infamy writing "God Dies," was finding *some* peace in Catholicism. The qualifier is only based upon the fact that nothing, or no one, ever gave her comfort for long. In director/

author/actor Elia Kazan's memoir, *A Life* (1988), he described a young Farmer as "having a special glow, a skin without flaw, lustrous eyes ---- a blonde you'd dream about. She also had a wry, and at times, rather disappointed manner, a [sad] twist of the mouth, which suited the part." It also suited the life ahead of her.

(Originally appeared in *TRACES of Indiana and Midwestern History*, Fall 2015, Wes D. Gehring Copyright.)

SYDNEY POLLACK:

An Author's Perspective

Sydney Pollack (left) and Dustin Hoffman in *Tootsie* (1982), with Pollack both directing and co-starring.

I have recently completed a biography of actor/director/producer Sydney Pollack (1934-2008). The filmmaker found his greatest success as the director of such celebrated pictures as *They Shoot Horses, Don't They?* (1969), *The Way We Were* (1973), *Three Days of the Condor* (1975), *Tootsie* (1982), and *Out of Africa* (1985). Indeed, *Africa* would give Pollack Oscars for both Directing and Producing the year's Best Picture. Plus, twenty odd years later the American Film Institute (AFI) would rate *Tootsie* as the country's second greatest comedy, after Billy Wilder's *Some Like It Hot* (1959).

So why a Pollack biography? There is a myriad of reasons. First, I have a pronounced admiration for his work, in all its facets. He initially acquired high profile status with *They Shoot Horses, Don't They?* (1969). This was the same date I started college and become *totally* immersed in film study for eight years (through graduate school). During this period Pollack helped jumpstart the last America film Renaissance — the 1970s. The rebirth rose from the death of the old Hollywood studio system, and the immense influence of the French New Wave movement, starting with Francois Truffaut's *400 Blows* (1959), and Jean-Paul Godard's *Breathless* (1960).

The three distinctive New Wave cinema breaks with traditional cinema are often showcased in Pollack's work — antiheroes over establishment heroes; a slice of life presentation, instead of a traditional narrative; and a conclusion which could be ambiguous, or even sad. Naturally, the conventional old school film has never gone away, because we all need escapist mind candy now and again. Yet, metaphorically, our lives are like movie rough cuts, capable of ending at any time (clutch each precious moment). As John Lennon observed in song, "Life is what happens when we're busy making other plans." I find Pollack's Americanization of the New Wave refreshingly real. There is no "art is where you get it right" security blanket philosophy. It is an honest pragmatic look at the abyss, not unlike a Kurt Vonnegut novel, or my favorite love song — George Harrison's "Something." The latter includes the hauntingly sincere lyrics, "You're asking me will my love grow, I don't know, I don't know." (Fittingly, this dates from the New Wave period, as does Vonnegut's best.)

Pollack's often kindship to this quasi-existentialism mindset was not hurt by growing up Jewish in a then less than liberal South Bend, Indiana. (Born in West Lafayette, his pharmacist father moved the young family to South Bend when Sydney was a preschooler.) Of course, his hometown hardly had a patent on racism, as he told a

1993 *South Bend Tribune* reporter: "It was [then] pretty standard to be anti-Semitic, just as it was to be anti-black," adding that South Bend suffered the same level of ignorance and intolerance as other towns of its size. "All prejudiced people don't believe they are prejudiced, unless they are Nazis ..."

In an earlier 1970 *Minneapolis Star Tribune* interview Pollack confessed: "I'm a tense guy. I was tense as a child; I'm tense today. Tense is a polite word for nervous." However, the article's author observed, "... there is no sign of tension in his hopeful voice. His anxiety is reflected only by the mound of chain-smoking cigarettes ..." Part of this was promoting a first hit movie. Would there be more? His then young life had already taught him one rarely works on a level playing field.

However, one could return to Pollack's youth and problems, which were hardly limited to Indiana. As the oldest child (he had a younger brother and sister who adored him), their father saw Sydney being a pharmacist. But Sydney wanted to be a new coin, not a re-issue. Moreover, he quite literally lived for the theatre, which his father scorned as a homosexual waste. Thankfully, one needs to pump the brakes momentarily, to address a strong boost Sydney took from South Bend. Pollack, like another contemporary Hoosier to Hollywood figure, James Dean (1931-1955), had a high school theatre teacher/director who made all the difference — in Sydney's case it was James L. Casaday (1907-1990). The two stayed in touch, and his teacher's *South Bend Tribune* obituary showcases the artistic breath and passion to which Pollack was exposed: "Mr. Casaday challenged his students with everything from the operas of Mozart to the modern works of [sometime filmmaker Jean] Cocteau, [Casaday] once spoke of his goals: 'I don't want to produce plays here that are run-of-the-mill high school trash. I want my kids to learn something that will give them a sincere appreciation of good theatre.'"

Casaday reinforced this intensity thoroughly. For example, all a young Pollack knew outside South Bend occurred when Casaday regularly took his students on Chicago theatre field trips. Indeed, even before the opening of Pollack's greatest triumph, *Out of Africa*, the director/producer remained impassioned about "Mr. Casaday" with a *Tribune* reporter: "It was amazing to come upon a man like him in a place like South Bend. I was lucky. God knows, I might be working in a drugstore now." (As a French New Wave addendum about cinematic change and Pollack — pivotal Truffaut also had a troubled youth turned around by a teacher mentor, writer Andrè Bazin.)

A second catalyst for a Pollack biography was how frequently he collaborated with my favorite actor/activist Robert Redford (1937). Fascinatingly, Redford had his initial moonshot moment the same year as Pollack — 1969, with *Butch Cassidy and the Sundance Kid*. However, the young men first met as actors in the low budget anti-war film, *War Hunt* (1962). They immediately bonded, with Redford later telling *Time* magazine, shortly after Pollack's death, they were "kindred spirits," wanting to do unique films, as Sydney was transitioning to directing. Years before, in a 1979 syndicated interview, Pollack more personally described that beginning: "He [Redford] was the only guy on the [*War Hunt*] set as quiet and scared as I was. We both had wives and young children, so we didn't bounce around like a lot of the other actors. Our families spent a lot of time together, and we got to be friends." Fittingly, the men were amazed at the provocative films then coming out of Europe, talking late many nights about movements like the French New Wave. As with many great directors, Redford eventually represented a frequent pivotal screen alter ego for Pollack. Thus, like John Ford (1895-1973) and John Wayne (1907-1979); or Martin Scorsese (1942) and Robert DeNiro (1943); Redford looms large in Pollack's filmography.

Ultimately, Pollack and Redford had nearly a fifty year friendship, with the actor being directed by Sydney in seven signature films. Their closest collaboration, which was so near an independent film Pollack mortgaged his house to make it (New Wave passion), was *Jeremiah Johnson* (1972). A surprise hit, it is a notable film for several personal reasons. For instance, it was shot in and around various Utah locations both men dearly loved (now synonymous with the Sundance Film Festival Institute). Also, though a frontier tale, *Jeremiah* was their most existentialistic work, via a subtextual anti-war attitude.

Carole Zucker's book on filmmakers, *Figures of Light* (1995), best captured the Pollack-Redford working relationship in an interview with the director during the production of *Havana* (1990): "… this is the seventh film I've done with [Redford]; we really don't have to say a whole hell of a lot to each other. Most of it is shorthand. He knows that in ... [many] scenes, whether it's *The Way We Were* or *Havana*, what I'm always pushing for is his vulnerability. The thing I want the most is for him to allow that to happen. I think it's fair to say that he's comfortable with me after this length of time and that there is a kind of trust. So, he will, sometimes, let himself be in a little more vulnerable way." This sort of familiarity made for a better film, and a more efficient one, too.

A third reason for writing this biography necessitates paraphrasing an old axiom I call my "scholarly salvaging" work — "I want to write/right something that has been lost and/or never even historically recognized about either an artist, or a single artwork." My research dives are so deep I risk a fate reminiscent of a line from a personally seminal novel, Michael Chabon's *Wonder Boys* (1996): "[He] climbed into a movie as into a time machine or a bottle of whiskey and set the dial for 'never come back.'" For me, intense period research is giving the past a future.

Okay, however, why Pollack? If you appreciate film, you know his successful career. So, what is all this "scholarly salvaging" about? It is the same reason I did a biography of Robert Wise (1914-2008, whose work ranged from gritty 1940s "film noir," to the multiple Oscar winning musicals *West Side Story* (1961) and *The Sound of Music*, 1965). Both artists were saddled with the left-handed compliment of creating films known for their "wonderful workmanship." For instance, Pollack's *New York Times* obituary said, in part: "The vitality of motion pictures has always been sustained by craftsmen [like Pollack] with a modicum of business sense and the ability to tell a good story." This is a polite way of saying he was not a real auteur.

Professional proficiency/craftmanship is no small achievement. However, Pollack, as with Wise, worked in several genres, and did not have an easily discernable visual style, versus a Tim Burton take on German Expressionism in films such as *Edward Scissorhands* (1990), *Sleepy Hollow* (1999), and *Sweeney Todd* (2007). Yet, of greater consequence, both Pollack and Wise put their cinematic stamp on a film through consistent themes and character. The real irony is the modern bastardization of the auteur theory. Again, this necessitates the deep dive of research. The aforementioned Truffaunt, pre-filmmaker, gave us the auteur theory, but his previously noted mentor, Bazin, essentially provided the template. And J. Dudley Andrew describes Bazin's philosophy thus, in his neglected *The Major Film Theories* (1976): "... an artist's vision should be ascertained from the selection he makes of reality, not from his transformation of reality." It is a continuation of any hoary joke about a vacuous person being easily distracted by bright, shiny objects. Thus, for many lazy viewers, auteurism stops at the visual ("Squirrel!"), with no contemplation of a rich multilayered text.

Very well; so what is a Pollack picture about? He strongly embraced T. S. Eliot's *Four Quartets* on life: "The purpose of all our wandering is to arrive at the place we started, and to know it for the first time." Accordingly, at the beginning of *Out of Africa*, Meryl Streep's Danish aristocrat relocates to the continent in 1913. Though a progressive during a colonial time, she still brings many baked in traditional values, from attempting to raise a crop not appropriate for the land, to wanting her romantic relationship with a free-spirited big-game hunter (Redford) to result in marriage. Years of wonderment and woe pass, but eventually her farm fails and her demands drive away her lover. Ultimately, with wheels up, she leaves this adored land; Streep realizes she should not, nor could not change Africa, or even her lover — an exercise in trying to nail down smoke. Pollack himself said in his 2000 voice-over DVD commentary of the re-issued film and Redford's character, "Passion — freedom versus obligation. If I say I love you … how much do I need to give-up?"

All this was very apparent from *Africa's* beginning when Redford's hunter, a transplanted European himself, had told Streep's Baroness: "We are not owners here." Though an aristocrat, too, he despised their arbitrary rules and the inherent racism of a class system. However, Streep's character had to come full circle to see it herself. Pollack would also shrink this Eliot Rosetta Stone to a word or phrase that represented the tale's "binding." For this film the binding was Streep's need for "possessiveness."

A variation of this possessiveness occurs in *Jeremiah Johnson*. Redford's title character attempts to escape this concept by becoming a 19th century mountain man. Like the tall tales it draws from, *Johnson* seems to be running from any number of past American "Manifest Destiny" conquest wars. As with *Africa*, the virgin American West and its native tribes had no concept of ownership. Only at *Jeremiah's* conclusion does Redford realize there is no escaping the white man's encroaching wars of possessiveness. This realization is bookended by meetings with an old mountain man called Bear Claw (Will Greer). At the beginning Greer gives the desperate to bolt Redford a tutorial on wilderness survival. The closing encounter strikes a Greer graduation note: "You [Redford] have learned well." More importantly, Jeremiah can finally articulate his Eliot moment: "It [civilized – life] ought to have been different." However, another umbrella binding could be added, one which encapsulates most Pollack pictures, "existentialism 101." Jeremiah has moved beyond the philosophy's "initial angst" and reached Kierkegaard (the father of existentialism) ultimate epiphany on an absurd world — s/he is responsible for giving meaning to their individual life, sans society … or religion. (As a Greer footnote, he was well cast. He had been blacklisted in the 1950s and went on to create an outdoor theatre near Topanga, California.)

Regardless, one could say a variation of Jeremiah exists a hundred odd years later at the close of the Pollack-Redford collaboration, *The Electric Horseman* (1979). Contemporary cowboy Redford ends the picture alone by choice somewhere in the remaining America West. His title character is done with civilization, so called, because he finally realizes society has been slowly killing him. Some critics called his character the "Existentialist Cowboy." And as an *Africa* addendum, in the Redford-Streep positive times the couple often discussed Kierkegaard's ironic obsession with hunters loving their prey, yet …

This transitions into another almost universal example of Pollack "binding" — the fleeting love story. While the director's screen couples seldom go the distance, he usually surprised people by observations like this Pollack excerpt from Laurent Tirard's *Moviemakers' Master Class* (2002): "I make movies … about relationships, mostly … I try to make films that raise questions more than give answers, films that might not really have a conclusion … because I don't like it when one person is right and one person is wrong … if that's the case, it's not worth making the movie …" For example, in the 2002 CBS broadcast *AFI's 100 Years … 100 Passions*, Pollack's favorite film, *Casablanca* (1942), topped the list. Let that sink in. That is a template for a Pollack relationship film. Fittingly, the director's *The Way We Were* was honored as the sixth greatest love story of all time, just above *Doctor Zhivago* (1965). None of these films hurt the Kleenex industry.

The Way was a commercial smash, but people forget it initially received mixed reviews. It was the first big budget Hollywood film to also address 1950s McCarthy blacklisting. Some critics wanted a political focus. For Pollack that was just part of the background of a relationship story. Michael Feeney Callan's definitive *Robert Redford: The Biography* (2011) recorded the actor speaking for both him and co-star Barbra Streisand as crediting Pollack's platitude: "This is first and foremost a love affair, and we conceded that and we trusted his instincts, and he was right."

A beguiling flip on *The Way* is the Pollack-Redford political thriller, *Three Days of the Condor*, driven by a love story with Faye Dunaway. Redford's title character plays a trusting CIA think tank researcher. One day it is his turn to pick up the lunch requests for the small department. But when he returns everyone has been murdered. He runs, calling the "company" for protocol on a safe CIA rescue. However, his retrieval "contact" attempts to shoot him. Shocked, he needs time to think in a safe haven. Thus, he randomly kidnaps Dunaway, and they return to her apartment and he explains his absurd plight: "I [and everyone in my department] just read books ... everything published ... we feed the plots, tricks, codes, into a computer. And the computer checks against actual CIA plans ... Who'd invent a job like that?" Call it Condor's sensitivity, appreciating her apartment's haunting black and white stills, the "Stockholm Syndrome" or, as Roger Ebert's wryly positive *Chicago Sun Times* review put it: "... perhaps his [Condor's] uncanny resemblance to Robert Redford" — soon has them in a save the bookworm affair.

Besides its existentialism core, including those powerful stills of an *empty* New York City, Pollack is also drawn to the "binding" of "trust." Initially, Condor could have been a carefree college kid playing at being a student-like patriot. He seems oblivious to the Watergate scandal (1972-1974) and the multitude of conspiracy theories. In contrast, Dunaway's character is in some sort of personal melt-down, from her obsession with taking moody pictures, to a boyfriend she is about to drop. Yet, by the story's open-ended disquieting conclusion, Condor has no trust, and she does. That is, because Dunaway has believed in a stranger's story and helped, at least for the time being — thwart an immediate danger, she feels empowered. Dunaway will give the boyfriend a second chance.

There is more, but this sampling of elements which hum through Pollack's work are linked to the broad brushstrokes of an auteur whose often big budget pictures are ironically anti-establishment and anti-war. His antiheroes are strong independent men and women often caught in a fuzzy existentialistic middle zone in which lasting love is a long shot. However, he also had the ability to inspire students like myself, back when the world was young, that they too could awaken to all their Christmases at once. After all, *Waiting for Godot* (1953) is an entertaining play, even though Godot never comes.

This segues into my final reason for writing this biography. After authoring many conventionally structured biographies, I aspired to profile Pollack in an imaginatively non-traditional manner. I would scrutinize his life and art through what could be called a "Pollack Portal" — keying upon ten of what I consider his most telling pictures: *They Shoot Horses, Don't They?*, *Jeremiah Johnson*, *The Way We Were*, *Three Days of the Condor*, *Bobby Deerfield* (1977), *The Electric Horseman*, *Absence of Malice* (1981), *Tootsie*, *Out of Africa*, and *Havana* (1990).

I was further encouraged in my personal challenge by having access to his private papers, which are housed in the Margaret Herrick Motion Picture Academy Library (Beverly Hills, California). For a biographer, this is like manna from heaven. When one chronicles a life it is partially about an "angle of vision" — what is the new perspective a biographer brings to the table? As already noted, a personal angle of vision was the salvaging auteur slant. However, no matter how much one knows about the person, in-depth analysis will often alter one's "angle of vision." Thus, one risks disappointment. Yet, as Pulitzer-Prize winning profiler Leon Edel's *Writing Lives* (1959) states; a good chronicler is "an artist under oath." This is especially true, when some criticize biographers for metaphorically breaking into a subject's "house" and "rearranging the furniture for a personal agenda." I found Pollack's house in order.

Since one can never know all the facts, an old profiler axiom to write by is a fidelity to the "best truth possible." Moreover, though all forms of writing are an introspective exercise, I concur with *New York Times* critic Megan O'Grady's belief that a biographer receives a double dip of personal insight. She states: "After all, it's often by looking back that we move the conversation forward, and by inhabiting the lives of others that we might glimpse pieces of our own." Given the impact Pollack had on my film foundation, my personal "looking back" perspective, after a long career, really makes the director's embracing of Eliot's *Four Quartets* especially pertinent to me.

Without trying to go clever on you, this is the time to cue the notability of Pollack's private papers. Many of my biographies have involved sifting through private papers. However, Pollack's collection is indisputably, for me, the most extraordinary, microscopic and telescopic simultaneously. With some difficulty I have whittled down a few quintessential examples. For instance, existentialism has been peppered throughout this essay. The philosophy pervades Pollack's work, with his first triumph an adaptation of Horace McCoy's brutal Depression novel, *They Shoot Horses, Don't They?* (1935, about sadistic dance marathons). While little known in America until the movie, for decades France considered the book a pioneering existentialist work. (Remember the French New Wave's influence on America's new age cinema.) While Pollack briefly acknowledged the movement in periodic interviews, nothing more elegantly makes the connection than a favorite "little piece of doggerel" he scribbled to an assistant during his *Absence of Malice* production (about a man wrongly accused of a crime): "The pendulum swings from side to side as ever it must. It swings to right and it swings to wrong. And it pauses at each a bit too long. But it never stops at the golden mean. And it never will 'til the world machine is [sic, scrapped] scraped in the cosmic dust."

This existentialistic tendency also infuses a random Pollack letter to a depressed Army fan during the exceptionally demanding on-location *Africa* shoot. Moreover, it showcases the sensitive acting coach tack he was long famous for prior to directing: "Having spent two years in the Army myself, I understand the depression you are dealing with now. Advice from other people means nothing, so I won't waste time giving any, except that I, like many others in the service, survived it. Perhaps what is being stored up as a result of the depression might be valuable to you sometime hence." Besides Pollack as mensch, it could be called a two-step tweaking of Camus — nobody gets out of here alive, but occasionally we stumble onto brief meaningful moments of clarity.

An additional selection, from an unclearly dated American film Institute (AFI) lecture, showcases both the challenges of filmmaking and his feminist bent in real life, too: "The director is a doctor. He has to deduce things backwards. I'll show my wife [Clair], who is very smart and knows the business [a successful actress turned architect], a rough cut and she'll say, 'You've got eighteen scenes where he is saying the same thing to her.' I'll say, what do you mean? There's just one scene. She'll say, 'There are eighteen.' Well, of course, there aren't eighteen, but it feels to her like there are, so I have to work out what's making her think there are eighteen ..." (Despite the fleeting nature of Pollack's film relationships, Sydney and Claire had been married nearly fifty years at the time of his death from cancer, 2008. Of course, the longevity was no doubt helped by the aforementioned note that this was a man who always needed to explore both sides of a conflict.)

Pollack's papers also impressively revealed he did as much production research as any driven biographer. For example, *Out of Africa* is based upon Karen Blixen's (Streep) autobiographical novel, written under the pen name Isak Dinesen, after her return to Denmark. It is clear that Pollack read everything she wrote, as well as anything on the less chronicled ephemeral lover, Denys Finch Hatton (Redford). Providentially, Pollack felt he had found a kindred spirit in a passage from the *Africa* text that has existentialistic overtones, as well as explaining why relationships of a nature are hard to sustain: "Perhaps he (Hatton/Redford) knew, as I didn't, that the Earth was made round so that we could not see too far down the road."

As with Pollack's omnipresent existentialism, his anti-war stance should be obvious, especially after his 1969 flawed but fascinating adaptation of William Eastlake's neglected 1965 novel, *Castle Keep*. (The work, in either medium, might be thought of as a cross between *Catch-22* and *Slaughterhouse-Five*.) However, thanks to Pollack's private papers, one finds his best articulation on war in an obscure quote from an obscure French magazine: "I believe it is possible to make films like *Jeremiah Johnson* and still speak about Vietnam as eloquently as showing agonizing soldiers and I believe these films are more satisfying from an aesthetic point of view."

My last Pollack papers item is as unique as all the rest, and revitalizing funny. It involves a congratulatory note from a celebrity. Nothing unusual about that in a special collection. However, in Pollack's material there is an inordinate number of letters from name personalities who obviously did not know him, and who also sound rejuvenatingly normal. The crème de la crème is an endearingly funny and realistic note from Jamie Lee Curtis: "Dear Mr. Pollack, I was having a bad day. My head was pounding and aching. My husband and I decided to brave Hollywood and go see *Out of Africa*. The traffic was lousy and the line long. There was a talkative couple in front of us fighting through the trailer. My head still hurt. Then it happened. Her voice [Streep's vo] came up and the colors and images flooded the screen and everything else disappeared. The movie is very special. Thank you. My head doesn't ache and my heart is so full. Please accept this as a fan letter. I am not used to writing them. All my best wishes, Jamie. P.S. I typed this."

As a Pollack biographer, if I can get across even a trifling sized sense of Curtis' engagingly honest directness, I will consider my efforts a success. Regardless, I feel that I have written myself home.

(Originally appeared as the cover article in *TRACES of Indiana and Midwestern History,* Summer 2022; Wes D. Gehring Copyright.)

PETER SELLERS AND HARRY LANGDON:

A Neglected Link

Harry Langdon in *Long Pants* (1927).

Quite possibly the most popular comedy figure in film today is the Blake Edwards' creation—Inspector Jacques Clouseau, star of the Pink Panther films. Clouseau (Peter Sellers), who has stumbled his way through five Panther films so far, would seem at first to be the perfect embodiment of the comic anti-hero—modern man's alter ego. That is, he is seemingly incompetent at every task, from operating mechanical objects (such as the all-powerful vacuum cleaner that attacks an oil painting in *The Return of the Pink Panther,* 1975), to his relationships with women (from the unfaithful wife of *The Pink Panther*, 1964), to his many failures at romance throughout the series.

Upon a closer examination, however, one is forced to admit that the persistent Clouseau usually proves to be a winner in his comic sleuthing, often through the mere fact of keeping his other world sanity. Critics Peter Lehman and William Luhr have explained this surprising success of Clouseau in the following manner:

> He survives, survives because, to an extent, he is much more attuned to the realities of existence in the modern world than they [his more rational enemies] are, because his very existence is a threat to all reason, all order.[1]

In other words, the only way to live and prosper in this illogical world, is to behave in a completely illogical manner. Thus, Lehman and Luhr note that in A *Shot in the Dark* (the second Panther film, 1964) Clouseau feels that the prime murder suspect is innocent, despite the fact that:

> Maria Gambrelli had a motive for the murder, had no alibi and was found on the scene holding the murder weapon. From this Clouseau concluded she was innocent.[2]

Needless to say, Ms. Gambrelli proves to be innocent.

Lehman and Luhr nicely capsulize the illogical logic of the detective by entitling their study: "I Suspect Everyone and I Suspect No One" – a Clouseau axiom from *A Shot in the Dark*. Their hypothesis is an interesting answer to the question of why Clouseau's unorthodox style proves so successful. However, what of those times when Clouseau is exercising no conscience strategy, unorthodox or otherwise? I am referring to the million and one assassination attempts on Clouseau that he manages to survive (physically as well as mentally), without even being aware of them. As the Clouseau/Panther series progresses, these attempted liquidations become the heart of the franchise.

This shift in emphasis, from stalking the stolen diamond (named, of course, the Pink Panther), to stalking Clouseau, occurs in *A Shot in the Dark*, with the introduction of Clouseau's supervisor—Chief Inspector Dreyfus (Herbert Lom). With the renewal of the series in the mid-'70s (*The Pink Panther* and *A Shot in the Dark* were both made in 1964), this shift in emphasis has been accelerated all the more.

Dreyfus, name sake no doubt to the equally misused Alfred Dreyfus of French history, cannot handle the eccentric style of his "star" detective and manages to go crazy in almost every picture since then. But this does not occur before Dreyfus, or the top hit men of the world (who are dispatched by Dreyfus in *The Pink Panther Strikes Again*, 1976) attempt to kill Clouseau countless times. In the latest film (*The Revenge of the Pink Panther*, 1978), Dreyfus' sanity is still being threatened by the presence of Clouseau but international drug chief Douvier is now directing the assassination attempts. Lehman and Luhr, only modestly ascribe it to a world growing all the more illogical. In contrast, I find the constant escapes from death by an unsuspecting Clouseau to be a throwback to the comedy persona of the silent comedian Harry Langdon.

Langdon, long canonized by James Agee in the latter's celebrated essay, "Comedy's Greatest Era," had a style which Edwards (whose films have always paid homage to silent comedy, and whose grandfather, J. Gordon Edwards, was a silent director) seems to borrow from in his creation of Clouseau. Langdon, like Clouseau, seems at first to be the perfect embodiment of the comic anti-hero. Granted no physical gifts, he seems completely at the mercy of adverse forces, be they man-made or natural.

His baby-like appearance of powdered face and small gestures reinforced this apparently helpless image. But this boy/man with the owlish blink, Langdon had one thing going for him that made all the difference in the world, what Frank Capra calls the "principle of the brick." Langdon might be saved by the brick falling on the cop, but it was *verboten* that he in anyway motivate the brick's fall.[3] Earlier, in "Comedy's Greatest Era," Capra had added—"If there was a rule for writing Langdon material, it was this: his only ally was God."[4] In correspondence with Capra, the director also compared the Landon persona to Jaroslav Hošek's darkly comic 1920s literary figure, "The Good Soldier Švejk" — caught up in World War I.[5] (Capra did the Langdon stories for the World War I picture *All Night Long*, 1924, and 1926's *Soldier Man*.) Capra would go on to essentially write and/or direct Landon's signature features — *The Strong Man, Tramp, Tramp, Tramp* (both 1926), and *Long Pants* (1927).

At the blackest of all moments, not unlike Clouseau constantly under the threat of assassination, the tide would suddenly turn in Langdon's favor. Thus, in *All Night Long* (1924) Langdon is a cowardly World War I soldier retreating from the bombardment of the enemy by climbing farther and farther up a pole. The shells inch closer, taking bites out of the wood as they climb with him. He suffers a direct hit and is blown away into the darkness. However, his unscheduled flight ends with a touchdown on an Allied general, saving not only Langdon's life but that of the endangered officer. Thus, through a further whim of the god of comedy, Langdon is given a promotion. (Woody Allen does a variation of this gag in the Napoleonic Wars sequence of 1975's *Love and Death*. He also received a promotion.)

The "principle of the brick" is quite applicable to Clouseau; at times in *The Pink Panther Strikes Again* the set is literally knee-deep in accidental assassination victims as Clouseau goes about his sleuthing, oblivious to any danger. Only with an ally as highly placed as God, could this bumbling detective carry on. Also, as with Langdon's unusual "explosion" promotion, where he really should have been killed, Clouseau not only survives danger but thrives on it.

There is more, however, to the Langdon-Clouseau analogy than the "principle of the brick." They are also alike in their approach to a rule of comedy that predates Hollywood, though it has long been highly honored there. It is simply called topping and is based on surprise. A comic situation and/or gag is established, and when that starts to pale, new variations on the old trick are added. For example, a trapdoor opens and our comic falls through—comic surprise. Next time the trapdoor opens and our comic walks right across the open space without falling through—comic surprise. The third time, ad infinitum, he falls and/or something new happens and the audience is again kept off balance.

Both Langdon and Clouseau, despite periodic rescues from above, are incompetent the majority of their screen time, from Langdon's lumberjack who cannot cut down a tree in *Boobs in the Woods* (1925, co-written by Capra), to Clouseau as a repairman who cannot fix anything in *The Return of the Pink Panther.*[5] They are comically brilliant in their bumbling (Clouseau's attempt to repair a doorbell being one of the highlights of the series). Yet they become even more comic (they top the laughter of their bumbling image) by pulling off major successes, such as Clouseau somehow realizing that prime suspect Mr. Gambrelli is innocent, or Langdon is becoming rich as a street musician because he plays so poorly people throw saleable junk in *Fiddlesticks* (1927). A third level topping often finds them slipping back into incompetency.

Lehman and Luhr are thus correct in focusing on the victory aspect of the Clouseau character (the successes of such an unlikely detective are indeed comic highlights). Yet, they neglect the fact that the comedy richness of those surprising successes is based on the fact that the viewer sees Clouseau as an incompetent in need of an deus ex machina act, à la Harry Langdon's persona.

Edwards often goes to the trouble of accenting that incompetency. This is best exemplified by the dual-focus narrative he constructs in *The Return of the Pink Panther*. Edwards cuts back and forth between the bumbling Inspector Clouseau and the handsome, capable retired jewel thief (Christopher Plummer) —who is also doing detective work to prove his innocence. Plummer's role, with all the nuances of the traditional, slick film hero, underlines the generally incompetent nature of Clouseau all the more, as well as showing that rational world alternatives are still possible in the world of these films.

A further accenting by Edwards occurs in the creation of Clouseau's Oriental servant, Cato. American literature contains many such relationships, where the hero's only friend is a companion-assistant of minority background, from Cooper's Natty Bumppo and Chingachgook, to the Lone Ranger and Tonto. The minority status of the sidekick underscores the outsider aspect of these heroes. But Clouseau (who needs all the help he can get) has a trusted companion that is a royal pain in the neck.

Clouseau, as if acknowledging this fact, has been known to call him my "little yellow swine." Cato's sole mission in life seems to be to surprise Clouseau and attempt to best him in the most comically destructive of karate duals. Thus, instead of assistance, the generally incompetent Clouseau has the added burden of needing to watch for a karate-mad servant coming out of the strangest places, e.g., in *The Return of the Pink Panther* Cato launched his attack from inside a refrigerator.

The comedy personas of both Langdon and Clouseau thus succeed only after an incompetent framework has been constructed around them. Then, when they win, it represents a great comic surprise, an act of God. And no matter how often we see the films, it remains fun for the student of humor, because it is such an incongruous pairing—incompetence and triumph.

(Originally presented at "The Athens Internation Film Festival," Ohio University, Athens, Ohio, April 1978. Published in Ball State University's *FORUM*, Autumn 1979; Wes D. Gehring Copyright.)

NOTES

1. Peter Lehman and William Luhr, "I Suspect Everyone and I Suspect No One: Blake Edward's Inspector Clouseau," "The Athens International Film Festival," Athens, Ohio, April 1978.
2. Ibid.
3. Frank Capra, *The Name Above the Title* (New York: Macmillan, 1971), 62.
4. James Agee, "Comedy's Greatest Era," in *Agee on Film, I* (1958; rpt. New York: Grosset & Dunlap, 1972), 14.
5. Wes D. Gehring, Late 1970s correspondence with Frank Capra (author's files).
6. See the author's PhD dissertation *Leo McCarey and the Comic Anti-hero in American Film*, 1978. [Later published by the *New York Times*' Arno Press in their series of outstanding film dissertations, 1980.]

CHAPLIN AND THE PROGRESSIVE ERA:

The Neglected Politics of a Clown

Chaplin's Tramp during the 1910s.

To link Charlie Chaplin's name with the term "politics" is to conjure up immediately the harassment the great comedian suffered (for alleged communist sympathies) during the Joseph McCarthy "red"–colored 1950s. Yet this harassment, which would eventually result in his self-imposed exile from the United States (1952), really touched upon little that was political in Chaplin's film career (his private life was slandered instead). In fact, preceding the non-political *Limelight* (1952), he had made only one film since 1940—"a comedy of murders" entitled *Monsieur Verdoux* (1947). And its poor box-office reception was due more to Joan Barry's long and messy paternity suit against him (women's groups boycotted the film in some areas), as well as Chaplin's retirement of his "tramp" character, than it was to his politics. Indeed, another "comedy of murders" had already proved highly successful earlier in the decade—in both the theatre and motion pictures—Joseph Kesselring's *Arsenic and Old Lace* (Frank Capra directed the film).

Dedicated witch-hunters who were out, then, to find evidence of Chaplin's political ties, communist or otherwise (in earlier features), were hard-pressed to find anything substantial. Excepting the anti-Nazi *Great Dictator* (1940), they found mere bits and pieces from which one could hardly construct a political philosophy, for example, the scene in *Modern Times* (1936) where the lumber truck loses its red flag and the tramp retrieves it and runs after the truck, to find himself inadvertently leading a workers' demonstration. To fall upon "redbaiting evidence" such as this shows how futile the search was. Moreover, it merely confirmed what any student of Chaplin's career had always shown, that the political stance of the man was at best that of a confirmed "ism" dabbler—a student of many causes but a follower of no single flag. And his films, beyond their common humanistic bent, were not really assignable to one of the traditional isms. Chaplin himself has said, "There are those who always attach social significance to my work. It has none. I leave such subjects for the lecture platform. To entertain is my first consideration."[1] Yet a political key of sorts did exist in the Chaplin filmography, and it was one actually hoary with American tradition. (See end notes.)

Those interested in discovering a consistent, viable political stance in Chaplin's work needed but to dig deeper, to the comedy shorts of the teens. More specifically, they needed to focus on the capping stage of the shorts—the twelve films he did for Mutual in 1916 and 1917—which his celebrated biographer, Theodore Huff, calls "Chaplin's most fertile years, his most sustained creative period."[2] Here, working in a much more disciplined manner than in the later features (which appeared only sporadically, every three to seven years), he fashioned twelve films in eighteen months. Only in such a situation (he was under a contract obligation to produce a certain number of films—but with full artistic freedom) has anything approaching a political philosophy surfaced in the work of Chaplin. It is a political philosophy embracing the Progressive Movement.

The Mutual period was, for several reasons, a period ripe for his political emergence. First, his earlier years in motion pictures had been something of an apprenticeship—focused more on learning his craft than on expressing a political perspective. Second, issues were in fact becoming more important to him. John McCabe notes that by 1916 "more serious matters begin to occupy Chaplin's thoughts than heretofore."[3] Third, this new company was a truly unique point in his career: "Of all his employers over the years, the Mutual company was the most agreeable to him. They were not dismayed by ... his growing tendency to introduce serious themes."[4] Fourth, Progressive politics was news. And it is quite natural for an artist, especially a comedy artist (who deals with a composite picture of the masses, versus the individual focus of the tragedian) to incorporate the topical into his work. Fifth and final, the majority of his work after the Mutual period was often years in the making and thus not open to topical politics. Moreover, with the election of Warren Harding (1920), politics in the next decade (Chaplin's most productive period after the teens) was no longer of premier importance in the country.

Chaplin's Mutual work fell at the close of a time that has come to be called the Progressive Era (1897-1920). This was a period when a great many Americans, largely from the middle class, led a broadly-based call for reform, from curbing the corruption of big city machines to the trust-busting of large corporations. At a time when organized bigness had started to dominate every facet of American life (industry, labor, and agriculture) the Progressive Movement was concerned "with improving the plight of the underprivileged individual and the quality of social life throughout the nation."[5]

Previous historians have noted the humanistic qualities of the Mutual work, but since Chaplin was from Britain (though he had already lived in this country a number of years when the Mutual films were made), his "Progressive tendencies" are usually explained away as more British than American in origin. Certainly his Dickensian childhood of poverty, as well as an adult fascination with the fictional world of that author, points toward this. Yet, because the parallels are so close between the American Progressive issues of the day and the themes of Chaplin's Mutual films, merely pointing to his British ancestry is to ask for a rather large coincidence. Moreover, before one cries foul at this besmirching of the *pure American* Progressive movement (by considering the American work of British-born Chaplin), it is best to keep in mind the recent work of "more urban-related historians such as Arthur Mann and J. Joseph Huthmacher [who] have ... emphasized ... the part that the British examples and the role the new immigrant groups played in the reform movement."[6]

Also, Chaplin adjusted quite readily to a country he found to be very much like himself—young and ambitious. In fact, Chaplin's close friend, writer Max Eastman, remembers the comedian saying: "Of course, I am essentially American. I feel American, and I don't feel British—that's the chief thing."[7]

Chaplin, moreover, seems to speak directly to these issues, as did a great many artists. In fact, celebrated Progressive historian David Shannon has stated:

> There was a tendency [during the Progressive Era] for the
> artist ... to create works that had a relevance to the problems
> facing society and thereby make formal culture more a living
> part of the American society than it had been in the previous
> generation.[8]

More specifically, Harry A. Grace's article entitled "Charlie Chaplin's Films and American Culture Patterns" has for its conclusion the statement that "Chaplin's films resemble the period of history in which they were produced."[9] My premise for this paper merely takes this observation one step further and examines the unique political parallels (which Chaplin was to keep fairly masked, sans *The Great Dictator* in his work after 1920) between his Mutual films and the Progressive Era. Thus, it would be more logical to call the always politically astute Chaplin an opportunist (in that he deals with Progressive issues during the high point of that movement) than to suggest that he was not aware of the "Progressive tendencies" in his work.

It is also important to keep in mind that Chaplin builds toward the Mutual issues in his earlier short films—they are not suddenly Progressive. His first year (1914) of filmmaking, under the tight rein of Mack Sennett (at Keystone), dealt with generally nonpolitical issues, such as bathing beauties and flirting husbands, and had lots of chases. It was Chaplin's apprenticeship, and issues would come only after he left Sennett.

In 1915, his acceptance of a lucrative contract from Essanay Film Company allowed him much more artistic freedom and a chance for more work of a political nature. Yet, it was not until nearly the close of his Essanay work in *Police* (March 1916), that he addressed himself to a Progressive subject. In this case, it was an attack on dereliction of duty by the police (in the face of strong middle-class need), and the propensity of the authorities to expect bribes.

The Essanay films, however, taken as a whole, are most important in terms of Progressive issues in that the urban theme takes precedence over the more rural and small-town penchants of his Sennett period. Thus, it seems significant that even in the pastoral setting of Chaplin's Essanay classic, *The Tramp* (1915), generally hailed as the first "tramp" film with pathos, Chaplin's rural sojourn is constantly interrupted by elements of the encroaching city—be they the speeding automobiles that endanger pedestrian Chaplin or the bullet wound he suffers from a gang of thieves. His next career move, to Mutual in 1916, found him prepared to focus more specifically on what were essentially Progressive issues.

In eleven of these twelve films he focuses on (possibly in the case of alcohol he capitalizes on) progressive issues. The films are best divided into five groups: those concerned with urban-corruption; the plight of the urban poor; the idle rich (not a specific concern of Progressives but a tangential area to both urban poverty and corruption, especially when contrasted with Chaplin's image of the poor); elitism; and alcohol.

Urban corruption is dealt with in his first two films for Mutual— *The Floorwalker* and *The Fireman*. They represent the continued interest of Chaplin in this theme, which he had begun at the close of his Essanay work with the previously mentioned *Police*. This trilogy points up the white-collar crime in the municipal services as well as the private sector. In *The Fireman* he plays an energetic but eccentric member of the fire department, run by his constant giant rival of the Mutual films—Eric Campbell. Campbell accepts a deal from a wealthy member of the city: he will allow this man's home to burn down in order to share in a large insurance policy. Chaplin, the honest fireman, is a true servant of the community, and he answers the alarm when it occurs.

In *The Floorwalker* he addresses himself to the private sector, examining corruption in business. His role is that of a prospective customer in a large city department store. Always inquisitive, he thoroughly examines practically every item in the store. While he plays the innocent downstairs, the store manager and floorwalker plan a robbery of their store upstairs. Because Chaplin resembles one of them, he is first implicated in, and then breaks up, the theft.

The second Progressive focus (the plight of the urban poor) occurs in *The Pawnshop*, *Easy Street*, and *The Immigrant*. This is best displayed in *Easy Street*, which, significantly enough, has long been considered "the most famous of the Chaplin Mutuals," as well as being his "most cleverly worked-out story."[10] (Art is never created in a vacuum, and Chaplin's concern for the urban poor parallels the period's "Ashcan School" of painting — which as the phrase suggests, put a spotlight on the struggling city dweller.)

In this film Chaplin plays a small-time thief reformed at a mission. And in a radical switch for his screen character, he joins the police force to help curb the area's robbery and violence. In his rounds he subdues the Easy Street bully—Eric Campbell—and begins to go above and beyond his duty as a cop on the beat. He visits the overcrowded poor with a church social worker, and at one point steals food for a desperate woman. His general portrayal of the skid-row neighborhood, here as well as in several other Mutual shorts, often borders upon the naturalism of Progressive Era writers such as Upton Sinclair or Stephen Crane—particularly the latter's *Maggie: A Girl of the Street*. For example, Chaplin's 1917 *Easy Street* contains a scene where a drug addict is about to put the needle in his arm. Documentary filmmaker and humanist Joris Ivens has even commented on the realistic quality of the Chaplin sets:

> There have been instances in fictional films where the real feeling of human misery in filthy surroundings was completely communicated. For example, in some of the interiors of Chaplin films.[11]

Certainly as early as *Police*, when he attempts to stay in a flophouse after his release from prison, Chaplin has an eye for the seedy detail the city presents to the poor.

Chaplin, of course, had known the deprivations of urban poverty as a child. Deserted by Chaplin's father, an overworked mother tried to keep her small family (Charlie and his half-brother, Sydney) together. Eventually it proved too much for her and the boys had to go first to a public workhouse, and then to an orphanage for homeless and/or destitute children. Chaplin has said that life at Hanwell (the orphanage) "was a forlorn existence. Sadness was in the air …. We were known as inmates of the 'booby hatch,' a slang term for workhouse."[12] The culmination of this tragedy was that Chaplin's mother (because of this poverty-induced family breakup) would be committed to a mental institution. She never fully recovered. All this happened to Chaplin before he was eight.

Third, in *The Count, The Rink,* and *The Adventurer*, usually through mistaken identity, Chaplin is able to join the upper crust and take pot-shots at its members. The most damning aspect of these vivid images of the privileged few is not comprised of single film episodes but rather of their cumulatively decadent whole then measured against the abject poverty Chaplin displays in his films of the other half. Chaplin seems to have underlined this approach by the manner in which he released his twelve Mutual films. One finds their release dates evenly balanced between the anti-rich films and those concerned with the underprivileged. Thus, *The Fireman* (June 1916) was the second Mutual film released. *The Count* (September 1916) was the fifth, *The Rink* (December 1916) was the eighth, and *The Adventurer* (October 1917) was the twelfth.[13] These anti-rich works appear at approximately three-film intervals. One sees Chaplin's portrayal of the idle rich as an influencing factor on Jean Renoir's 1939 classic *The Rules of the Game*. The director was very much a Chaplin disciple. Progressive period, or not, the comedian could also project, as did Renoir, that sometimes there could be little difference between the classes, à la Renoir's famous observation, "Everyone has their reasons."

If one then sees the twelve films as a whole, with their regular intertwining of both the privileged and underprivileged, one is reminded of the intellectual editing process called the contrast-cut. Historian Gerald Mast's example of this cut, drawn from Soviet Cinema of the 1920s, is equally true of what Chaplin's slowed-down metaphorical variation on this technique (from film to film instead of shot-to-shot) accomplishes in his Mutual films:

> The director cuts from the dinner table of a poor man, who eats only a few pieces of bread, to the table of a rich man laden with meats, candles, and wine. The contrast of the two tables comments on the injustice of the fact that two such tables can exist at the same time.[14]

Certainly, fun at the expense of the rich is not something to be limited to any one period. But in the context of Chaplin's other Mutual work, it seems a fair addition to his subliminal Progressive statement. Moreover, each period's approach to a subject is often different—in the Progressive teens the protagonist (in this case Chaplin) is often poor, and the superiority of the rich is something to be scorned. In contrast, during the Depression American film comedy often found the protagonists to be both rich *and likeable*, made winsome by their screwball and/or incompetent nature—players such as Carole Lombard and Cary Grant.

These screwball comedies came at a time (1934) when the American political and economic system was being severely tested by the Depression. People did not want their comedy too disruptive, especially after the initial efforts of the New Deal, something Andrew Bergman has noted with the failure, at this time, of the Marx Brothers' best and most anarchistic film comedy—*Duck Soup*.[15] Thus, Bergman later notes that the screwball comedy, especially with its class comradery:

> became a means of unifying what had been splintered and divided. Their "whackiness" cemented social classes and broken marriages; personal relations were smoothed and

social discontent quieted ... Screwball comedy was implosive: It worked to pull things together.[16]

Chaplin's Mutual films, on the other hand, could be called *explosive* in nature. They drew attention to problems in American society, especially the unequal distribution of wealth. Yet, their politics was well received because they were made at a time (Progressive Era) when America was actively searching out its weaknesses. America, bolstered by the justness of Theodore Roosevelt's "New Nationalism" and Woodrow Wilson's "New Freedom," could more easily handle criticism from the film arts. In fact, for a time (during the peace conference in 1919, after the close of World War I) America tried to bring Progressivism to the world, via President Wilson's Fourteen Points.[17] American humorist Finley Peter Dunne, writing during the Progressive Era, capsulized nicely this almost aggressive tendency for change when he wrote (under the guise of his crackerbarrel figure, Mr. Dooley):

Th' noise ye hear is not th' first gun iv revolution. It's on' y th' people iv th' United States batin' a carpet.[18]

Fourth, despite Chaplin's moving contrasts of the rich and poor, he harbored certain elitist tendencies typical of most Progressives. This was reflected best at the time by the "lack of any significant Progressive labor legislation" and the contempt with which the middle class looked upon such union techniques as the strike.[19] It seems that only the enlightened middle-class Progressive could assist the underprivileged; the underprivileged could not and should not try to accomplish change alone. (History now reveals a much darker side to Wilson.)

Chaplin's *Behind the Screen* takes just such an anti-union stance. The film finds him and Campbell as fellow carpenters who refuse to join a strike, and even hire an additional worker. The strikers, who have given no real reason for walking off the job, are portrayed as long-haired anarchists more interested in destroying the work site than returning to employment. Predictably, Chaplin outsmarts their plan and is able to break their strike. But it was concerns like these (the underprivileged asserting themselves) that at times made the Progressives seem a bit reactionary. They wanted what was best for the have-nots but according to Progressive standards. Thus, John Buenker notes that a large number of Progressives, from "the upper and middle classes, aimed at removing the machinery of government as far as possible from the great mass of voters because they held the latter responsible for the failure of government to cope with the problems of modern America."[20]

Fifth, in *One A. M.* and *The Cure* Chaplin deals with another Progressive issue of the day—alcohol. In fact, by the time of Chaplin's Mutual films the subject was even more topical because of our entry into the war (alcohol was needed for war-related industries). Arthur Ekirch notes that Progressives "welcomed the war's encouragement of ... prohibition of alcoholic beverages."[21] And they did get results. In 1917 Congress passed the Lever Act (limiting the production of whiskey) and the Eighteenth Amendment—Prohibition (submitting it to the states for ratification). Plus, the push for Prohibition was also linked to the suffragette movement. (By 1918 some women over the age of 30 who met certain property qualifications could vote.) Interestingly, Chaplin's longtime leading lady during this period (Edna Purviance, and real life love interest), was often his career's most assertive heroine, except for *Modern Times* later gamine, Paulette Goddard.

Comedy based on the drunk or alcoholic can, of course, be found in almost any period. Indeed, Chaplin himself uses the comic drunk throughout much of his career. But *One A.M.* and *The Cure* are of special significance, because it is only in these two works that Chaplin ever devotes an entire film to the subject of alcohol. Moreover, the two films can be naturally paired for a commentary on the misuse of alcohol. *One A.M.* (made first) chronicles something of a comic nightmare as Chaplin returns to the most surrealistic of homes after a night on the town. *The Cure* studies the other end of the alcoholic dilemma—Chaplin's comic look at the drying-out process in a sanitarium.

The films are delightfully funny, but in both there is an underlying sense that alcohol is not in the best interest of society, something his later, shorter alcohol film references do not allow time for. Moreover, it seems appropriate that at this time the Progressive push should not only inspire Chaplin to seize upon a topical issues but also possibly reflect, in an indirect manner (as is comedy's method with any message), Chaplin's "understandable aversion to alcohol, which had brought such tragedy to his family."[22] Without unduly forcing the issue, we might keep in mind that Chaplin later commented extensively on the adverse effects of alcohol in his autobiography. He noted the waste it brought to talent: "Many an artist was ruined by drink—my father was one of them. He died of alcoholic excess at the age of thirty-seven." And he saw the change it could bring to those around such an individual, such as the relationship between a normally gentle, forgiving mother and her child: "In later years, whenever angry with me, she would ruefully say, 'You'll finish up in the gutter like your father.'"[23] Thus, Chaplin had been taught many lessons on the misuse of alcohol by the time he was an adult. They might, in fact, be summed up by another comment from Chaplin's mother (uncovered by film historian Roger Manvell), after she stopped her boy from selling flowers in a saloon: "Drink killed your father, and money from such a source will only bring us bad luck."[24]

All this is not to say, of course that everything Chaplin did at Mutual fitted smoothly into the Progressive mold. For example, in *The Immigrants* he plays upon the irony in the promise of America and the Statue of Liberty juxtaposed against the cattle-like treatment the newcomers receive on their arrival in the new land. In this film, Chaplin takes a big-city problem too far for many Progressives—the plight of the underprivileged immigrant. The typical Progressive was Nativist in viewpoint and felt immigration restriction was the answer to many problems (legislation along these lines was eventually passed in the early 1920s). Yet, it is only fitting that Chaplin, the most famous immigrant of the day, should express the plight of these less fortunate immigrants.

It should be noted, however, that even here Chaplin makes entreaties to the Progressives' anti-immigration stance, playing upon their belief that immigrants were inherently inferior. Other than the innocent heroine (Edna Purviance) and her mother, the rest of the immigrant passengers are portrayed in a largely negative light (as comedy antagonists for Chaplin). This entails gambling, fighting (including the drawing of a pistol), and robbing an elderly woman. Moreover, once Chaplin's immigrant character is in New York he has no job and no money. And it is only through the kindness of an artist that he receives employment as a model, which one assumes can only be temporary. To many Progressives this would represent an example of why they felt the immigrant was inferior, and thus a drag on American society.

In the final analysis, then, Chaplin's Mutual films represent a neglected comic survey of several Progressive issues at the very close of the era. Occurring too late to be called Progressive muckraking, in the tradition of Sinclair's *The Jungle* or Ida Tarbell's *History of the Standard Oil Company*, the Mutual films were instead a final summing up of what the Progressive Movement had tried to be. And with regard to Chaplin's career they mark an equally important moment of neglect—a rare time when he allowed a definite political stance to emerge, for any length of time, in his work. Interestingly enough, in 1919 Chaplin actually took a more direct Progressive issue in real life, when he joined Douglas Fairbanks, Mary Pickford, and D. W. Griffith in forming United Artists. This allowed them to control their own cinema interests — escaping the big business demands of the growing studio system. An anti-union period crack on United Artists' "birth" suggested "the lunatics have taken over the asylum." (However, comedy connoisseurs might go back to an Edgar Allan Poe darkly comic story, "The System of Doctor Terr and Professor Fether," 1845, for the true roots of the phrase.)

Be that as it may, before long the curtain of success—a mixture of increased leisure and the necessary mystique fame requires—would separate Chaplin from all but the most spontaneous of pointed political positions (such as the close of *The Great Dictator*, where he steps out of character and gives an anti-Nazi speech directly to the viewer). Still, even in the early 1920s, on the eve of his first feature, one can hear Chaplin self-consciously testing politics nestled in double-talk, when he is asked by a reporter:

"Are you a Bolshevik?"

"I am an artist. I am interested in life. Bolshevism is a new phase of life. I must be interested in it."[25]

(Originally appeared in a special film-focused issue of *Indiana Social Studies Quarterly*, Autumn 1981; Wes D. Gehring Copyright.)

Notes

1. Theodore Huff, *Charlie Chaplin* (1951; rpt. New York: Arno Press & New York Times, 1972). p. 256.
2. Ibid., p. 65.
3. John McCabe, *Charlie Chaplin* (Garden City, New York: Doubleday & Company, Inc., 1978). p. 77.
4. Ibid., p. 95.
5. George Mowry, *The Progressive Era, 1900-20: The Reform Persuasion* (1958; rpt. Washington, D. C.: American Historical Association, 1972). p. 12.
6. Ibid., p. 31.
7. Max Eastman, *Heroes I Have Known: Twelve Who Lived Great Lives* (New York: Simon and Schuster, 1942). p. 200.
8. David Shannon, *20th Century America: The Progressive Era, 1900-1917* (1963; rpt. Chicago: Rand McNally College Publishing Company, 1974), p. 115.
9. Harry A. Grace, "Charlie Chaplin's Films and American Culture Patterns," *Journal of Aesthetics and Art Criticism*, June 1952, p. 350.
10. Huff, p. 77.
11. Joris Ivens, *The Camera and I* (New York: International Publishers, 1969), p. 88.
12. Charles Chaplin, *My Autobiography* (1964; rpt. New York: Pocket Books, Inc., 1966). p. 22.
13. Isabel Quigly, *Charlie Chaplin: Early Comedies* (New York: E. P. Dutton and Co., Inc., 1968), p. 158.
14. Gerald Mast, *A Short History of the Movies* (Indianapolis: Bobbs-Merrill Company, Inc., 1976), p. 184.
15. Andrew Bergman, *We're in the Money: Depression America and Its Films* (1971; rpt. New York: Harper and Row, 1972), p. 37.
16. Ibid., pp. 133-134.
17. Lecture by Professor Dykstra, History Class on the Progressive Era, University of Iowa, Iowa City, Fall 1975.

18. Finley Peter Dunne, "Mr. Dooley on National Housecleaning," in *The Progressive Years,* ed. Otis Pease (New York: George Braziller, 1962). p. 304.

19. Mowry, p. 26.

20. John D. Buenker, *Urban Liberalism and Progressive Reform* (New York: Charles Scribner's Sons, 1973), p. 119.

21. Arthur A. Ekitch. Jr., *Progressivism in America: A Study of the Era from Theodore Roosevelt to Woodrow Wilson* (New York: New Viewpoints, 1974), p. 270.

22. Huff, p. 65.

23. Chaplin, pp. 7,10.

24. Roger Manvell, *Chaplin* (Boston: Little, Brown and Company, 1974), p. 49.

25. Charlie Chaplin, *My Trip Abroad* (New York: Harper & Brothers, 1922). p. 8.

GEORGE CLOONEY'S

Midnight Sky

George Clooney at the beginning.

Since my favorite actor/activist/sometime director Robert Redford (1937) has essentially retired, George Clooney (1961) now occupies that spot. As well as occasionally directing, Clooney, like Redford, is an activist, too. Another parallel is that both men honed their acting skills on the small screen. However, Clooney's television apprenticeship was much longer. The program which finally made him the dog that caught the car occurred with his starring role on *ER* (1994-1997).

As a film professor in an overly PC period, I teach my students to attempt getting past the private politics of a performer, if the movie in which s/he appears is of cultural, or historical importance. That being said, it is much easier to embrace a filmmaker whose private time is often spent on activities to which one has strong beliefs, be it Redford's environmentalism, or encouraging young filmmakers, à la his Sundance Institute, to Clooney keying on a myriad of African tragedies, including genocide and starvation.

Naturally, this link between the actor and the viewer is further reinforced if the artist's true passions bleed into the work. For example, one could argue that Redford's signature film is 1976's *All the President's Men*, which was produced through his Wildwood Enterprises, while the same case could be made for Clooney's *Good Night, and Good Luck* (2005, which the actor also directed and co-authored).

Fittingly, both pictures address an internal threat to American democracy. *All the President's Men* is a journalistic thriller about the unraveling of Watergate. *Good Night and Good Luck*, which uses legendary broadcaster Edward R. Murrow's (1908-1965) sign off close as a title, examines his pivotal contribution in bringing down red-baiting Senator Joseph McCarthy (1908-1957).

Obviously, not every movie in an actor's career moves the goal posts. Clooney is no different. He will always have *From Dusk to Dawn* (1996) and *Batman & Robin* (1997) on his resume. While neither is a bad film, the former movie comes close. Indeed, Leonard

Maltin's retitling of the Quentin Tarantino-scripted picture, *Natural Born Vampires*, says it all.

Clooney's collaborations with Steven Soderbergh have also been uneven, ranging from the excellent caper picture *Out of Sight* (1998) and the stylistic film noir *The Good German* (2006), to two pedestrian (2004, 2006) sequels to 2001's entertaining Rat Pack homage/loose remake of 1960's *Ocean's Eleven*. In contrast, his batting average is higher when playing broad dark comedy with the Coen Brothers, such as that left-handed *Odyssey*, *O Brother, Where Art Thou?* (2000) and *Burn After Reading* (2008). In these cases, this handsome leading man plays comic stupid with a vein of sensitivity not in Jim Carrey's *Dumb & Dumber* (1994, and its 2003 sequel) performing tool kit. One could liken it to comparing Laurel & Hardy with the Three Stooges. That is, underneath the slapstick lies a nuanced meditation on people.

Unfortunately, Clooney has rationed what propelled him to the big screen — melodramatic romantic comedy. Arguably, his best screen example comes early with lovely Michelle Pfeiffer and *One Fine Day* (1996). However, there is a bittersweet romantic comedy backstory in the poignant Jason Reitman directed *Up in the Air* (2009). However, this latter picture makes the perfect transition to what Clooney does best — topical moving pictures that demand engagement.

In *Up in the Air* Clooney works for a company that handles mass firings during the recession that followed President George W. Bush's administration. This involves constant travel for Clooney's character, who tries to distance himself from his gut-wrenching obligations. Naturally, it showcases how this damages his personal life. However, the picture proves most timely in a constant sticking the landing manner by having all the *Up in the Air* victims being played by amateurs who had also recently been fired.

The aforementioned *Good Night, and Good Luck* was another of these well timed classic pictures. Though ostensibly about the blacklisting blight of 1950s McCarthyism, the picture was also an alarm for potential similar seismic dangers in early twentieth century America. As with *Up in the Air*, the latter picture resonated with the public, and the critics. Indeed, Clooney was also nominated for both a Best Director Oscar, and authoring the Best Original Screenplay (with Grant Heslow).

Good Night obviously also shares a high quality connection with Clooney's *Syriana* (2005), which actually was completed before *Good Night*, but was delayed by a head injury he received during a mock torture scene. Clooney's character, which generated a Best Supporting Actor Oscar, is caught up in a multilayered political thriller centered around American Middle East oil interests. It is rare in its ability to juggle a complex story with a balanced grey area mix of corruption and conscience. The added *Syriana* and *Good Night* link, beyond being cautionary tales, is the filmmaker's innate public service passion.

As the son of a broadcast journalist (Nick Clooney), the actor has always been fascinated by current events. In a 15 October 2005 National Public Radio (NPR) interview George Clooney made a *Good Night* statement which could double as his catalyst for making topical pictures, "I feel as if my job — as an entertainer — [is] to try to raise the debate [over topical issues], not to answer the question … I don't know the answers. I just thought it was a good thing to ask the question."

Clooney's public service zealousness again brings one back to *Good Night*. The aforementioned head injury making *Syriana* was so serious he could not receive insurance clearance to make the Murrow movie. Thus, he mortgaged his Hollywood home and refused a writing and directing salary. (The Hollywood Guilds forced him to be paid a minimum of one dollar for each task.)

Regardless, this is neither an attempt to scrutinize his every picture, nor create a Saint George essay. The actor is an extremely well-paid star who relishes his Italian Villa, and occasionally makes, to use that teetering motion with your hand — "so-so" movies, some of which have been noted. However, before examining his most recent attempt to address a current pressing issue, Clooney deserves to have one additional quality movie plucked from his filmography.

In this film Clooney plausibly gives his preeminent performance — the frazzled father of *The Descendants* (2011), for which he received a Best Actor Oscar nomination. The universal relevancy here is just holding on to the funny/sad Kafka on wheels nature of life. Clooney is a successful lawyer whose wife's accident results in a coma. Suddenly he has to be a *Mr. Mom* (1983), which teeters closer to *Kramer vs. Kramer* (1979) squared. That is, while in the latter picture Dustin Hoffman must only perform a balancing act with a little boy, in *Descendants* Clooney has two older daughters, one of which is channeling James Dean teenage angst.

However, Clooney is somehow navigating this "perfect storm," to punningly reference one of his earlier hits, when he discovers his wife had been cheating — a most thoughtless act. However, sadly — welcome to too many households. Yet, the degree of difficulty topper is that his large family owns an extremely valuable piece of property which has to be sold. Is a potential win fall not a good thing? Yes and no. Since the final family financial decision is George's, this has screaming into the pillow potential. However, his character and the movie realistically gerrymander their way through a relatable look at one variation of the "human comedy" — hard-bought impressions of life.

Before plunging into Clooney's latest sensitive cinema examination of a current troubling topic, one must add a final fan clause. In essays examining a favorite contemporary filmmaker, such cases often have ephemeral elements beyond the work and general philosophy of said artist. In such scenarios, one inadvertently bumps into random traces of self. That is, at times Clooney and I are strangely on the same wavelength. A scholarly writer might remain silent as a fish on the topic, lest some satirist ape Groucho Marx's *A Night at the Opera* (1935) crack, "Boogie boogie!" However, just as academics can be fans, it is vacuous to not mention these links. It is as instantly evident in periodic self-reflection as the snapping shut of a switch blade. Moreover, it represents a perfect segue to the original catalyst for this essay. So please, some indulgement.

Through the years in print interviews and on talk shows, such as a recent *Late Night* with Stephen Colbert, Clooney has talked of the important transitory tactile nature of letter writing. He bemoans its increasing rareness and he personally continues to both write and treasure letters he has saved; both from famous people, *and* individuals who will never have biographies written about them. That could be me talking.

On another occasion, several years ago, *GQ* magazine did a special Hollywood issue in which stars picked their yesteryear favorite, and then were showcased in a photo shoot tribute. Clooney picked Clark Gable, whose former California home he lives in when Stateside. As in the 1930s, Gable was "King" in my childhood home. Clooney also was in the aforementioned "Rat Pack" movies, both because he thought they were "beyond cool" (frequently cited), professionally *and* personally. Early in his career he stayed with his famous aunt, Rosemary Clooney, and met them, with Martin being the most laid-back. Bingo. In my youth, Martin and Gable were special.

In addition, Clooney is frequently on record as feeling blessed over having a career compass, given not everyone has a calling. Ditto again. Of course, while my light is a small candle, and his is literally a Hollywood klieg light, I would not have gotten through this ongoing Covid-19 nightmare without my writing.

There are other links, but the most recent and intriguing Clooney coupling occurs on his new science fiction film *The Midnight Sky*. However, a brief setup is necessary. Last term several of my college film students wrote term papers on recent apocalyptic movies. I was struck by the mob mentality and self-centeredness of their screen characters clinging to survival. It seemed such a contrast with an end of the world high school paper I had done decades before — Nevil Shutes' 1957 bestselling novel *On the Beach*, and its 1959 screen adaptation, had been my focus.

Written at the height of the Cold War, what had impressed me about *Beach* was how civilized Shute's doomed victims responded to the end. If one is not familiar with the story, it opens after a nuclear apocalyptic war has occurred. Little information is given, other than a domino-like scenario, à la the beginning of World War I, only now with countless nuclear strikes.

So extreme is the radiation fallout, everyone in the world has died except people living in and around Australia. However, global air currents will soon terminate everyone in the Southern Hemisphere. The central character is a United States submarine Captain named Towers, whose ship finds itself in Melbourne, the world's most southern major city. Regardless, the nature of the civility is best suggested by the adaptation casting of Gregory Peck as Powers. His performance could double as a template for his future Oscar winning Attica Finch in *To Kill a Mockingbird* (1962).

Other key *Beach* characters are few, and include a young Australian naval officer, his naïve wife and baby, a cynical scientist/professor, and a potential one-time party girl love interest for the captain. There is little hysteria, and little hope. Early on Towers does take his ship north along the American West Coast to investigate a mysterious Seattle radio signal, and measure radiation levels. Both dash any lingering pipe dream.

The Australian government issues voluntary suicide pills, which most people only resort to at the end, choosing to live their lives like there will be limitless tomorrows. Gardens are planted, naval regulations are followed, and Peck's Tower even buys gifts for his wife and children in dead America. His well-named character becomes very close to the young woman, but he keeps their friendship platonic. I remember *the* Catholic magazine of the time, *The Catholic Digest*, giving it a split decision review, celebrating the sanctity of marriage, but condemning suicide.

Contemplating writing a topical paper, I reread *Beach* and rescreened the adaptation, wondering if I could discover a more recent such civilized take on the subject for an essay comparison.

Almost simultaneously I discovered Clooney had adapted the 2016 end of the world novel *Good Morning, Midnight*. Retitled *The Midnight Sky*, it went into limited theatrical release over Christmas 2020, and became Netflix available in January 2021.

While I waited for *Midnight Sky* cable availability, I read this most civilized apocalyptic novel. Based upon past Clooney films, since he was a co-star, doing uncredited writing, *and* directing, this signaled high quality personal potential, especially given he had been off the screen for four years. If it would be a close adaptation, I marveled that my quirky Clooney connection was continuing. However, here is where it gets hair on the back of the neck standing up strange (cue the *Twilight Zone* music). Not only was it close to *Good Morning*, but for a nanosecond near the middle of the picture there is a pivotal in-film *Beach* clip.

I have written articles on the significance of movie film footnotes. For a consummate filmmaker such moments are Rosetta Stones, not random acts. Fittingly, changes in the Clooney adaptation are best filtered through *Beach*. Sadly, many contemporary critics are like my students. If it is from a black and white picture done *way back* in the mid-twentieth century, they do not exist. A long ago science fiction film to them is Clooney's cameo in Sandra Bullock's tour de force *Gravity* (2013). This qualifies as being aggressively illiterate, since the importance of *Beach* has continued to be acknowledged throughout the years. For example, the 12 October 1986 *New York Times* called it "the most haunting evocation we have of a world dying of radiation after an atomic war." Moreover, Margaret MacMillan's recent critically acclaimed book, *WAR: How Conflict Shaped Us* (2020), lists *Beach* as the first significant artistic warning of a nuclear war.

Regardless, in *Midnight Sky* Augustine (Clooney) is a world famous scientist dying of cancer at an Artic observatory. It is 2049 and "three weeks after the event." Both the novel and the film are even more obscure than *Beach* about the cataclysmic event. During a rushed Arctic camp doomed evacuation, a little girl has maybe been left behind. The frantic mother is assured the child boarded an earlier flight. Regardless, it is fitting a dying of cancer Clooney is soon Arctic alone.

Augustine has lived a self-centered loner life dedicated to finding a humanly hospitable world in space. His dying regret is having turned away from scientist Jean Sullivan (Sophia Ruddle) thirty odd years before. She was pregnant at the time, but recognized his work would always come first. Thus, she had not shared her condition. The child grows up to be astronaut Dr. "Sully" Sullivan (Felicity Jones). The now world famous Augustine only stumbled upon his fatherhood seven or eight years after the split, when his nomadic research path briefly crossed Jean's.

"Sully" never knows Augustine is her father. In the novel he had anonymously sent her expensive space related gifts, until he lost track of Jean and the child. In the film Jean had simply told Sully her father was a great man who had an important mission to accomplish. Sully became a scientist/astronaut both because of a moon rock Augustine had once given Jean, and the awe with which she and her colleagues held Augustine's work. Indeed, this is how their lives finally intersect. Sully and several other scientist/astronauts are returning from a two year space mission from an habitable Jupiter moon (K-23) which Augustine discovered.

The film story really starts when Clooney's character discovers that the thought to be missing little girl (Cavoilinn Spingall) is hiding at the arctic control center. A concerned Clooney initially attempts to contact the station's recently departed scientists and staff. However, there is no response, just as the world seems to have shut down. Briefly falling back on being a lifetime loner, he is frustrated to be responsible for a child. However, her puppy dog-like underfoot presence soon allows Augustine a joy he has never allowed himself, the gladness which comes from allowing someone into his world. It softens the aforementioned regret, and even energizes his weakened condition. He is needed. The child is all but speechless, and shares her name by drawing an "Iris" flower.

The *Midnight* story fluctuates between Clooney and the returning space vehicle. Pregnant Sully (with the ship's commander, David Oyelowa), and the rest of the crew are increasingly concerned about NASA's silence. Clooney is equally upset about not being able to contact what at first seems to be several possible incoming ships … to warn them. However, what soon becomes clear is his fixation on this craft. Yet, at this point viewers neither know it is indirectly his mission, nor given his Einstein-like space status, realize he would be aware it is the only ship in deep space.

The communication situation at Augustine's present location is not strong enough to reach the K-23 craft. So he and the child take what equipment they can and head further north to a better equipped weather station. A grueling two day snowmobile trip, it necessitates making camp one night, and includes everything from the inherent beauty of the setting, to a near fatal accident in which a portion of a seemingly frozen lake gives way. Clooney and the child bond. In the novel the attraction of better equipment is the only reason to head north. In the film Clooney borrows the added *Beach* incentive from the slowly spreading radiation fallout having reached their original camp.

The K-23 ship is having communication problems, too. A meteorite shower has destroyed exterior communication equipment. So Sully and astronaut Maya (Tiffany Boone) also have a dangerous journey to make — the need to walk in space. The exterior hardware is repaired but another meteorite storm occurs, and Maya dies. It is an especially difficult loss, from her being the youngest and most popular crew member, to the ironically beautiful yet deadly view of blood bubbles beginning to appear in her helmet. (It has been said that "Every good story contains the duality found in Pandora's Box: horror and beauty; awfulness and awe.")

Eventually contact is made between Augustine and Sully twice, with the final conversation having her reveal both his influence on her and affirming his prediction that the Jupiter moon would be habitable — "Like landing in Oz in sexy red colors for the first time [from a black and white world]." Only at the end does the viewer discover Sully's given name is *Iris*. This emotional ending impact sends the viewer scrambling to reconfigure and re-examine what has come before. It is a gateway to a place which was not obviously visible before. However, at some point Augustine has made the connection, saying, "It's very nice to finally meet you." Then his second chance little girl is gone, a figment of his imagination, or a gift from God — though Clooney is an agnostic? I only make the religious reference because of Clooney's Biblical-like conclusion, and a character name (Augustine) that suggests the driven so-named Catholic saint (354-430), obsessed with the search for inner truth. Augustine is also derived from the Latin word "to increase."

The ending and some story points differ from the novel, but the *Beach* influence is often present. In the novel, straws are drawn for the following choice: "Short for a life sentence in space [without the power to return to K-23]. Long for an uncertain descent [to Earth]." There are not enough re-entry pods, if everyone had wanted to roll the dice. A non-pregnant Sully originally draws a short straw, but the others decide that she and the commander should return to an uncertain earth, since they have fallen in love. If the two survive, the story has Adam and Eve implications.

Clooney makes his Eden ending much more definite. Sully is pregnant, and she and her ship commander partner *can* turn back to the Earth-like K-23. Plus, with a bow to *Beach*, Mitchell (Kyle Chandler), the space ship pilot, like Gregory Peck, will return to his implied dead family. (He is the one who had been watching the in-film *Beach* clip.) Scientist Sanchez (Damian Bichir), the oldest crew member, will accompany Mitchell back. Because Sanchez had once lost a young daughter who would have been Maya's age, he had always felt a fatherly affection towards her. Thus, his real and metaphorical family situation parallels Mitchell's.

Clooney's awareness of just who his little Iris represented, however, had been an accumulative affect, as it was in the novel. For example, even at the book's midpoint, Augustine "realizes she [Iris] was replicating the meal he'd made them last night. He felt a kernel of pride that she had paid attention, that he had taught her something useful without even intending to. *Perhaps this is how fathers feel*, he thought."

With the touching surprise twist ending, the movie and book invite a second look. What was most telling for me was the in print Sully had more parallels with Augustine. While she was not dying, the Earth bound Iris had been in regret mode, too. Like her father, Sully had been so science driven she had also walked away from a relationship and a daughter. At the close she is ready for a do over with Mitchell. Clooney has traded this for a more upbeat close.

Regardless, there is no exact time one can say when Clooney knew who, or what Iris represented. The quiet little girl was often drawing, and one of her pictures prompted Clooney to say he once knew someone who looked like that. One knows he means Jean, because viewers periodically see her in Augustine flashbacks. Yet, between the film having immediately established a missing child, periodic Clooney recollections, and the astronauts frequently exercising the ability during downtime to almost enter into cherished virtual reality scenarios, the "now" is sometimes hard to pin down.

Be that as it may, the universality of *Midnight Sky* grew in post-production. In an Associated Press (AP) 7 January 2021 interview with Jake Coyle, Clooney said he had originally embraced the seemingly obvious *Midnight Sky* message: "of what regret can do to you. I thought of what he's [Augustine] really dying of is not cancer but regret. It's killing him … when you get older, it's [regret as] a cancer."

However, the *Midnight Sky* shooting wrapped just prior to the Covid-19 outbreak. Naturally, like most things in the world, Clooney's work was thrown into topsyturvydom. But as the final editing took place, a more comprehensive meaning appeared. In a 20 December 2020 NPR interview with Lula Garcia-Navarro, Clooney stated what the film is even more about is: "our desperate need to be home, or to be with the people we love and be in contact with them. And sometimes we forget that, and all of a sudden you take it away so you can't be in touch. I think we are all going through a lot of that. And you're at least reminded [by the film] of how lucky you are to have somebody in your life that you love that much."

Entertainment Weekly's 19 December 2020 *Midnight Sky* descriptive review said it best, "[this] dystopian drama whose fluctuating tone — grim, with flickers of hopeful sentiment — feels almost comfortingly familiar, if a little on the nose for 2020."

SEINFELD, MEET MR. BENCHLEY

And Literary Friends

The Extraordinary Robert Benchley stumbles about the Disney lot in *The Reluctant Dragon* (1941).

The *Seinfeld* television situation comedy (1989-1998) is one of the small screen's most celebrated programs. For example, IMDB (Internet Movie/TV Database) ranks it as history's third greatest comedy, with the *Simpsons* at number one. The "Ranker" (American Ranking Service) also places it at three, but with *The Office* (American version) topping the bill. Moreover, *Rolling Stone* magazine grades it fifth of *all* television programing, giving *The Sopranos* the pinnacle position.

With such kudos, there is no debating its pop culture significance. The *Seinfeld* setting is Manhattan's Upper West Side and follows the misadventures of title character comedian "Jerry" Seinfeld and his three closest friends, former girlfriend Elaine (Julia Louis-Dreyfus), George Constanza (Jason Alexander), and goofy apartment neighbor Cosmos Kramer (Michael Richards). Much of the action takes place in Jerry's apartment, and a diner just around the corner. Most of the segments stay in the upscale neighborhood, like such quintessential episodes involving the "Soup Nazi" deli owner (odd food ordering etiquette), or the "Chinese Restaurant" (waiting in line).

With everyone having vague or often changing jobs (other than Seinfeld's stand up constant), everyone seems to be living beyond their means, á la Woody Allen New York-based movies. This especially applies to Richard's grubby Kramer. His trademark explosive entrances to Jerry's apartment were inspired by his comedy idol, Art Carney. Art too had a signature entrance as Jackie Gleason's equally eccentric neighbor on TV's pioneering *Honeymooners* (1955-56, but more often this was an ongoing sketch on Gleason's various variety shows). Also like Carney's Norton, Kramer looks like he might have also had a job in the sewer. Plus, he shared Norton's and Gleason's bus driving Ralph Kamden's ongoing get rich schemes. Richard's character represents *Seinfeld*'s only sitcom series throwback. Jerry and his other friends were more contemporary in their self-centeredness.

Seinfeld has often been described as "a show about nothing," as in the minutiae of daily life. However, in 2014, sixteen years after the show ended, though naturally it lives on in high profile syndication, the comedian denied on Reddit (a news and discussion website) the minutiae catalyst and expressed surprise over this explanation. The irony is that for years he had given that explanation on late night talk shows. Moreover, for added PR during *Seinfeld*'s original run, episode three of season four was directly suggested to have been inspired by the minutiae motivation of the program. Entitled "The Pitch" (first aired September 16, 1992), it involved Jerry and George attempting to sell to a network a program about comic mundaneness. Thus, the overwhelming comedy incitement since 1990 has been minutiae.

Why? Starting in the decades before the 20th century mankind's position in the cosmos had manifestly declined. In 1859, Darwin's (1809-1882) book *On the Origin of Species* (evolution) unquestionably dampened *Genesis*' statement about man being "made in the image of God." Consistent with Darwin, Karl Marx's (1818-1883) three-volume *Das Kapital* (1867-1883) suggested societies developed through class conflict — Capitalism was a goner. Uniform with these negative human projections, the founder of psychoanalysis, Sigmund Freud (1856-1939), ultimately postulated that individuals were not even aware of a subconscious which drove their lives.

In 1895 prolific English writer H. G. Wells wrote the pioneering anti-utopian novel *The Time Machine*. Many gifted authors followed with their own dire projections, including E. M. Forster's *The Machine Stops* (1909), Aldous Huxley's *Brave New World* (1932), C. S. Lewis' *Out of the Silent Planet* (1938), George Orwell's *1984*, (1948), Ray Bradbury's *Fahrenheit 451* (1954), and on and on. Since the time of Plato's (427 B.C. -327 B.C.) *The Republic* (360 B.C.), writers had been composing hopeful utopian works about the coming times. Now the best and brightest were chronicling a frightful future. This did not portend well for thinking humor, unless one removed the guard rails and embraced dark comedy.

The result has been the humor of minutiae — a head in the ground distraction from what had and/or was about to happen. Plus, the 20th century delivered. World War I (1914-1918), known as "the war to end all wars," guaranteed a more disturbing sequel, with a depression "prologue." How best to describe the first "act?" Critic Deirdre Donahue said of World War I, "The extraordinary carnage .... did not just kill men. The violence destroyed accepted ideas about valor, duty, class, human behavior, and whether the future even mattered." Then the Second World War added a Holocaust and the creation of a weapon which moved its most central scientist, J. Robert Oppenheimer, to quote Hindu scripture, "I am become death, the destroyer of worlds."

At this point one could say, "Well done; thank you for letting the air out of a lie. However, it is important to show the next generation where our humor really came from. After all, *the* Orwellian *1984* message born out chillingly in recent years is an untruth repeated enough times becomes "the truth." Moreover, I am constantly correcting my college students that Seinfeld did not create comedy minutiae. A brief comedy tutorial seems necessary. Call it a public service with jokes.

Predating the haunting 20th century, American humor was originally anchored to what one might best generalize as the populist crackerbarrel type, a personae going back to Benjamin Franklin's character Poor Richard. It's basic template was a rational world navigable by common sense. The latter component was attached to age — the school of hard knocks. This figure came with practical axioms, too. These ranged from the hoary, "A penny saved is a penny earned," to Franklin's strictly off the record actual explanation for inventing bifocals, "So one could both see the woman in one's arms, while watching the door for her husband."

Regardless, given the crackerbarrel figure's working class wisdom, there was often a tendency to address political issues. For example, America's last national figure in this tradition, Will Rogers, would often prick what he felt was disorganized national leadership.

For example, one of his especially biting and well-known observations noted, "When Congress makes a joke it's a law. And when they make a law it's a joke."

Rogers was that rare example of a crackerbarrel figure in the early 20th century. However, his most popular films were set in the past, such as *Judge Priest* and *Steamboat 'Round the Bend* (both 1935). The implication was that this mindset was only applicable to an earlier, simpler time. Of course, one should note that it is uncommon for any comedy type to completely disappear. Thus, a case can be made for the long running *Andy Griffith Show* (1960-1968) showcasing an American Solomon in the crackerbarrel mold of a never neverland called Mayberry.

However, the pivotal example of the transition of crackerbarrel humor morphing into the antiheroic mundane modern scene can be seen in Kin Hubbard's nationally syndicated character, Abe Martin. At the time of Hubbard's 1930 death, Rogers declared him "America's greatest humorist." Martin's early observations were pure crackerbarrel, such as "How'd you like t' be marooned in Napoleon, Indianny, an' dependin' on th' Congress to git you out?" Yet, very soon he was anticipating, in a down home manner, a key component of a later pivotal arbitrator of American modern humor — the *New Yorker* minutiae (founded in 1925). Thus, when Hubbard's Martin moved to observations like, "Two can live as cheaply as one ... just not as long," or "Marriages are made in Heaven, an' very few o' them ever git back t' th' factory," he was onto a future fundamental *New Yorker* perspective — the "battle of the sexes."

Celebrated 20th century American humorists who found a home at the *New Yorker*, especially James Thurber, S. J. Perelman, Robert Benchley, and Will Cuppy hovered over the sexual card domination of the male and/or general antiheroic surreal situations. Both characteristics are at the core of Thurber's signature short story, "The Secret Life of Walter Mitty." The heyday of these writers ushered in what literature came to call the "Little Man" [comic antihero]. While these writers dominated the first half of the 20th century, the "Little Man" has never gone away, from Charles Schulz's Charlie Brown to Woody Allen's comic antiheroes, "Relationships are like the Middle East; there is no solution."

A central element of going from crackerbarrel to antiheroic minutiae humor involved elevating the importance of women, and invariably giving them the upper humor hand in varying ways. Feminists appreciated the higher profile, but were increasingly unhappy with some of the comedy types. First, there was the dominating wife guarding against a husband wanting to slip out for a beer with the "boys," or governing boys themselves.

However, like most stereotypes, there was a basis in reality, and studies documented it in all fun formats, from newspapers comic strips to the movies. Entertaining references, such as Henry Jenkin's *What Made Pistachio Nuts? Early Sound Comedy and the Vaudeville Aesthetic* (1992), and Steve Seidman's *Comedian Comedy: A Tradition in Hollywood* (1981) chronicled a male fear at this time of matriarchal power in antiheroic humor having multiple causes. This ranged from the *Little Man* evolution paralleling the rise of the women's movement, to maternal domination in immigrant families — research chronicled women adjusted better to change. Entertainment evidence included pioneering newspaper comic strips, like the Irish *Bringing Up Father* (also known as *Jiggs & Maggie*), and the martinet German mother attempting to maintain order in *The Katzenjammer Kids* (briefly known as *Hans and Fritz*, or *The Captain and the Kids* during our WWI conflict with Germany).

Given my Irish-German background, these were still high profile strips in both of my grandparents' homes, with hard bound volumes of the comics in the family libraries. Naturally, period variations of the strips were soon found in vaudeville and the movies. In fact, the early 1910s birth of *Bringing Up Father* was also essentially the template for American's first international film comedy star, the large round John Bunny. His short subjects invariably had him attempting a fifth columnist rebellion against his Olive Oyl-like thin screen wife (Flora Finch), and were known as "Bunnyfinches."

For students of early American sound film comedy, the *Bringing Up* scenario is no doubt most associated with Laurel & Hardy and W. C. Fields — with the latter very much in the Bunny mold, with Fields even referencing him in *The Bank Dick* (1940). Indeed, the real life antiheroic youth of the Marx Brothers documents this maternal domination, perfectly meshed with their children of immigrants status. Their dominating German/Jewish mother Minnie Marx controlled her husband and the boys like any episode of *The Katzenjammer Kids*. Moreover, she created and managed what became the Marx Brothers, whether her sons wanted show business careers or not. Groucho's son, Arthur (named after his brother Arthur "Harpo" Marx), later turned her puppeteer force of nature into a hit Broadway play, *Minnie's Boys* (1970). While Shelley Winters' title role performance could chew the furniture a bit, if one saw the production it seemed fitting for Minnie the comic legend. Moreover, as Jenkins noted, whether referencing Laurel & Hardy and Fields, or literature's *Little Man* syndrome, the 1930s Depression further empowered this matriarchal clout. "Because husbands' increasing dependence upon their wives to provide additional or even primary income for the family ... [represents] a rapid deterioration of the father's status."

A second feminine controlling factor adhered itself to defining them as a comically frustrating irrational survival instinct. That is, the modern world was ever more absurd, yet men continued to attempt to navigate in a rational way. This was folly, or as a Cuppy essay title collection so succinctly put it, *How to Become Extinct* (1941, also paralleling America's entry into World War II). In contrast, an irrational woman in an irrational world was right at home. Liken it to our Covid-19 shot, one's vaccine has a trace amount of the virus. This contributed to cinema's screwball comedy genre, including films like *My Man Godfrey* (1936) and *Bringing Up Baby* (1938).

Even earlier than this the newspaper comic strips and vaudeville had a variation of this phenomenon on steroids and generally referenced it as "Dumb Dora" couples, jump-started by a popular newspaper strip of the same name (1924-1936). While at the time there were dozens of vaudeville Dora duos, the coupling is now most synonymous with the nearly fifty-year comedy couple George Burns (1896-1996) & Gracie Allen (1895-1964).

In the post-WWII era and the birthing of existentialism and Samuel Beckett's *Waiting for Godot* (1953), women were now just as likely to be victimized, and/or assume what for today would be a more PC presence. Yet, even when one thinks of 1950s pioneering TV programs, screwball comedy lived on in the zany domestic (yet cool New York) setting of "I Love Lucy" (1951-1957), the "Dora" twosome carried on with *Burns & Allen*'s TV show (1950-1958), and the controlling wife/ultimate winner was at the heart of *The Honeymooners*, despite Ralph's blustering.

Regardless, in the latter half of the 20th century, and early 2000s, American humor, when both men and women were equally sentenced to a sliding scale of bozos and bottom feeders, another early 1900 antiheroic minutiae component further surfaced. Fittingly, it also had roots in the amalgamation of both the *Little Man* movement and dominating female eccentricities. The modern world just seemed absurd, whether the illogic was women driven or not.

Consequently, while the Marx Brothers' world might have been created by the all-powerful Minnie, their routines, whether on stage or in the movies, were surrealistic in tone, be it their own verbal slapstick, or whatever ludicrous things Harpo produced from his trench coat. Salvador Dali loved the Marx Brothers, to the point of later producing Harpo-inspired art work. Pioneering Dadaist and surrealist Man Ray considered W. C. Fields' *Million Dollar Legs* (1932, in which the comedian plays the president of a mythological European county "a surrealistic masterpiece"), and predated by a year the Marx's own masterpiece, *Duck Soup*, in which Groucho heads another mythological country.

Beckett also loved the personality comedians of the first half of the 20th century, and incorporated them into his work. For example, the first production of *Godot* (1953) featured Burt Lahr (*The Wizard of Oz*'s cowardly lion) as one of two pivotal clown-like characters stood-up by God. Much later Mike Nichols cast Steve Martin and Robin Williams as this duo (Estragon and Vladimir) in his underrated 2015 production of *Godot*. Even if existentialism and dark comedy embrace Kafka's meaning of life as "you die," that is no reason to not have some laughs killing time with mundane merriment before time kills you.

Of course, long before *Seinfeld* minutiae, American "comedy about nothing" had three additional components to distract from life's disturbing ultimate dead end, beyond the battle of the sexes, the "Little Man," and life's inherent absurdity. One might label them as angrily overreacting to minor issues, distractingly pointless games, and simply embracing the absurdity. All can be best exemplified by arguably the 20th century's still most relevant humorist, Robert Benchley. Here is how Thurber described his work, "One of the greatest fears of the humorous writer is that he has spent three weeks writing something done faster and better by Benchley in 1919." S. J. Perelman, *New Yorker* essayist, Marx Brothers screenwriter, and author of the Oscar-winning screenplay for 1956's *Around the World in 80 Days*, said of Benchley, "A good stuffy way to describe him would be to say that 'he occupies a unique position in American humor.' Benchley occupies nothing of the sort, he is top dog."

Regardless, a Benchley take on the comic overreaction might best be taken from his essay "Rapping the Wrapper," from one of his anthologies, which invariably have absurdist titles, *From Bad to Worse or Comforting Thoughts About the Bison* (1934). It states, "There used to be an advertisement which read: 'We couldn't improve the product, so we improved the wrapper.' That's fine, provided you *do* improve the wrapper. But there is such a thing as improving the wrapper so that nobody can get at the product. It may be a perfectly dandy wrapper, airtight, watertight and germ-proof, but if the buyer has to send it to a garage to get it off, something is wrong somewhere." In this case, Benchley's vexation is directed at a package of mints. However, substitute that product for opening a new overly sealed DVD, and everything applies. Indeed, I once broke a DVD in the opening process.

Under "distractingly pointless games," one need go no further than *From Bad to Worse*'s essay, "How to Break 90 in Croquet." (Croquet was very popular among New York's 1920s "Algonquin Round Table" wits, which most famously included Alexander Woollcott, Dorothy Parker, Benchley, and a less than quiet Harpo). Benchley's piece describes croquet as "a daredevil, madcap sort of sports, it is true, but then these are dangerous days." (If croquet outings outside Gotham were not possible, Benchley and company resorted to rooftop games. Regardless, one wonders if his "dangerous days" reference included any falling wooden croquet balls and passing pedestrians.)

Benchley's surrender to pure absurdity is best showcased in the essay, "Carnival Week In Sunny Las Los," from his anthology *The Treasurer's Report and Other Aspects of Community Singing* (1930). He finds himself in yet another of the period's fictitious lands. Benchley describes the country's native drink known as *wheero*; it is so strong one need only pour some in an open saucer on a window sill "and inhale deeply from across the room. In about eight seconds the top of the inhaler's head rises slowly and in a dignified manner until it reaches the ceiling ... The teeth then drop out and arrange themselves on the floor to spell 'Portage High School, 1930,' the eyes roll upward and backward, and a strange odor of burning rubber fills the room ..."

All these examples of nearly a century worth of American comic minutiae are merely a modest survey of how *Seinfeld* did not begin "a show about nothing." Brilliant yes, but not groundbreaking. It is past time to correct history. Anything else would be like the following absurdist joke at the expense of the series, "Eating cereal in the dark is *disturbing*, another thing [breakfast food obsessed] *Seinfeld* forgot.

(First appearance. Original journal placement was at a recently defunct publication. Wes D. Gehring Copyright © 2022.)

PART FOUR:

A LIGHTER SIDE

IF THE SHOE FITS

Chaplin even incorporated his signature shoes into his autograph.

As a film professor I teach my students to scrutinize the screen closely to better "read" a movie. For example, is there a snippet of another film within the film? These are rarely accidents. To illustrate, there is the briefest cinema informational in-joke early from Martin McDonagh's Oscar winning dark comedy *In Bruges* (2008). A British hit man (Brendan Gleason) is watching the opening of Orson Welles' *Touch of Evil* (1958). If one ever wondered about the profession's possible viewing habits — Welles' beginning depicts a hit man planting a car bomb.

However, playful or pivotal, plot points need not be as brief as a film fragment, or a burning Rosebud finale. Sometimes key misè-en-scencè (objects in the film frame) can be almost ever present, something as simple as shoes. Indeed, pop culture claims nothing defines one more than foot apparel.

Alfred Hitchcock films frequently play upon this perspective, such as the corpse's Technicolor bright shiny new shoes which open *The Trouble With Harry* (1955), not to mention the title character's even more dazzling two-tone blue and red socks. Said corpse will be buried and dug up throughout the movie. However, the Hitchcock's pièce de resistance, with regard to shoes, starts the director's *Strangers on a Train* (1951). This is the picture in which the ever so charismatic man/child mama's boy Bruno (Robert Walker) proposes a crisscross exchange of random (fail-safe) murders to Farley Granger's professional tennis-playing Guy. The duo meet murder plot point cute. Walker's psychopathic encounters Granger's famous athlete on a train. However, viewers first follow a comic crisscross path of just their shoe ware in boarding.

Bruno's loafers are expensive but gaudy two-tone gunboats, while the modest Guy wears a nondescript pair, as lackluster as he is, despite being the star tennis player. Both end up in the train's club car; their shoes accidently touch, and Bruno starts a conversation which entertainingly leads to his crisscross pitch. (By this time we are in full figure mode.) He proposes to kill Guy's adulterous money hungry estranged wife, if the straight arrow athlete murders the charismatic villain's hated father. It is as brassy basic as Bruno's eyesore shoes, or garish monogrammed tie.

Given this character's defining piece of apparel, it should come as no surprise that shoes are often also the focus of the traditional arts, delineating everything from class, or innocent romanticism. Indeed, both are combined in the *Cinderella* folk tale, which is also sometimes entitled "The Little Glass Slipper." The young girl is as transparently pure and victim-in-waiting fragile as the see through slippers.

Moreover, arguably the Western world's most identifiable painter, Vincent van Gogh (1853-1890), was obsessed with the subject, including depicting "A Pair of Old Shoes," "A Pair of Leather Clogs," "Three Pairs of Shoes" ... I am particularly partial to these paintings, because they remind me of my maternal grandfather's farming work boots, which were similarly showcased just inside his home's side door — "hard bought" impressions of life.

However, if blue collar is not one's first foot entre to art, think of Edgar Dega's (1834-1917) countless Impressionist paintings of ballet slippered (toe shoe clad) ballerinas. Yet, like van Gogh, such Degas canvases as "Dancer Adjusting Her Shoes," "Dancer Fixing her Slipper," "Dancers Tying Shoes" ... suggests his sometimes snapshot imagery (paralleling the birth of photography) recognizes the work behind the artifice.

Regardless, Degas epitomizes the quintessential segue back to cinema's most eminent movie on the subject — Michael Powell and Emeric Pressburger's *The Red Shoes* (1948), about an aspiring ballerina (lovely Moira Shearer's film debut), torn between dance and love. It is essentially a variation upon the Hans Christian Anderson fairy tale about a young girl's pair of red slippers that will not allow her to stop dancing.

Besides having those red slippers constantly front and center, à la Dorothy's (Judy Garland) *Wizard of Oz* (1939) slippers, *The Red Shoes* did not go lightly on that sprinkling of interpretation and evaluations. It poses the question of dance (art) versus love/life. Thus, is the tragic close to be blamed on the power of the iconic shoes, or a ballerina's suicide when pressured to leave dance? Now before anyone goes all #metoo on the subject, à la a man is never asked that question, repeat after me, "However timeless the art, it is still subject to being time-bound."

Moreover, despite this particular female stereotype, a pertinent any gender perspective has also always existed. With regard to dance, it is most poignantly depicted in Bob Fosse's dark comedy musical/quasi biography *All That Jazz* (1979). Though a hedonist with the most complicated of personal lives, when his brilliant alter ego choreographer/director Joe Gideon is asked by Death to define life he can only say "Work." As Gene Fowler movingly described another self-destructive set of artists in *Minutes of the Last Meeting* (1954), "They were their own executioners." Drama critic Ashton Stevens put it more poetically, when describing a Fowler cast that included W. C. Fields and John Barrymore, "Nobody can run downhill as fast as a thoroughbred."

Regardless, even Dorothy's red shoes had the power to go home, if she had only clicked her heals together three times and repeated, "There's no place like home (like you do); she then voluntarily leaves Oz's stain-glass Technicolor poppy fields for black and white Kansas. (This is what comes of being smacked by wooden shudders during a tornado, unless one loves Topeka in the springtime.)

Of course, the use of shoes in a movie can also occupy a middle ground. That is, not always present, but then appearing with show stopping heartache. This might best be rendered by a scene in the dark comedy light *JoJo Rabbit*, (2019, Oscar winner for Best Adapted screenplay). At the end of World War II a ten-year-old German boy, title character Roman Griffin, is part of a comically disorganized Nazi youth group. Plus, he even has a buffoonish Hitler as an imaginary friend (played by the film's writer/director, Taika Waititi)! As JoJo is beginning to realize the political lies which engulf him, he realizes his beloved mother (Scarlett Johansson) is both hiding a Jewish girl in their attic, and performing other vague fifth columnist activities. The latter factor would explain her frequent absence. However, there is one striking mother-son sequence in the village. In the distance several resistance leaders hang from a public square scaffolding as a Nazi warning, but Johansson's Rosie makes it clear to JoJo these victims are heroes.

The beautiful mother is not overdressed, but one momentarily notes her stylish shoes. However, there is so much to unpack in the sequence the shoes hardly register. Soon JoJo has befriended the Jewish girl, even covered for her by claiming she is a sister. With the war so close to ending, it appears the trio will survive. Yet, understandably, the still unnerved little boy, not watching his path on an errand, bumps his head into something in the town square. As JoJo turns, he realizes it is his mother's shoes. She has become among the last resistance leaders hung, before the Allies free the village.

The director, however, does not tilt the camera above the shoes that the crying boy so desperately hugs. In Waititi's voice over commentary (Movies Anywhere's *JoJo Rabbit* Blu-Ray DVD, 2020), he expresses there was no need to produce redundant horror.) For both a little boy and an audience, those mere shoes have symbolized a light gone dark. Moreover, to paraphrase director Carol Reed on his darkly comic film noir, *The Third Man* (1949), "A sequence should end as it has to. I don't think anything in life ends *right*."

As long as pop culture nihilism is on the table, via Johansson's pretty shoes, one is reminded of Guillermo del Toro's dark fairy tale, *Pan's Labyrinth* (2006). Again, a closing scene turns upon some lovely shoes. This much honored filmmaker enjoys toying with his agnostic nature by often intertwining the parallels between religion and mythology. Thus, the finale of *Pan's Labyrinth* is either the death of a young girl, or her rebirth to a former life as a princess of the underworld. However one "reads" it, the fact that the last vision of the child alive has him accenting Dorothy's *magic Oz* red slippers seemly satirizes any hopeful religious references that pepper this twisted folk tale.

Anyone drawn to the art of Chaplin, with his Tramp figure being arguably cinema's most iconic figure, must realize he utilizes his clodhoppers at both ends of the comedy and/or symbolic spectrum. First, the oversized shoes are ever present to visually define his comic hobo station. Indeed, historians have even discussed various explanations connecting the shoes to the eccentric walk. These theories vary from the simple explanation that the Tramp walks that way to just keep the oversized boots on, to many Chaplin chronicles suggesting the gait was borrowed from a "splayfooted" Chaplin childhood acquaintance — a deformity characterized by abnormally flat and turned-out feet. Richard Attenborough's biography film *Chaplin* (1992, with Robert Downey, Jr. in the title role) also embraces this explanation. However, the most fascinating frame-to-frame exposition on Chaplin's footwear comes from French film theorist Andre Bazin. As a realist, art is defined by ambiguity (the randomness of life). Thus, Bazin celebrated a Tramp walk that seemed capable of going left or right instantaneously. (See Bazin's *What Is Cinema?*, and *What Is Cinema, II?*, both 1967.)

Second, Chaplin sometimes took the gunboat portion of his Tramp "uniform" to single symbolically elevated sequences. For example, in his greatest film, *The Gold Rush* (1925, the work for which he most wanted to be remembered), those boots are displayed in conceivably his career's two most extraordinary sketches. The initial example plays to the comedian's much quoted perspective on humor, "Life is a tragedy when seen in close-up, but a comedy in long-shot." The older Chaplin, however, was just as likely to reduce it to a cynical aside, "In the end, everything is a gag."

The first *Gold Rush* sequence in question has a starving Charlie cooking one of his oversized boots for a Thanksgiving supper. He is snowbound somewhere in the frozen Klondike with fellow victimized prospector Mack Swain. The catalyst for both the film and this bit draw upon the Donner Party tragedy (1846-1847), in which a pioneer wagon train was stranded in the Sierra Nevada mountain range and ultimately resorted to cannibalism. (He had also read Mark Twain's "Cannibalism on a Train.") While researching the project, Chaplin found one survivor's diary documenting cooking a moccasin. (Later Swain also has comic thoughts of eating the Tramp.)

Despite its macabre origins, Chaplin's character inspiringly mimes his way through the meal, with a series of brilliant visual puns. These range from twisting shoe laces around a fork like so much spaghetti, to offering Swain a pull upon a twisted shoe nail as if it were a wishbone. Chaplin has taken a defining element of his Tramp wardrobe (even his elaborate autograph included his large shoes), and used it as a poignant centerpiece for a study in dark comedy light.

The second pivotal *Gold Rush* sequence dependent upon the Tramp's "shoes" are not really shoes at all. The routine occurs in a New Year's Eve performance called the "Oceana Roll," or the "Dance of the Dinner Rolls." Charlie has been stood up for a meal he prepared for his love interest, a saloon girl (Georgia Hale), and her friends. Falling asleep at the table, his dream shows him entertaining them. Sticking two dinner rolls with forks, a foreshortening close-up again allows the magic of a Chaplin metamorphosis to perform the most enchanting dance with these miniature "shoes." Indeed, when the *Gold Rush* premiered in Berlin the audience stormed the projection booth and had the operator repeatedly rewind the film and show the "dance" again and again.

What makes these two memorable moments doubly interesting are their origins. The first pulls laughter from an actual tragedy. The second example, without minimizing the Tramp's pain when he realizes this most ephemeral of dances only occurred in a dream, is that it was one of the comedian's most popular dinner party routines throughout his life. Consequently, once again an artist has defined an event, or himself through the use of a pair of shoes.

Much of the shoe imagery I have noted in this piece, like van Gogh's canvases, Charlie's boots, the worn slippers of Degas' dancers ... speak to humbleness. Indeed, even the bright exceptions accent their otherworldliness. I am reminded of George Harrison's songwriting struggles to emerge from the huge shadow of fellow Beatles, John and Paul. Fittingly, one of George's first written vinyl solos, on the "B" side of "The Ballad of John and Yoko," was called "Old Brown Shoes." Thus, while many people *seem* to be content on metaphorically steel rail explanations, tattooed behind my eyelids is still a belief about most people that coincides with a 1969 observation by comedian George Gobel. He stated, on an evening when he had to follow Bob Hope and Dean Martin on one of Johnny Carson's most extraordinary shows, "Did you ever get the feeling that the world was a tuxedo and you were a pair of brown shoes?"

NEIGHBORHOOD BASEBALL,

Or What Were Mantle and Maris

Doing In a Cary Grant Picture?

Babe Ruth (left) and Gary Cooper as Lou Gehrig in *Pride of the Yankees* (1942).

It's baseball time again, and today's game has become a technical art form. There are designated hitters and runners and six kinds of relief pitchers. Managers make with space-age communication to the bullpen, scouts in the team press box and carryout pizza places.

Until the "Show" players swing metal bats at automatic pitching machines, while bat boys are now responsible for extension cords and fans must respond to the "bonk" of the bat. Even the physical setting of the game has been revolutionized, with enclosed air-conditioned stadiums, where the Astro-turf infield is vacuumed twice a week, instead of mowed. (My greenkeeper-like dad says the real grass will come back someday. We can hope.)

All this is not to deny baseball progress, but I can't help thinking about how baseball was played when I was a kid. We used a vacant lot two blocks from my house. It was huge but for some reason we played on the extreme northeast corner. I guess we stayed because the base paths were already worn out from countless neighborhood pickup games. Having well-defined base paths was especially important; it made it seem like a real diamond. (Actually, more like the proverbial "diamond in the rough." Sorry, it was just there.)

Home plate was anything handy: a discarded T-shirt, Jim Franklin's glove, Larry Jones' little brother ... The backstop was a piece of plywood we had "borrowed" from a housing development down the street. We braced it up with three 2-by-4s and Tim Smithy's iron-rimmed Schwinn. The base paths were a little crooked, but all the bases were pretty much across from another — something not to be taken lightly.

Another reason I guess we stayed there was because the constant playing had kept the infield from growing over with weeds and discarded junk. However, that was not to say that an infield grounder might not go for a triple because it did a crazy bounce off a discarded Chef-Boyardee can lurking in the underbrush. You slid into a base at your own risk.

Yet, playing in the infield wasn't too bad except for the pitcher. Actually, being pitcher was popular until Fats Gifford got a line-drive off his nose, and they rushed him to the hospital, and we had to quit playing because it was his ball. Of course, the "mound" was only about six inches high because whenever anyone pitched he kept kicking the "hill," like in the major leagues. Also, it was a little off to the right because we had utilized several gopher mounds in a clump. The really bad positions were right field and catcher. Our right field was the shortest in the world. It made Yankee Stadium's comparable short "right field porch" seem like a distant planet. (The Yankee's had originally designed the stadium "that Ruth built" to make it easier for lefty Babe to hit home runs ... as if he needed any help.)

Regardless, a left-handed midget could have hit a homer every time on our diamond. The neighboring "Big Show Drive-In" fence cut it off short, and if that wasn't enough, the remainder of it was full of these six-to-eight-feet piles of dirt — remains from some sewer pipe job done years ago. Evidently, sometime before my gang of friends started playing there other kids built underground hideaways between said piles. They'd connected a few by covering them with tree limbs, veiled the limbs with cardboard, and then topped the whole mess with dirt.

They'd done such a great job you'd never know they were there. As a matter of fact, we didn't know either, until Randy Sparks disappeared circling under a routine pop fly to right. One second he was backing up, and then there was just a little puff of dust. It was like Johnny Carson's "mystic" character "Carnac the Magnificent" was in the area making right fielders disappear. (My comedy/sports loving dad never put a TV curfew on me when Carson or baseball was involved. In fact, the first "Late Show" I ever saw was Lou Gehrig's story, *Pride of the Yankees* (1942). It was also the first time I ever saw my dad tear up. Of course, I can't vouch for when I was born. The Gehrig bio picture is sometimes considered the first "male weepie" film.

Regardless, playing catcher was a position *nobody* wanted. We had no protective equipment. Not only that, every kid had about sixty-eleven bad hitting habits at whatever we were using for a plate. Everyone seemed to throw their bat if they made contact. For example Larry was afraid of the ball, so he'd back up just before each pitch and often lay-out the catcher with some wild swing.

Moreover, that was just the beginning. Mosquito Johnson was the only boy in the neighborhood with spikes. When at bat he used to stretch his right leg back with the pitch for added power, and always stepped on the catcher's feet. Bob "Tarzan" Breem had a habit of throwing off his cast iron batting helmet, for extra speed, if he got a hit. Naturally, the catcher usually got it in the puss.

Tarzan's heavy duty helmet was rare for the time. However, his parents told him he had to wear it because he was always getting beaned by the pitcher. He wasn't dumb or spooked by a pitch. He just liked to "hang in there" like they said on TV and "wait out that curve." Very few of us even knew how to throw a curve, let alone hit one. But he was stubborn, and we didn't want to hurt his feelings. So we just kept inadvertently beaning him.

Back then we always watched the *TV Game of the Week*, with Dizzy Dean and Pee Wee Reese as announcers. Both were former All-Star players, Dean was equally famous for mangling the English language. Once chided for using the word "ain't" on the air too much, he responded, "A lot of folks who ain't sayin' 'ain't,' ain't eatin."

My dad was especially fond of Dizzy. He felt Dean handled every situation right. At the time there were umpteen Alou brothers playing in the National League, and the youngest was named Jesus. Well, Pop didn't think it would sound right if Dizzy had to say something like "Jesus struck out." (Something tells me the real Jesus would have been more prone to do a "sacrifice" bunt ....) Anyway, so Dad was always happy when Dizzy would announce him as "J. Alou."

Even after our gang watched a TV game we'd immediately head for the diamond. Every kid had a bat and a glove with a pocket black from rubbing too much softening oil in it. Sometimes balls would come back stained and slippery after a catch. The leather straps connecting the glove fingers were usually broken, too, and if you didn't catch the ball right in the pocket it'd shoot through the leather fingers. A lot of the boys got smacked in the face. Plus, we all had our personal Little League hat on, coming in every possible shade... but acceptable.

Most kids had their own bats — usually slightly broken. We never threw bats away when we could fix them with a couple of nails and a coat of paint. It was neat then to paint the bat black and put white adhesive tape on it for a grip. The bats were painted black because a good hit would then make a white mark on it. And with several such marks you'd be hailed as a "slugger." Everyone had a few battered hardballs, but no one wanted to use his because we always lost one or two a game in the distant tall grass.

One boy had a catcher's glove and mask, but hated sharing them. Rowland Jacob had a complete baseball outfit his mother had bought at Sears for $17.95, with "approved by Ted Williams" stamped on the box. But that was unusual in our group.

Most kids played in T-shirts and jeans with tennis shoes. Idiots went barefoot and sissies wore sandals. Really lucky boys had cool T-shirts with the wording "New York Yankee" or "Chicago Cubs" across their scrawny chests. Mine said "Fairchild Funeral Parlor"; it was my Little League sponsor. The summer I remember most was 1961. Mickey "the Mick" Mantle and Roger Maris (the Yankee "M & M Boys") battled most of the season to try and top Babe Ruth's 60 home run record. It seemed like every day that summer someone, even strangers, would ask you, did one of them hit another dinger. Maris ultimately got to 61 on the last day of the season. While Mickey was my favorite player, and the reason I played his center field position, I was happy for Maris. However, a lot of others were displeased. I didn't fully understand it at the time until my dad taught me the word petty.

Regardless, the following year the M & M Boys received all kinds of promotional appearances. Indeed, I even saw them in Cary Grant's movie *A Touch of Mink* (1962). Interestingly, a few years later, when Mantle retired, he observed, "I've often wondered how a man who knew he was going to die [Lou Gehrig] could stand here [at Yankee Stadium] and say he was 'the luckiest man on the face of the earth,' but now I guess I know how he felt." Even for us kids, baseball was just that special.

For instance, in the fall we'd play every night after school until supper. Then mothers on back stoops would pierce the air with the names of a baker's dozen or so little wayward ball players, minus of course, such playing handles as "Mosquito" and "Tarzan." (That's how I first learned Mosquito's real name was Tyrone Barton Alan, but I didn't hold it against him.)

A few times after supper we even tried to play by flashlight, but it was not successful. Thus, despite Yogi Berra's most famous saying, "It ain't over until it's over," when all those neighborhood mothers made with that deafening chorus of names, it was over.

That was baseball when I was a kid.

(The original version, call it a "director's cut," of an article which first appeared in the *Indianapolis Star Magazine*, May 4, 1980; Wes D. Gehring Copyright.)

DARN TEN SPEEDS:

How to Become Extinct

Will Cuppy could have been anticipating 10-speeds when he wrote *How to Become Extinct* (1941).

While I was in a film graduate program, with a minor in "totally freaked out," my undergraduate sister Sue inadvertently did a dicey thing to me. Going home for part of the summer break, she asked me to double as her storage unit. I was staying behind to try the other side of the desk ... my first solo teaching.

Helping her wasn't a problem ... except for one thing. She had me babysit her men's 10 – speed bike. However, don't worry, this will not turn into a deep dish discussion of the tragic neo-realism classic *The Bicycle Thiefs*. Yet, I do wonder if Will Cuppy had the early 10–speed in mind when he wrote *How to Become Extinct?* Regardless, though Sue did not have a bike dealership herself she accidently performed a classic method of sly salesmanship. This goes all the way back to the pioneering 19th century humorist Thomas Chandler Haliburton. His signature "Down East" clockmaker/peddler *Sam Slick* traveled about weighed down by his assorted timepieces.

He often sold his wares by merely leaving a clock or two, as a favor, with "non-customers." It was just to lighten "his load" he said, until he could go to the next village and return. Then, as now, the darn thing soon became indispensable. Thinking they were just doing a good deed, there was often a sale. I fell into the same pattern and bought a 10-speed.

So far, what is the problem, if the product is so indispensable? Well, so many 10-speeds, following so quickly on the old traditional balloon tired heavy one speed, presented some unique problems to go with the fun. I feel it necessary to document some of the trials and tribulations that the trailblazing 10-speed owners went through ... hazards history has forgotten.

First, why were the tires so narrow? The gaps between the bars of many street drainage gutter openings were often greater than that of the 10-speed tires. One could be sailing along, happy as could be, when all of a sudden there was — instant stop, *if* you managed to hang on. But some owners just continued to sail along, unencumbered by the bike — sorry looking apprentice Superman in a kryptonite world.

If you had managed to hold on, you instantly found yourself pointing straight down, eyes bugging out, hands in a death grip with the bike handles, teeth nearly chewing on the oh so close handlebars, your yet to be informed legs still pumping away, and one thought pulsated through the brain — snipers. Many victims remained in this pose for several minutes; they were sometimes heard to mumble discombobulated words that sounded like: "mommy," "brain hurt," "bike path," "vasectomy," or the more conventional "What the —!"

Also, because of the unique appearance of the accident: back wheel still spinning high in the air, the front wheel firmly anchored in the street grating bars up to the axle, and the rider now a frozen form against the sky — passing people didn't help. They took the thing to be some sort of modern sculpture, commenting in passing things like, "Note the eternal symmetry of the spinning wheel," "I prefer more representational art," "Could you imagine 'The Thinker' on a 10-speed?," and the more neutral, "A remarkable lack of pigeon doo-doo." Regardless, I don't think this is what critics had in mind when they suggest, "Art is where *you* arise above yourself."

Second, why did the early 10-speed have such a high pitched braking squeak? It was not unlike the sound of a cat in a blender. This resulted in pedestrian cases of the heaby jeebies, crying small children, and yelping canines suddenly in search of earplugs. Moreover, many dogs needed to be rehousebroken, with the occasional need for some sort of couch therapy. Personally, the sound reminded me of actress Jean "I can't stand it!" Hagen's voice in *Singin' in the Rain,* or maybe Mickey Mouse on helium. This often caused self-conscience riders to minimize braking and trying to take corners at warp speed — often resulting in more modern art/ crash sites.

Third, why did those 10-speed companies make the racing "toe straps" so easy to drop down and lock your foot onto the pedal when one was just out for a casual supposedly relaxing ride? One usually wasn't aware it had happened ... at first. Thus, you would coast up to a stop sign, unaware that your feet were essentially strapped to the pedals. As one slowed and the rider was not able to plant his or her feet on the pavement, suddenly gravity took over. You would invariably fall against a shiny sports car whose owner was waxing it between lights. The sound of metal handlebars hitting any part of his man/child toy usually resulted in several possibilities ... all bad for the cyclist. There was the standard smack to the face, or the ever popular pushing you into the car on the other side. This then resulted in now two apoplectic automobile folks (with steam coming out their ears) giving you a good stomping.

If you happened to be back a bit from the stop sign, next to a seated passenger, there were more hazards. If the window was down and the commuter was a woman, when gravity struck it would appear like you were making a pass (innocently leaning through the window) and she would scratch your eyes out. Next, though you would not see it owing to blindness, a boyfriend passenger might exit said vehicle and make like Muhammad Ali all over you. If the window was up when the "lean" occurred the cyclist *merely* suffered a mild concussion, because silly us, back then we often did not wear helmets.

One was maybe "lucky," with the term used lightly, if the cyclist was on the outside lane and had the presence of mind to jerk towards the ditch side of the road. Then one was "only" looking at cuts and bruises and possible lacerations from discarded broken bottles or other sharp discarded ditch objects. Of course, there was the chance of landing in road kill or the ever present poison ivy. However, erase lucky if the cyclist smacked his head on a rock and rolled into the ditch; you could be MIA out of sight. In the other occasions, even with people beating on you, the cyclist would be seen and eventually helped ... after a possible initial robbery. But if conked out in the tall grass, it might be quite a spell before some passing candy striper came to the rescue. It gives an added twist to the punch line of an old joke — "Do you know the hardest thing about learning to ride a bike: the road."

Fourth, why were those early 10-speed seats made out of surplus Army gun turrets? I still have never sat on a more uncomfortable object, and that includes everything from cement curbs during huddles playing street football, to a cast iron porch railing I was once planted on during a family photo back when the world was young. Moreover, while I am not a medical doctor, I have since read studies that if you rode on those portable anvils too long ... well, you didn't need to worry about a big family. Indeed, that's why if you see any vintage newsreel footage of professional racers standing as they strain along for seemingly more power, it was a cover. Their heinie, or in just plain street talk, their butt had said, "Enough already!"

Fifth, while bugs smacking one on the face had always been a biking hazard, the added speeds of those 10-speeds were an additional bug hassle, especially if it was a Cicada summer. Consequently, the thoughtful manufacturer might have also included a little booklet of short replies when friends (so called) kidded you about an insect covered face, from a career directed, "I plan to be an entomologist (study bugs ... must I explain everything?)," to the healthy food fact, "I just chew them up; they are all protein you know."

There's more, but I think you get the idea. However, I believe that the Shakespearean saying about "neither a borrower nor a lender be" should also have a corollary, or an appendage (which always sounds suggestive to me) "that misadventures learned from someone's storage unit does *not* give you thoughtful hidden depth." Besides, if it is hidden, what's so good about it?

Regardless, I still regularly see my sister ... but we just go on long *walks* ...

(The original version, call it a "director's cut," of an article which first appeared in the *Indianapolis Star Magazine*, April, 1979; Wes D. Gehring Copyright.)

WES' TRIP TO 1970s BEATLES LAND:

Covid Colored Memories

Wes at *the* Zebra crossing on his Beatles inspired adventure.

Shortly after Covid-19 hit, I was flying out of Los Angeles following my annual spring break research trip—an historian's version of a vacation. As flight attendants were sanitizing everything in sight I felt like Will Smith in an un-filmed prologue to *I Am Legend* (2007) —in which he appears to be the only survivor on Manhattan Island following a horrifying plague. Actually, that last phrase was redundant — "plague" more than says enough.

Regardless, while I write to my young grandkids weekly, at that time I started to compose episodes to them about a game changing backpacking trip I took to England one summer—thus the juvenile title. In our family the Beatles occupy a very high perch, and I thought I could share in little people language what the trip and the Beatles meant to me. They gave me my love of words, and the summer adventure proved I could depend on myself. Therefore, I hoped to share some modest life lessons. The year was 1970, and the 1960s had been an English pop culture decade, from the Beatles and the "British Invasion," to Sean Connery as *the* James Bond. Country music legend Roger "King of the Road" Miller pretty much said it all in his 1965 Grammy-winning song, "England Swings."

However, the initial catalyst for my essays was just an exercise to keep me in my grandkids' minds, loosely built around a Beatles-inspired escapade, after my freshman year of college. Of course, like most people. I felt Covid would be a brief isolation. Now, after 27 weekly installments and counting, I wonder if the stories will turn into something to remember me by. Hopefully, that is just my Irish heritage beyond the pale side talking. If not, to quote then vice-president Harry Truman upon hearing that FDR was dead, "Jesus Christ and General Jackson," I had to do something.

Be that as it may, as with most writers. I fully embrace the Nora Ephron (1941-2012) family mantra — "Everything Is Copy!" As the child of scriptwriters (including the 1957 Katharine Hepburn and Spencer Tracy *Desk Set*), and the most talented of her scribbling siblings, nothing was sacred. For Ephron, that included chronicling a messy divorce from Carl Bernstein (yes, that Bernstein) in the 1983 novel *Heartburn*, and plucking relationship fodder from friends for her award-winning 1989 script, *When Harry Met Sally*.

Consequently, I started thinking maybe this could be a book. After all, I was hardly unique in missing my little people. Moreover, in today's helicopter parent/smart phone-obsessed society, many of my college students seemed fascinated by my ancient history travel story. Naturally, they were incredulous that anyone would savor dropping off the grid — make that the pre-grid — and enjoy it.

Yet, while I mock their media mania over minutia, it is not a broadside against youth. Indeed, this personal adventure at 19 is a defense of the Teflon nature of being young. Yes, I generally agree with Oscar Wilde's "Youth is wasted on the young" more each year. However, one could also quote a less well-known rebuttal from Karin Blixen's novelized memoir, 1937's *Out of Africa*: "The earth was made round so we could not see far down the road." Risk-taking naiveté can sometimes be a good thing, too. For example, to paraphrase Orson Welles on his 1941 masterpiece, *Citizen Kane*, a first film shot when he was only 26, "Anything revolutionary about it was simply because I was too young to know it couldn't be done." As a stand-up comic fond of fracturing axioms once said, "Fools rush in ... and get all the good seats."

Moreover, if truth be told, this story for my grandkids, which my daughters seem to be enjoying, too, was a random English trip which was not fully appreciated at the time. As John Lennon once said, "Life is what happens when you're busy making other plans." I am reminded of "Moonlight" Graham's (Burt Lancaster) 1989 *Field of Dream* insight about his achingly brief Major League moment: "We just don't recognize life's most significant moments *while* they're happening. Back then I *thought*, 'Well, there'll be *other days*.' I didn't realize that was the *only* day." Naturally the "Big Show," if only for a half inning, trumps my teen adventure, but still I now attach that sort of feeling towards it.

Regardless, while the idea to chronicle this journey has been pinballing around in my mind for a long time, it has now taken on an anti-travel pandemic, potential check-out time remember Grandpa dimension. There is also the challenge of writing in a new format.

However, I am not going to rush the tale, especially since each installment triggers new memories. I want to enjoy the significance of the escapade. In fact, I see this writing caper as a negation of a normally all too true observation from Milan Kundera's 1984 *The Unbearable Lightness of Being*: "We live everything as it comes, without warning, like an actor going on cold." However, in this case, I get to chronicle the formerly script-less rehearsal of a personally memorable piece of time.

Moreover, I find my subject choice increasingly consequential in new ways, such as attempting a scaled down version of Mark Twain's *Innocents Abroad*— (1869, I know I'm no Samuel Clemens, but one should always set the bar high), *and* connecting to my grandkids in a different way. The episodes thus far are loose and connected by simply being a Beatles driven road trip. There is even one or two with a fairytale-like perspective. As my friend Mark and I killed time in New York waiting for our flight (all road trips require a sidekick — it's in all the handbooks — it shows personal growth), we beelined to Times Square, like you do.

In that installment I wrote about meeting a *giant*. Back in 1970, Jack Dempsey still had his restaurant on Times Square off Broadway, between 49th and 50th Streets. He always sat in a corner booth, and we were able to go in and shake the hand of a childhood hero. While long of tooth, he was still imposing, and his hands were huge. Plus, all roads back then seemed to lead to the Beatles. When he asked what we were doing in New York and we got over the shock of him caring to ask, he offered the information that the first time the Beatles came over (1964) they were supposed to meet Sonny Listen (then the heavyweight champion), but he refused, calling them "sissy boys." However, he added "Clay met them" [Cassius Clay soon beat Listen for the title, though he had been known as Mohammad Ali for years by 1970]. I couldn't see Dempsey being an Ali fan, but I thought it was generous of him to share the story. Yet, there were others to see the icon, so we left, not thinking to ask for an autograph.

As with Dempsey, the Beatles and 1960s England were equally ripe for storytelling enhancement. Here was history's most identifiable band, and they suddenly reinvented themselves as the vibrant multicolored *Sgt. Pepper's Lonely Hearts' Club Band*. Not only is it still *Rolling Stone* magazine's number one album, the group temporarily freeze-framed themselves into history with the inspired Madame Tussauds Wax Museum-like cover. (Was it Beatles payback that Liston was the only boxer included on the pop culture hall-of-fame cover?) Regardless, then they pivoted on a dime, and took everyone on *A Magical Mystery Tour*, with leader John Lennon next declaring "I Am the Walrus." As an artist heavily influenced by Lewis Carroll, sometimes a fairy tale aura could be suggested by merely quoting John's lyrics, or passages in the eccentric short stories of his early books, *In His Own Write*, and *A Spaniard in the Works* (both 1964). There can hardly be any doubt that John's "I Am the Walrus" was influenced by Carroll's poem "The Walrus and the Carpenter."

Consequently, "Wes Goes ..." has already taken several twists, but then so did Shel Silverstein's *Where the Sidewalk Ends*, though I do not think I am up to writing any of his country western songs, like Johnny Cash's "A Boy Named Sue." Be that as it may, as a film professor, there will naturally be film references, because as Steve Martin observed in *Grand Canyon* (1991): "You don't watch enough movies, all of life's riddles are answered in the movies."

So far the weekly installments have already noted that while everyone talks about the Beatles' early 1964 appearance on the *Ed Sullivan Show*, today not enough attention is paid to their first film later that year, *A Hard Day's Night*. It was a groundbreaking critical and commercial hit, with arguably the decade's most significant movie critic, The *Village Voice*'s Andrew Sarris (who brought the auteur theory to America) calling the film a "juke box *Citizen Kane*." Forty years later *Time* magazine rated *A Hard Day's Night* as one of the 100 greatest films ever made. Moreover, what is now forgotten, is that if the Beatles had been so inclined, critics felt they could have done a cinema variation on the Marx Brothers. Their twist was being a reverse take on the earlier comedy team. That is, the Marxes acted surreal in a sane world, while the Beatles attempted to maintain sanity in a world gone mad, either by their mere appearance, or against a growing backdrop of social unrest. Indeed, historians now suggest their early 1964 success was further fueled by a depressed America looking for some distracting joy after the November 1963 assassination of President John F. Kennedy.

Be that as it may, viewing a revival of *A Hard Day's Night* on the trip was even a tutorial on English screenings. At that time in their film theatres, one often paid different prices depending on where one sat. Plus, smoking was allowed, but many theatres had no treats up front. However, no worries. Like an American ball game, there were "barkers" inside the seating area selling sweets — except they were usually pretty young "birds" — like the nightclub cigarette girls in old black and white movies.

Strangely enough, several things on the trip seemed to underline that the adventure was inspired by the Beatles. I had made arrangements for Mark and me to periodically pick fruit at a camp just outside of Norwich — a city near the breadbasket of England, about 100 miles north of London. The place was like a home base — sort of a revolving door migrant camp. We would work a week or two, and then take off for parts unknown ... returning whenever we wanted. The pay was poor but we got to know the locals and the rather primitive living conditions were free. Anyway, the place was called "Strawberry Fields." Plus, a modest nearby amusement park gave us backstories on some Beatles songs, such as "Helter Skelter" was a giant slide, and an arcade game section that was called "Penny Lane."

If a book does happen it will probably produce an ironic twist on my grandkids, not unlike what once occurred with my daughters, Sarah and Emily. They grew up with me writing a great deal of books, but that was just what Dad did. No big deal. However, during their obsessive young "Star Wars" period, I happened to be doing a book on dark comedy, which involved a brief correspondence with Alex Guinness. He had done several brilliant dark comedies for Britain's Ealing Studio, including *Kind Hearts and Coronets* (1949) and *The Ladykillers* (1956), with the latter film later remade by the Coen Brothers (2004, with Tom Hanks). Thus, despite all my writing, only then did I get some attention; they found out I was corresponding with *Obi-Wan Kenobi!*

While the books have continued, if anything comes of "*Wes Goes to 1970 Beatles Land,*" one can bet the house and all the silverware that that will be the one "grandpa g" book my grandkids will remember me by. Well, I guess that was the original purpose.

(Reprinted with permission from *USA Today Magazine*, January 2021. Copyright © 2021 by "The Society for the Advancement of Education, Inc. All Rights Reserved.")

TIME TRAVEL

Applied to Various Comedy Genres:

There Are *No* Guilty Pleasures

The lovely other worldly Veronica Lake and Fredric March in *I Married a Witch* (1942).

Each Sunday the *New York Times*' "Book Review" section does an opening page interview with a prominent author. Except for rare occasions when a non-author celebrity pitches their children's book, this is my pivotal *Times* piece — akin to a child being aware there is going to be ice cream. Regardless, the questions obviously vary depending upon the author. However, the interviews always include a few standard queries. Probably the most popular one asks, "Does your reading ever involve any 'guilty pleasure' subjects?"

This is seldom a jump ball situation. Most authors answer the same way I would, "Guilty pleasure reading does not exist." This go-to response is that no matter what authors are currently research reading for their next book, something from their downtime scrutiny invariably finds its way into their work. It is a narrower variation on Nora *When Harry Met Sally* Ephron's philosophy, "Everything is copy." That is, who knows what will inspire and/or impact one's current manuscript. One can never back the wrong horse.

These introductory comments serve as a lead-in for what follows. *If* you put a dull butter knife to my neck and forced a guilty pleasure reading/screening topic from me it would be time travel stories, anything from H.G. Wells' classic novella, *The Time Machine* (1895, which kicked off the phenomenon), to John Cusack's 2010 film *The Hot Tub Time Machine*. (Actually, I might feel a little guilty about that one, though it was popular enough for a sequel.)

Regardless, though my time tripping fascination has had a longer "everything is copy" gestation period, it too is now having a creative impact upon my humor activist work. I am currently writing what will be my career opus — an overview of American film comedy, with a modest print humor foundation.

Consequently, as I examine various comedy subgenres, each include excellent time tripping examples. For instance, Mark Twain's *Connecticut Yankee in King Arthur's Court* (1889) is essentially a personality comedian pinballing back in time — Will Rogers played the title character in the 1931 film. However, many of the following references will be cross listed as compound genres with science fiction, or fantasy. For instance, personality comedy is alive and well in the *Back to the Future* franchise (1985, 1989, 1990), though some might initially label it science fiction, too. Regardless, the first and best installment finds Marty McFly (Michael J. Fox) as a contemporary teenager (1985) accidently sent back to

November 5, 1955. This is the date his sometime comic partner, Christopher Lloyd's zany scientist with the Einstein hair, first decided to create time travel. However, by hooking up with Lloyd's younger self, Marty not only manages to get "back to the future" (by way of a comedy minded DeLorean car, no less), he also oversees a fix to his 1985 dysfunctional family.

Another compound personality comedy example with an unusual teaming would be Will Smith and Tommy Lee Jones in *Men in Black 3* (2012). Smith has to go back to 1969 and rescue a younger version of his partner (James Brolin) from an assassination. As a necessary footnote here, keep in mind that comic time travel is a no problem bank shot with the "butterfly effect" — in which a small change in one state of a deterministic nonlinear system can result in large differences in a later state.

In contrast, applying the "butterfly effect" to a serious time tripping story is like a bad day in Bosnia. Maybe the definitive example is Stephen King's novel *11/22/63*. The author spends 1100-plus pages chronicling how going back to rescue President Kennedy ends up in a future where language fails, and Ingmar Bergman silence begins. Indeed, in 2022, Netflix began streaming an extremely popular Ryan Reynolds time travel film, "The Adam Project," in which the ultimate mission is to save the future by destroying the ability to time trip.

Other personality comedies involving time travel with a twist would include Woody Allen's *Sleeper* (1973) and Bill Murray in *Groundhog Day* (1993). As the former film opens Allen's character realizes he died during routine surgery and was cryogenically frozen and forgotten. When fully defrosted he reveals he had a premonition this would happen, since he had found a parking place near the hospital. Still in shock, he adds, "I can't believe this. My doctor said I'd be up and around in five days. He was off by 199 years."

Groundhog Day is about being stuck in time, and while arguably Murray's greatest comedy, it has been credited with being a compound genre with everything from science fiction to the art house film. The latter link occurs because after surviving several suicides from going through the same day in the same small town innumerable times, he decides to turn his "sentence" into a self-improvement exercise. When Murray finally becomes "unstuck," his obnoxious cynic has become an accomplished mensch, with a promising chance at romance.

This nicely segues for a transition to romantic comedy. I would start with the film *Kate & Leopold* (2001) for two reasons, beyond being an entertaining tale. First, it stars (with Hugh Jackman) one of the genre's most iconic heroines, Meg Ryan. Though not in a league with her performance in Ephron's aforementioned written *When Harry Met Sally*, it becomes a satisfying Ryan romantic comedy tetrad with *Sleepless in Seattle* (1993), and *You've Got Mail* (1998). Indeed, *Kate & Leopold* creates an insurmountable trio topper — following love into the 19th century for a bonus royal marriage to Jackman's Duke of Albany. How this happens merges into my second reason. The Duke finds himself in 1876 New York sketching the nearly completed Brooklyn Bridge. He spots a figure with an amazingly small camera (Liev Schreiber). The photographer turns out to be his time tripping future great-great- grandson doing family research. Schreiber has discovered the existence of a gravitational time portal which is periodically operational by jumping off the bridge.

Yes, I know this seems a stretch, but it is the crutch of my second time travel revelation. Schreiber heads to the bridges' exit portal; Jackson misreads it as a fall. In attempting to save him, this portal returns both to the 21st century. In other words, time travel stories minimize how Einstein's scientific hocus pocus is possible. It is like an old-fashioned musical in which people just burst into song — a great deal of suspension of disbelief is required. Seldom does one even get close to H.G. Wells' sketchy time machine description. All one now needs is a simple phrase, like a "rip in the fabric of time," or a "time portal," with an occasional "black hole" thrown in to get things rolling.

In fact, *The Time Traveler's Wife* (2009), from Audrey Niffengger's 2003 novel, practically brushes off the whole process. She merely blames it on a rare genetic disorder of the title character's (Rachel McAdams) librarian husband (Eric Bona). However, this story adds a dicey curve. Her husband has no control over when or where he travels — talk about messing up dinner plans. Plus, these unplanned exits have another negative component. One arrives nude. This could even cause trouble for a magician in Bagdad. Thankfully, the husband usually reaches a location in which his nakedness is tastefully obscured, such as among shrubbery. (The subject of poison ivy never comes up.)

Regardless, when noting romantic comedy and time travel, the natural pivot is to screwball comedy (American farce). The genre's greatest contributor here is the short lived but prolific American fantasy novelist, Thorne Smith (1892-1934). The pivotal example would be his last work, the posthumously published *Passionate Witch* (1941, finished by Norman Matson). It was made into the celebrated time tripping screwball comedy, *I Married a Witch* (1942), with Veronica Lake as the most enchanting of 17th century witches.

Lake's Jennifer has been burned at the stake for her craft, with a tree planted over her grave to create a sort of ethereal prison. Puritan Jonathan Wooley (Fredric March) had denounced Lake, resulting in her curse on his male descendants to be forever unlucky in love. When lightening splits open the tree 250 years later, her spirit is freed. After assuming a lovely human form, she searches out contemporary Wooley (also March) for further torment. However, a screwball twist finds her falling in love with him. (Smith's novel was later the inspiration for the popular television series *Bewitched*, 1964-1972).

Another time tripping screwball comedy, possibly inspired by the sexy ghosts of Thorne Smith's 1926 novel *Topper*, is *The Ghost Goes West* (1935). In 18th century Scotland Murdoch Glourie (Robert Donat) would rather engage in wooing women than war against his wealthy clan's arch rivals, the MacClaggans. In an act of cowardice and cartoon-like stupidity, Murdoch dies when his gun powder barrel hiding place explodes. His then equally dead dad curses him to haunt their Glourie Castle until he can make a MacClaggan admit the superiority of Murdoch's family.

Flash forward to the 20th century and the current owner of the castle, debt-ridden Donald Glourie (also Donat). Consequently, he sells the ancestral home to screwball comedy's favorite American nouveau rich businessman, Eugene Pallette, who is abroad with his family. The sale's catalyst is that Pallette's daughter is attracted to Murdoch's ghost, thinking he is actually Donald, given Donat plays both parts.

Pallette's ostentatious character naturally has the castle taken apart and rebuilt in Florida, like you do, and both Donat characters are obligated to go along. Murdoch must follow the curse, and only Donald can supervise the reconstruction. Serendipitously, there is a Floridian MacClaggan against which the curse can be lifted, and Donald is engaged to Pallette's daughter. As for the free ghostly Murdoch, given his sensuous parallels with Smith's ghosts, he is no doubt still "haunting" Miami Beach.

A natural time tripping transition from screwball comedy is to dark humor. How so? Despite the former genre eventually ending with a loving couple, most of the time is spent trashing love. With dark comedy, everything is trashed. The point of the genre is that there is no point. Growing up in the 1960s, when most of my friends forever had a Kurt Vonnegut paperback in their jean back pocket, the novelist's *Slaughterhouse-Five or The Children's Crusade: A Duty-Dance with Death* (1969) immediately comes to mind, as well as its 1972 film adaptation.

The lead character, Billy Pilgrim, is constantly coming unstuck in time. However, while he has no control over when this happens, his antiheroic situation is different from *The Time Traveler's Wife* in two distinct ways. He thankfully neither arrives naked, nor is the setting new to him. Each re-entry is some point in his life, ranging from an American prisoner of war surviving the 1945 firebombing of Dresden, to being in a future alien exhibit on the planet Tralfamadore. Since Vonnegut was at Dresden, the story has a further genre compounding of labels beyond dark comedy, including "semi-autobiographical science fiction," and "anti-war fiction," subtextually attacking the Vietnam War.

While there are additional time tripping dark comedies, the most mesmerizing is Sydney Pollack's 1969 adaptation of the William Eastlake novel *Castle Keep* (1965). Set in and around a European castle, Pollack creates a Vietnam War dark comedy by shooting a theatre of the absurd look at the conflict through the prism of having an allegedly World War II film pinball through time and space with seemingly several wars existing simultaneously. This ranges from Nazis and paintings of Middle Age soldiers storming castle walls via crude ladders, to Burt Lancaster directing troops from a cavalry officer's white horse — suggesting the eternal worthlessness of war. It also poses the question as to whether this is some horrific nonexistent nightmare. Indeed, in some interview sessions Pollack even suggested questioning the reality of *Castle Keep*. Regardless, the best in-film comment occurs early — Peter Falk's soldier says, "Maybe we've come to the wrong war." And always keep in mind, it is impossible to discuss war and morality in the same sentence.

This time travel trek through American film comedy and/or print humor must close with its final genre, populism. The opposite of black comedy, populism is so positive it is sometimes even known as a "fantasy of good will." Though the original foundation of American humor, its iconic film example is Frank Capra time tripping *It's a Wonderful Life* (1946). Based upon Philip Van Doren Stern's short story, *The Greatest Gift*, one might better credit Charles Dickens' novella *A Christmas Carol*. In this case, the time tripping is made possible by some hard working angels. (In the original script they are led by a heavenly Benjamin Franklin.)

Since *Life*'s longtime annual holiday screening makes little explanation necessary, it has a logical time tripping companion,

Field of Dreams" (1989). The film is based upon W. P. Kinsella's novel *Shoeless Joe* (1982), which he started at the famous University of Iowa's Writer's Workshop — thus the story's Iowa setting. Adapted to film and directed by Phil Alden Robinson as *Field of Dreams*, the frequently cited goal was to make an *It's a Wonderful Life* baseball film.

Again, it is so well known, little narrative rehashing seems necessary. Moreover, as with Capra's film, the time tripping sequences often occur as if from on high, starting with an Iowa farmer (Kevin Costner) hearing a biblical-like voice in his corn field, "If you build it [a baseball field] he will come." Eventually, several further voice cues and varied surprise time twists reveal just who "he" is. The film has had such an ongoing impact that even the conclusion of the aforementioned hit anti-time travel movie, *The Adam Project*, essentially closes with a variation on *Fields*'s ending.

Consequently, this is my personal proof there are no reading "guilty pleasures." Moreover, my next project is tentatively even a comic time travel manual for if the phenomenon becomes real and one needs helpful hints. For example, what would be the best policy when you are booked for a certain year, and your luggage goes to 1946? Can you select an alternate year, if you are forced into an unexpected layover...and so on?

AN ELDERHOSTEL FILM CLASS:

VS.

A Hospice *Waiting* List:

Is the Premise of Hospice Understood?

Horsefeathers' oversexed Groucho (right) showcasing the only college
class of personal interest — anatomy.

[Editor's Note: In the late 20th Century it was popular
for older summer vacationers to take a brief "Road"
Scholar class during their travels.]

I've just been spoiled for a week. No, I neither briefly joined the Beatles, nor got to play centerfield for the Yankees. Likewise, I didn't get a sweepstakes check from Johnny Carson's sidekick Ed McMahon either, despite, of course, deserving it immensely.

What's all the noise about, then, you ask? Well, I just completed teaching an Elderhostel film comedy class at Ball State University (Muncie, Indiana), where I am a professor. And these older, generally retired students are wonderfully unretiring in class. Yet, like Rodney Dangerfield, they "don't get no respect." Two different couples even claimed grown children wanted to put them on a hospice "waiting list." Do their kids understand the premise of a hospice?

Regardless, I felt like a teacher again. These folks were actually agitatedly happy to be in a classroom. The first day I thought I was headlining a concert. These nontraditional students asked questions, and — pssst, don't let this get around — they even requested additional reading material, not to mention applauding at the close of lectures! Honest. Granted, today's professors have to be part-time entertainers to keep students engaged. However, for a week I really was always tempted to look behind me.

Well no, I didn't get any roses, and no coins were thrown, but twice during my first lecture I had to stop and pinch myself just to make sure I wasn't having one of my "hurrah for teachers" dreams. You know, the one where outstanding graduating almost professors are drafted by various high profile schools for seven figure numbers, no-cut contracts, with additional product endorsements for things like BIC pens, pencil boxes, and the ever popular White-Out.

Now, I'm not suggesting that my normal, younger brand of college students are apathetic — implying it yes, but not saying it. I am reminded of the Marx Brothers film *Horsefeathers* (1932), where Groucho (America's favorite King Leer) is a college president (yes, you heard right) in favor of expanding the football stadium at the expense of needed dorms. When this Marxist leader is asked just where the students will sleep, he responds "Where they've always slept — in the classroom!"

This is not to say my college students sleep in class. However, I always have a few who appear to be getting in the snooze mode. In the academic world it is technically referred to as the "glazed doughnut look." Indeed, I am certain several could lead symposiums in catnapping, or imitating a whiskey coma.

These are the same students who, after being absent, always ask, "Did I miss anything important?" It is as if to reduce the rigors of getting a Ph.D, and trust me, rigors is a polite word for it, to a boardgame. (By the way, the best reply to this question is, "Nothing *you* would have understood." But use the reply sparingly until after you receive tenure, because as is commonly known, "Tenure means never having to say you're sorry.")

Anyway, there were no "glazed doughnuts" among the Elderhostel group. In fact, their continuing drive to learn reminds me of that old definition of an ant — always busy, yet always finding time to go on a picnic. With regard to a comparable academic movie experience, the film *Education Rita* (1983) comes to mind. Though Julie Walter's delightful nontraditional title character was much younger than my Elderhostel group, the movie tag inspired by her hungry mind was equally fitting for my recent experience, "Sometimes students end up being the best teachers."

Of course, people are always suspicious of diabetically wonderful experiences. Well, if you want a flaw, the group's fire drill exit times were probably not quite up to speed. Oh, and a teacher in a stuffed shirt — I mean in a nearby classroom — complained about periodic loud laughter, especially during a screening of Chaplin's *The Gold Rush* (1925). One sequence was so popular, "The Dance of the Dinner Rolls," I had to show it twice. "Charlie" is seated at a supper table, and by jabbing two bread rolls with his forks, and a foreshortening of camera placement, he performs the most delightful number with seemingly little feet.

I told the class it was history repeating itself, because upon the film's initial release the Berlin audience had stormed the projection booth and demanded that the sequence also be repeated. Regardless, other than such outbursts of *rowdiness*, it really was an ideal class, or to paraphrase Shakespeare, "like an ongoing good deed in a naughty world."

(Originally appeared in the 600,000 readership of the *Elderhostel* journal, January 1989; Wes D. Gehring Copyright.)

MUST PRAISE IMMEDIATELY

Result in the "Sky Is falling"?

Babe Ruth allowed his bat to generate all the attention he needed.

While doing research, I recently had a moon shot moment I would like to share. Except I neither want to jinx myself or come off sounding like those vain shiny people. Thus, while I attempt to make a normalization of a potentially demoralization situation, let me briefly pivot from vanity and curse concerns to some family background explanations. Afterall, Freud allows us to blame everything on our parents. Mine were antiheroically superstitious, and felt good news was a trigger for bad.

Of course, narcissistic problems often lesson with age thanks to mirrors. However, the rumor Methuselah was my younger brother is false. He was a second cousin on Dad's side. (I sensed you wanted to know.) Regardless, "A long time ago in a galaxy far, far away ..." I was taught "to keep my own doorstep clean, and otherwise button-up, unless I had something positive to say." This is hard if you are a class clown, especially if someone is aggressively illiterate.

That was my mom's mantra. As a youngster the "doorstep" metaphor confused me. So my dad translated the equation into our special language of "sports speech." Consequently, to paraphrase him, "If you score a touchdown, you do not go all hot dog in the end zone. That implies one has done a unique thing. However, if you then calmly give the ball to the referee, it implies this is business as usual — a much stronger statement. Along the same lines, if you hit a home run, you modestly trot around the base path with your head down. Naturally, avoid tripping over bases, but keep in mind you have just humiliated the pitcher. Do not rub it in by acting crazy happy. Otherwise, he might 'put it in your ear' the next time you come to bat. He still might, but it lessens the chances."

For example, in *The Pride of the Yankees*, Gary Cooper's portrayal of Lou Gehrig never showed him going all demented after a four-bagger. As the Yankee's later great manager Casey Stengel used to say, "You can look it up." Naturally, in later years when I was lucky enough to hit a run home, or score a touchdown, this was my guide.

Of course, back then my father's advice was *the* norm. If I had gone ballistic after either such accomplishment, my coaches would have gone all Bobby Knight (another phrase for ballistic) on me. Still, one learns more by emulating one's heroes. I was a running back in high school, which was the position of my favorite NFL player, Gale Sayers. In *Brian's Song* (1971), the "male weepy" about the cancer death of his close friend and teammate, Brian Piccolo (the league's first black and white road roommates), Sayers never went

TD peculiar. (As an antiheroic footnote, back then even the position was only called a *half*back.)

Still, with the possible exception of Jim Brown, Sayers was the best running back ever (let's not argue). Indeed, once one of the most iconic of comedians (PC police are hovering nearby, so I must lose his name), actually built a routine around Sayers. The comic said, in part, "The catalyst for Sayers' greatness was his stop and go speed. Though faster than Wile E. Coyote's Road Runner nemesis, Sayers could break on a dime, give you nine cents change, and immediately return to 'beep beep' speed."

Regardless, returning to the risk of a cursed ego foundation, I am not unaware of signs, except maybe on back-to-back roundabouts. For example, I'm a lapsed Methodist, whose philosophy is now more of a "cling to the wreckage" outlook. It is like one of Mel Brooks' 2,000 year-old-man observations (as interviewed by Carl Reiner). Brooks' ancient one claimed, "At one time everyone worshipped a guy named Phil. However, Phil then got hit by lightning. Consequently, we figured there was something out there bigger than Phil."

I too think there is something out there bigger than Phil ... who provides signs, and of course, our conscience. (My mother crafted my gift for guilt.) Arguably, Mark Twain's funniest short story is "The Carnival of Crime in Connecticut," in which he kills his conscience and finds true happiness. Since I have yet to master that comic crime, the most memorable sign I have received about not becoming self-centered involved a seemingly *Ferris Bueller's Day Off* (1986) like moment. I had just lettered in football as a high school freshman and was wearing my varsity jacket for the first time. In that era this was a big deal. I had had it on for all of five minutes and sadly I had allowed some show-off vanity to briefly creep in. I was anxiously waiting for the morning school bus. (At that time only rich kids had cars; my family had *one* tired, very used Chevy.) Seconds before the bus door opened a bird the size of a Buick flew over and did a dump down the front of my new jacket that looked like an *Animal House* (1978) film trailer for the food fight sequence.

Over time I began to do some antiheroic family research, which I will limit to story bookends. Both sides of my family are Irish, but we have none of the distinguishing physical Irish trademarks. That is, there is neither any reddish blonde hair, nor freckled fair-skin and blue eyes among us. We all have dark complexions, dark hair, and brown eyes. It was what I had always suspected even before I and several family members each took one of those Ancestry DNA tests — there's a lot of unaccounted for Spanish links. Why?

Back in 1588, *cocky* world power Spain was at war with England, and their giant armada decided to take the long way around the British Isles for a surprise attack — big mistake. Ask anyone. Ugly storms took out much of the fleet. One could not see one's hand in front of one's face, not that there is much pleasure in that. Regardless, many Spanish sailors either drowned, or were washed ashore in Ireland. After that some swashbuckling Errol Flynn *Sea Hawk* (1940) type knocked off the remaining Spanish armada. (However, I digress — a major part of the academic life.) Anyway, with mass transit being a bit dicey back in 1588, many of my waterlogged Spanish ancestors stuck around and intermingled with the native Irish. This makes my clan what is called "Black Irish." Luckily, the Irish were hardly fond of England either. See Jonathan Swift's "A Modest Proposal," which documents England's negative to the Irish "Beyond the pale" philosophy. (Must I explain everything?)

Okay, flash forward to my October 1950 birth. This is the same month and year when Charlie Brown first started to appear. Thus, I feel like my antihero credentials are complete, especially given a dark comedy 1976 strip in which Snoopy is sitting atop his doghouse with his typewriter. "I hear you're writing a book on theology," Charlie Brown says to him, "I hope you have a good title." Snoopy thinks, "I have the perfect title ... 'Has It Ever Occurred to You that You Might Be Wrong?'"

Well, along related lines, it is finally time for my Nervous Nellie press release. My book *Genre-Busting Dark Comedies of the 1970s* logs in at #38 on "Book Authority's (CNN and Forbes) 100 Best Comedy Books of All Time," as recommended by Russell Brand, Bill Gates, Seth Logan, Sheryl Sandberg, [Chief Operating Officer of Facebook] and 79 other judges." Yes, I double checked, too. Because while it is not a humor book per say, talks about comedy told with some degree of wit qualified. Consequently, even if my antiheroic, superstitious, cling to the wreckage heritage now jinks me, at least I had a moment of balanced fairness. How so? For years I had to fight mainstream publications which found me too scholarly, and scholarly journals which felt I was too mainstream. Ironically, my simple goal was just an intelligent audience. Oh, and I felt especially justified that both *Peanuts'* writer (Snoopy/Schulz) and I should both fixate on 1970s dark comedy. So there I have said it ... but I feel like a "knock wood" comment close.

WORDSMITHING: Or How a Single

Phrase Can Be a Catalyst

For a Book — "It's a Mystery"

The review phrase "Mr. Deed Goes to Yankee Stadium" was literally the catalyst for this book ... and title.

In the past I have written about the "found essay." For example, in doing a column about sound movies helping derail Buster Keaton's career, I came across so many stage actor interviews comparing theatre work to early sound pictures I could not resist writing about it.

However, sometimes a single phrase can inspire a biography. Granted, one usually has interests in that area. Still, it no doubt seems ironic, since with cinema shouldn't the catalyst be a picture? After all, images can be visceral shards of glass, like the freeze frame ending of Francois Truffaut's *The Four Hundred Blows* (1959). In this autobiographical work, Truffaut's sad alter ego (the boy Jean-Pierre Léaud) has run away from a reform school but is stopped by the ocean. The neglected child turns back from the sea as he is about to be caught.

In the pivot he looks directly at the camera, breaking the fourth wall. The unloved child had always wanted to see the ocean, but now it seems to have betrayed him ---- he has nowhere to run. However, his perplexed yet haunting eyes really seem to be indicting the viewer. How could society have so abandoned him?

This is a freeze frame grenade. Since a still is just one image in a film composed of thousands of images, to isolate one automatically pushes it towards the potential for art. One has an image transformed into a possible postcard of perceptions. Yet, despite such multiplicity in a film frame, I remain more effected by wordsmithing. For instance, I was researching an article on baseball legend Lou Gehrig and came across a *Pride of the Yankees* (1942) review with a passing reference to *Mr. Deeds Goes to Yankee Stadium*, à la Frank Capra's populist classic, "Mr. Deeds Goes to Town" (1936).

There was an epiphany, like all the gears in a clock had clicked together. I immediately saw how Capra's democratic populism was so inherent to baseball, with its pastoral linear progression. Plus, one had to wait for *the* star to bat. There was neither the unfair constant feeding of the ball to a Michael Jordan, nor football's dark comedy chaos after the ball was hiked. Soon I had written such a book, and used that title ---- *Mr. Deeds Goes to Yankee Stadium: Baseball Films in the Capra Tradition*. Sure, I already knew a great deal about the subject, but it was like that off-hand reference had seared my thought process.

The same thing occurred when I was doing a biography of James Dean, the cult legend from the early Eisenhower era. American teens were then just bobbing bottles on a sea of indecision. When the metaphorical car wreck that is life became a James Dean reality, youth mourned itself. However, despite how his short life had already known sadness, I was disillusioned by research revealing how he had overplayed his alleged angst-ridden youth. Plus, the close of his posthumous released film *Giant* (1956) demonstrated he could not play anything but his stuck in amber troubled youth. To paraphrase Humphrey Bogart's dark comedy comment at the time, "Dean's death had been a great career move."

However, the Dean research had overlapped with another "rebel without a cause" ---- Steve McQueen. The actor had admired Dean, and there was even a Hoosier connection. Paradoxically, or maybe not so paradoxically, both had been born in white bread Indiana. Yet, the long-suffering youth that Dean had so falsely played up and marketed as his screen persona was the total entirety of Steve McQueen's *Four Hundred Blows*-like youth. Moreover, when I discovered why the actor felt a special connection to the war title of one of his seminal films, I knew I was going to do a McQueen biography and use that moniker ---- *The Great Escape* (1963). That title represented to McQueen what movies had meant to his life. Otherwise, his existence would probably have been one of petty crime and periodic jail time, or worse.

My third biography inspired title harkens back to when I was ten or twelve, long before helicopter parents. In summer one merely hopped on your Schwinn and the day was yours. I often biked a goodly distance to an old, yet alluring Paramount theatre in downtown Cedar Rapids. (The city always disappointed visiting cousins, because they thought they were going to "See the rabbits.")

Regardless, after the movie my next stop was a Catholic mission/ used book store.

One day I discovered a Robert Benchley anthology entitled *From Bad to Worse Or Comforting Thoughts About the Bison* (1934). I laughed so loud a nun shushed me. (Can they shush a little lapsed Methodist?) I proceeded to plop down on the floor and giggle through the whole book. I had discovered my favorite humorist. This was the man that inspired James "Walter Mitty" Thurber to observe, "One of the greatest fears of the humorist writer is that he has spent three weeks writing something done faster and better by Benchley in 1919." That title still produces a smile, and many years later I was befriended by his daughter-in-law Marjorie, who shared many stories about "Mr. B," as well as giving me access to his private papers. The result was *"Mr. B" Or Comforting Thoughts About the Bison: A Critical Biography of Robert Benchley.*

Consequently, though a picture might be worth a thousand words, a simple phrase can assemble an ocean of words between covers.

(Reprinted with permission from *USA Today Magazine*, May 2022. Copyright © 2022 by "The Society for the Advancement of Education, Inc. All Rights Reserved.")

MOVIE MUSIC With a Twist:

I Think That's What Killed Curly

From left to right, *Young Frankenstein* (1974) cast members: Marty Feldman, Cloris Leachman, Gene Wilder, and Teri Garr.

Movies have never been without music. Even in the silent era, large cities had orchestras accompanying these pioneering pictures (sometimes even with a sound effects person), while smaller towns and/or theatres had an assisting piano player. Moreover, for most of film's history audiences have thought of cinema related songs as having been either directly written for the film, or previous recorded numbers creatively reassembled for the story's soundtrack.

Examples of the former would include Henry Mancini and Johnny Mercer writing the haunting "Moon River" theme song for Blake Edward's *Breakfast at Tiffney*'s (1961). Audrey Hepburn's untrained voice rendition of the song is so apt for a small-town runaway to New York. Other tunes written directly for the screen are countless, from John Lennon's "Help" (1964), for the Beatles film of the same name, to Dolly Parton's "9 to 5," which also doubled as the 1980 title of the movie.

Previously recorded soundtrack songs illustrations immediately reveal my aging Baby boomer roots. For instance, Dennis Hopper's *Easy Rider* (1969) strings together classic rock numbers, especially it signatures road song, Steppenwolf's "Born to Be Wild." Along the same lines, *Big Chill* (1983) writer/director Lawrence Kasdan wanted the rock soundtrack to be evocative of the film's boomer college years. Kasdan's picks ranged from Motown to the Rolling Stones' eulogy to life, "You Can't Always Get What You Want" — the perfect song for a 1960s crowd later brought together for a friend's funeral.

All these musical samples help explain how one part of Hollywood sausage is made, as well as being examples of songs which continue to stand on their own. However, at this point, I would like to call an audible on the subject of music and movies. Have you ever considered the musical misdirection of songs inspired by movies and/or movie actors? There are more than one would think, and the songs often come with backstories of greater interest and/or insight than the traditional movie music process just described. It also doubles as a more focused use of screenwriter/director Nora Ephron's mantra, "Everything is copy." That is, whereas Ephron used all of one's life experiences for artistic inspiration, this pivot is strictly anchored in films.

To start, one might come full circle back to *Breakfast at Tiffany's*. In 1993 the band Deep Blue Something released a song named after the movie. Their "Breakfast at *Tiffney's*" number was their only hit, but what a hit. It charted highly in top 100 record lists worldwide. Composer Todd Pipes was an Audrey Hepburn fan, and the song was inspired by *Tiffany's* and the actress' 1953 *Roman Holiday*, for which she won a Best Actress Oscar.

The lyrics are about a naïve young man about to lose his girlfriend. He uses their mutual love of the film to hopefully keep them together. However, the song stumbles upon an engaging subtext. Truman Capote, who wrote the novella upon which the film is based, credited the title to a native New Yorker joke. There was a time if you asked an out-of-towner what was Gotham's most glamorous restaurant, he would reply — Tiffany's. The film's opening gently spoofs this phenomenon. Since the jewelry store was never a restaurant, Audrey Hepburn's high priced call girl stops there at dawn (after a night on the town), prepared with a Danish and coffee. Eating from a paper bag, and dressed in her now iconic Hubert De Givenchy "little black dress," she breakfasts outside Tiffney's while admiring the window display's diamond baubles. However, she had once been a small-town outsider, too.

As a fluid transition to another movie inspired song linked to a legendary actress one has "Bette Davis Eyes." The mega-star of Hollywood's golden age was the stimulus for Jackie DeShannon and Donna Weiss to write the 1974 song. It proved to be a modest hit for DeShannon. However, Kim Carnes' 1981 "Bette Davis Eyes" cover made one check disbelief at the door. The song spent nine nonconsecutive weeks at the top of America's "Billboard Hot 100." Not surprisingly, it was 1981's biggest hit, winning Grammy Awards for both Song and Record of the Year.

Plus, the backstory for "Bette Davis Eyes" is poignant, without feeling like you have been swallowed by a rainbow. The then 73-year-old actress was euphoric over the song. Despite two Oscars and countless classic films, this musical gem "made me seem cool to my grandchildren ... [by making me] a part of modern times." The appreciative Davis sent thank you letters to DeShannon, Weiss, and Carnes when the record became a hit. She later followed this up with roses to the trio after the Grammy wins.

Given my age, I grew-up in an era of wall-to-wall Westerns, both on TV and in the movies. At the time, Bob Hope joked, "I have to brush hay off my set just so I can turn it on." Fittingly, according to both the American and British Institutes, the greatest and most influential Western of this era, or any other, was John Ford's *The Searchers* (1956, with John Wayne). Certainly, this runaway train of a Western would inspire one song.

It proved a Da Vinci Code film for a teenage Texan who wanted to be a rock 'n roll star, Buddy Holly. He attended the film, and heard Wayne frequently observing, "That'll be the day," wherever anyone suggested doing something inconsistent with his character's cowboy code. Shortly after seeing the picture Holly co-wrote the song "That'll Be the Day" (with Jerry Allison). The following year he formed a back-up group, The Crickets (with Allison on drums), and their release of "Day" was certified *Gold* by the Recording Industry of America (RIAA). This meant it had sold a million records just in the United States. (This was such a massive number that in 1958 RIAA redesignated *Gold* status to 500,000 records sold.)

Again, the later context dwarfs the original event. While a mere twenty-two-year-old Holly tragically died in a 1959 plane crash, he managed to record nearly two dozen songs which "charted" in the United States and/or Great Britain. The latter fact is especially important, since his influence in England was mammoth. The first song recorded (a demo-tape) by The Quarrymen, a Liverpool band formed by John Lennon in 1956, which evolved into the Beatles (1960), was "Day." Moreover, their new insect name was inspired by Holly's Crickets. The American's style, the fact he wrote his own songs, and even his glasses (Lennon was half-blind without his) was a major effect on the Beatles.

Holly's impact on the Rolling Stones was equally important. Their first major hit in the United Kingdom was a 1964 cover of Holly's "Not Fade Away." Indeed, that song was the A-side of the band's first American single (45 record). Plus, another soon-to-be-major British group were completely transparent on the impact of this pioneering Texas rock 'n roller. In 1962 this band named itself The Hollies. Its talented co-founder, Graham Nash, would later form Crosby, Stills & Nash, just in time for Woodstock. Regardless, the

Hollies were a major band of the era, with hits like "Carrie Anne" (echoes of Holly's "Peggy Sue"?), "He Ain't Heavy, He's My Brother," and "Long Cool Woman in a Black Dress."

Later in America Holly's first hit and most popular song would assume special historical status. It was inducted into the Grammy Hall of Fame in 1998. Next "Day" was placed in the National Recording Registry, a list of sound recordings that "are culturally, historically, aesthetically important, and/or inform or reflect life in the United States," in 2005. This more than merits London Holly fan Robert Plant unleashing his Led Zeppelin wail.

Given Holly having moved the needle into rock 'n roll's "British Invasion" of America, it brings to mind a Beatles song which was inspired by a movie far distant from the Western genre. While early Beatles' music had Lennon-McCarthy credits, John was usually the dominate composer. Appropriately, one of the group's pre-American hits was drawn from John's childhood. His parent's tumultuous relationship meant he was largely raised by his mother's (Julia) sister, Aunt Mimi. Shortly after the musically inclined Julia came back into his teenage life, she was struck and killed by a car on Liverpool walk. Obviously, the young man cherished any mother memories he had, essentially after losing her twice; he even naming his first son Julia*n*

As an adult John revered a bedtime song Julia had sung to him from Walt Disney's 1937 film *Snow White And the Seven Dwarfs*. "I'm Wishing" is the first song featured in this, or any Disney animated feature. Snow White quiets the morning doves and via the song she shares "I'm wishing (I'm wishing) for the one I love to find me." However, in wanting to hold the doves' attention, the song begins, "Want to know a secret?" This is the genesis for John's later Beatle love song, "Do You Want To Know A Secret?"

For some American rock music balance one might provide a segue to Aerosmith, one of *the* American groups formed as the Beatles split, and fronted by Steven Tyler. According to a 2014 *Wall Street Journal* interview with Tyler and bandmate Joe Perry, the group had reached a creative block, and decided to attend the Mel Brooks/Gene Wilder parody picture, *Young Frankenstein* (1974). Early in the movie Aerosmith was gifted with a comic sequence which produced arguably their signature song.

When young Dr. Frankenstein (Gene Wilder) inherits the family's Transylvania estate, he is met at the train station by pop-eyed hunchbacked servant Igor/"Eye-Gore" (Marty Feldman). As his soon to be assistant Igor helps with the luggage, Feldman provides the doctor with a short stick/cane and asks him to "walk this way," which produces a comic hunched-over stride. "Walk this way" is an old music hall/vaudeville bit that has occurred in many variations. Indeed, one of the earliest renderings is equal parts verbal. A heavy-set woman goes into a drugstore and asks for some talcum powder. The bowlegged clerk says, "walk this way," and the woman responds, "If I could walk that way I wouldn't need talcum powder!" However, the bit's most frequent movie modification involves a butler, or a servant like Feldman, with a comic gait greeting a guest and requesting s/he "walk this way" (follow him). Examples include William Powell in *After the Thin Man*, (1936), and Dudley Moore in *Arthur* (1980).

Long after the release of *Young Frankenstein*, *Bookseller* magazine (September 13, 2011) shared a period quote from Feldman, "It's a terribly old joke. I [improvised] it to make the crew laugh and Mel Brooks said, 'Let's shoot it' ... [Wilder and I] both said, 'Mel please take that out,' but he left it in. He said, 'I think it's funny. Audiences will laugh at it.' Gene and I were both wrong. Mel was right."

Regardless, Aerosmith and Tyler were immediately inspired to write "Walk this Way," which was such a hit it jumpstarted the group's 1970s career. However, the number fueled yet another Aerosmith comeback of historical importance when they re-recorded it as a 1980s duet with the Run-DMC hip hop/rap group. The now much bigger hit became the first rap song to be played on mainstream radio. Both versions are now in the Grammy Hall of Fame.

There are several other examples I could note, such as the 1984 novelty number "The Curly Shuffle," a tongue-in-cheek homage to the Three Stooges' "Curly" Howard by the one hit wonder group, Jump 'N the Saddle Band. Okay, so maybe the long delay in producing "The Curly Shuffle" did not contribute to his premature death. However, it would not have hurt if this underappreciated comedian would have experienced the love generated by a song peppered with his trademark lines, including: "woob-woob-woob!," "nyuk-nyuk-nyuk!," and "soitenlyly!" Be that as it may, I believe my modest two-part goal has been accomplished. First, it turns "movie music" inside out for new often more interesting perspectives. Secondly, it embraces a loopy film aficionado belief best articulated in Kasdan's *Grand Canyon* (1991). Late in the movie Steve Martin's filmmaker character asks his friend (Kevin Kline) if he has ever seen Preston Sturges' *Sullivan's Travels* (1941). The movie chronicles a film director (Joel McCrea) who has just gone through a life altering experience — not unlike what has recently occurred to Martin. The epiphany of *Travels* is essentially, order is not making sense of life, but rather not allowing the chaos to destroy you.

It also predates the similar insightfully brave title of Joan Didion's definitive essay collection, *We Tell Ourselves Stories in Order to Live*. Regardless, when Kline's character answers "no" to Martin's question, the latter responds, "You haven't seen enough movies. All of life's riddles are answered in the movies." Whether one buys this, or not, movies stories, musical or not, can briefly provide a brief intermission.

HOMAGE TO A HUMORIST:

With a Gin Twist

Light Armour is a lovely pun for the writing of this parodist.

I am writing a book on American film comedy, with a modest foundation in print humor. I am splitting the subject into comedic subgenres, with the current focus on parody. One's first response here might be Mel Brooks' *Blazing Saddles* and *Young Frankenstein* (both 1974). However, for me, I initially think of Richard Armour (1906-1989), an academic turned poet and parody artist. His poems are not unlike those of Ogden Nash. For example, his ode to mustard has often been credited to Nash: "Nothing attacks/ the mustards from wieners/as much as the slacks/just back from the cleaners."

Yes, his poetry essentially parodies serious verse. Regardless, I first fell in love with his spoofing of serious English texts, such as *The Classics Reclassified* (1960, where he also documents the importance of not being educated if you want to be a famous author), and *American Lit Relit* (1964, which asks the burning question — has poetry been dead since 1882? I can't tell you; you'll just have to buy the book).

I discovered him as a child in a used bookstore, a funny friend between two covers. Later as a young professor I was lucky enough to meet Armour at "The First International Humor Conference" (1979, Los Angeles). Fittingly, he was receiving a lifetime achievement award — a large platter (undoubtedly plated) which seemed an odd gift for a humorist, though it could undoubtedly have been pawned. I would have opted for a bust of Mark Twain, or better yet, a slightly silly Shakespeare sculpture, since another Armour text classic is *Twisted Tales From Shakespeare* (1957). Afterall, there needs to be more thought put into an award for a humorist capable of writing in a preface, "The reader will *not* encounter any half-truths, but may occasionally encounter a truth-and-a-half."

Armour was disarmingly pleasant to be around, which is frequently *not* the case with many prominent humorists. (Don't you hate it when you discover your idol could've been the model for Hannibal the Cannibal?) As a sometimes scholar he told me that he wore two outfits — cap and gown, and cap and bells. I later found out Armour told everyone that line. However, I didn't care; he could have just given me the brush. I would have.

I will always remember his egalitarian nature, plus his perception that I was a young scholar chafing at how boringly serious academia was addressing humor. To paraphrase his most memorable aside to me, "Whatever the writing, one wants to deliver the insight with the intimacy of a comic diarist." That was a Da Vinci Code moment for me. As if this was not enough, it actually got better. My meeting highlight was making him laugh — a comic hero I discovered at twelve in the wilds of Cedar Rapids, Iowa. Be that as it may, I knew the laugh to be true because it occurred just as Armour was sipping his gin and tonic. Honest, like in an old slapstick movie — I was the partial recipient of that drink ... sort of an accidental "Gin Fizz."

What was the joke? It was some manna from the sky. The conference was in a section of Los Angeles called "Little Tokyo;" the new Japanese hotel in which it was held had a special travel department in which guests could book and/or check on their flights. Just before meeting for drinks, I had stopped to see if my Indianapolis flight for the following day was still as scheduled, adding the carrier was "TWA" (Trans World Airlines). It was a huge airline at the time, thanks to its expansion by onetime corporate director Howard Hughes.

However, when I told the young staffer "TWA," there was a pause, and she asked me to spell it. Sometimes humor is just given to you, with a gin mist. Nonetheless, after a brief handkerchief cleanup, Armour told me I must promise to use that line in a future book. Well, it is finally a perfect fit for the print and film humor text I am writing.

Consequently, as a final thank you tribute to Armour, let me close by affectionately mimicking his parody style. I am confident that you will learn and chuckle from my forthcoming book, and/or chuckle at learning from it. Others might have accomplished more with their lives, but at least I wrote a lot of stuff down.

— Professor Gehring, somewhere off the coast of Indiana

(Reprinted with permission from *USA Today Magazine*, November 2022. Copyright © 2022 by "The Society for the Advancement of Education, Inc. All Rights Reserved.")